Remington & Russell

The Sid Richardson Collection

REMINGTON & RUSSELL

by Brian W. Dippie

University of Texas Press 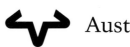 Austin

Publication of this book was made possible by
a grant from the Sid W. Richardson Foundation.

Printed in Japan
First Edition, 1982

Requests for permission to reproduce material
from this work should be sent to Permissions,
University of Texas Press, Box 7819, Austin,
Texas 78712.

LIBRARY OF CONGRESS
CATALOGING IN PUBLICATION DATA

Dippie, Brian W.
  Remington & Russell.

  Bibliography: p.
  1. Remington, Frederic, 1861–1909—Catalogs. 2. Russell, Charles M. (Charles Marion),
1864–1926—Catalogs. 3. West (N.Y.) in art—
Catalogs. 4. Richardson, Sid, 1891–1959—Art
collections—Catalogs. I. Title.
ND237.R36A4   1982   758'.9978   82-2594
ISBN 0-292-77027-8   AACR2

Dedicated to my grandmothers,
Margaret Dippie and Nora Brander,
and the memory of my grandfathers,
Thomas Dippie and William Brander

Contents

Other Western Painters

Introduction

SID W. RICHARDSON, like his friend Amon Carter, sought respite from the pressures of his many business activities in a particularly western form of recreation. He collected western art. Born in Athens, Texas, in 1891, Richardson attended Baylor University at Waco before entering the oil business in 1913. Thereafter, oil, cattle, and land underlay a career that paralleled the boom-and-bust nature of the petroleum industry in its turbulent, formative years. Sid Richardson's fortune crashed along with the nation's economy in the early 1930s, but he simply started over and built himself back up. He had a genius for making deals and, an acquaintance recalled, "the spirit of the chase"—both qualities that served him well when he decided to collect western art. Things were on the upswing for Richardson when he startled Bertram M. Newhouse, president of the Newhouse Galleries in New York City, with a question and an offer: Could the Newhouse Galleries form a collection of western pictures for him? If so, go out and buy them and he would pay the price. Bert Newhouse still cherishes the memory of the trust that Richardson, "the finest natural gentleman I ever knew," reposed in him. Richardson operated on loyalty, and Newhouse Galleries remained his principal dealer from 1942 to 1947, when he acquired the majority of his paintings. Clyde Newhouse, who was sent by his father into the field to locate what was available, remembers the sense of excitement with which Richardson, busy as he was, "took up the chase." There was an element of gamble in collecting western art at a time when it was not established as it is today, and this added zest to the pursuit. As oilmen like Richardson and Frank Phillips,

Thomas Gilcrease, and R. W. Norton won the twentieth-century West, Clyde Newhouse believes, the paintings that showed the earlier winning of the West became important to them. Themselves part of the western legend of freewheeling enterprise, through their collections they established a lasting link to the romantic legends of an older West.

Certainly Sid Richardson enjoyed his western paintings. He favored the works of Frederic Remington and Charles M. Russell and was still acquiring an occasional new piece until shortly before his death in 1959. "Anybody can paint a horse on four legs, but it takes a real eye to paint them in violent motion," he once told his nephew. "All parts of the horse must be in proper position, and Remington and Russell are the fellows who can do it." Their paintings hung in his rooms at the Fort Worth Club and on the walls of his home on San José Island,[1] off Rockport, Texas, and Bert Newhouse recalls that a visit with Richardson always involved an appreciative inspection and discussion of the art with which he had surrounded himself. Nor did Richardson confine his collection to Remington and Russell. While he collected none of the pre–Civil War western documentarians (George Catlin, Karl Bodmer, Alfred Jacob Miller, Paul Kane, and Charles Wimar, for example), he did acquire works by such lesser known, late nineteenth-century realists as Gilbert Gaul, Peter Moran, and Charles F. Browne. He showed no interest in western landscape art (Albert Bierstadt or Thomas Moran)

---

1. Although San José was the name given to this island by the Spanish, it was long known as St. Joseph Island. In 1973 the Texas Legislature restored the original name.

or the tranquil scenes typical of the southwestern school centered in Taos and Santa Fe, but he did collect paintings by Oscar E. Berninghaus, Frank Tenney Johnson, William R. Leigh, and Edwin W. Deming that involved action or suspense. Richardson obviously liked the "Wild West school" best. He acquired one oil by Charles Schreyvogel but concentrated on Remington and Russell. It was a decision whose wisdom time has confirmed; Remington and Russell remain today what they were in their own day, the "titans of Western art."[2]

Frederic Sackrider Remington was born in the town of Canton in northern New York on October 4, 1861. His boyhood fostered a lifelong love of horses and the out-of-doors, while his father's tales of action as a cavalry officer in the Civil War filled his head with pictures and inspired a passion for things military that found a western focus with the annihilation of General George Armstrong Custer's command on the Little Bighorn River during the nation's Centennial Year, 1876. At the age of fourteen Remington was smitten with the urge to go West and see for himself the blue-clad cavalrymen, bronze-skinned Indians, and buckskin-garbed frontier scouts who peopled his fantasies. But his was a family of some prominence—his father owned the Canton newspaper and, a staunch Republican, had secured a patronage plum, U.S. collector of the port of Ogdensburg, New York, on the St. Lawrence River. Naturally the Remingtons expected Frederic to attend college and prepare himself for a business career. Instead, he passed a

year and a half at Yale playing football and studying art. He obviously never relinquished his youthful ambition to see the West, for when he came into a small advance on his inheritance after his father's death, he was off to Montana in August 1881 for a few months' stay. Although he tried to settle into a clerkship in Albany on his return to New York, he remained restless and eager to see more of the West. The opportunity came in February 1883. With the balance of his inheritance in hand, he was off again, this time to Kansas, where he purchased a sheep ranch and, for the only time in his life, made the West his home. He did not stay long—about a year—and was never keen thereafter to reveal that he had been a sheepman, not a cattleman. Thus, a journalist in 1907 described him as a "stockman on a ranch" and spoke in glowing generalities about his experiences, lumping his Kansas sojourn with the many reportorial excursions he made to the West through the 1890s to fabricate a portrait of Remington, the complete westerner:

. . . this blond, youngish giant who sat idly smoking a cigarette and looking as if he had led a sheltered existence between walls and amid refined surroundings all his life was once a ranger on the limitless prairies, a hard-riding, rough-living, free-fighting cow-puncher,—for do not lose sight of the fact that Frederic Remington has put himself and his own experiences in very nearly every picture he has drawn or painted. "He rides like a Comanche," said one of his friends speaking of Remington's early career. "He knows as much about horses and cattle as any man alive. And so he

2. J. Frank Dobie, "Titans of Western Art," *American Scene* 5, no. 4 (1964): 4–9.

should, for he spent most of his youth in the saddle, rounding up mavericks, chasing and being chased by red men and hobnobbing with scouts, pioneers, miners and the picturesque freebooters of the plains."[3]

Nonsense like this created the false impression that Remington's art always drew directly upon personal experience. In fact, his major easel paintings were tributes to the Wild West of fantasy. They drew on the artist's experience for their sense of place and authentic details, but on his imagination for their subject matter. Remington's achievement was to fuse observation and imagination so seamlessly that his contemporaries assumed he had actually witnessed what he painted, and a journalist writing in 1892, at a time when Remington's reputation as the supreme illustrator of western life was recent but already secure, was acute in remarking: "In his pictures of life on the plains, and of Indian fighting, he has almost created a new field in illustration, so fresh and novel are his characterizations . . . It is a fact that admits of no question that Eastern people have formed their conceptions of what the Far-Western life is like, more from what they have seen in Mr. Remington's pictures than from any other source, and if they went to the West or to Mexico they would expect to see men and places looking exactly as Mr. Remington has drawn them."[4]

Remington illustrated for the major periodicals of the day—*Century Magazine, Harper's Weekly, Harper's New Monthly Magazine*—and lesser journals as well. By the end of the century, as reproductive processes and photographic technology reached new sophistication, the illustrator's role as a purveyor of information became obsolete, marooning those who were satisfied in the role but freeing others like Remington who wanted to go their own independent ways.[5] Since 1888 he had been exhibiting in major art shows, seeking recognition as something more than an illustrator, an artist in the recognized sense of the term at the time. He also held sales of his work and competed for prizes. In 1891 he was elected an associate of the National Academy of Design. But he never quite made the breakthrough he was seeking until he turned to sculpting in 1895 and discovered an unexpected talent. "I am to endure in bronze . . . —I am modeling—I find I do well—I am doing a cow boy on a bucking broncho and I am going to rattle down through all the ages," he wrote with characteristic enthusiasm.[6] The public liked what he was doing, and Remington toyed with abandoning painting altogether to glory in the joys of "mud." His color sense, he readily conceded, was suspect, while form was his forte. Sculpting seemed the answer, clay a medium in which he could express

3. Perriton Maxwell, "Frederic Remington—Most Typical of American Artists," *Pearson's Magazine* 18 (October 1907): 403.

4. William A. Coffin, "American Illustration of To-day" (Third Paper), *Scribner's Magazine* 11 (March 1892): 348.

5. Estelle Jussim, *Visual Communication and the Graphic Arts: Photographic Technologies in the Nineteenth Century*, pp. 211–214, 235–236.

6. Frederic Remington to Owen Wister, [January 1895], in Ben Merchant Vorpahl, *My Dear Wister—: The Frederic Remington–Owen Wister Letters*, p. 160.

himself fully while earning critical respect as well, though some dismissed his bronzes as illustrations in three dimensions.

By 1901 the painter in Remington also came out fighting. He would teach himself how to see all over again, letting his color sense develop naturally. A contract with *Collier's Weekly* gave him the freedom to paint what he wanted, with *Collier's* reserving exclusive reproduction rights. In return, he would receive an annual fee. This arrangement removed monetary worries and allowed him to work at his painting. His technique evolved dramatically during the last five years of his life as he abandoned the crisp, linear illustrative style that had served him so well for two decades to concentrate on mood, color, and light—sunlight, moonlight, and firelight. His later oils present a vision consistent with the flat assertion that *his* West was dead. "I mean just this: The West is no longer the West of picturesque and stirring events," he explained. "Romance and adventure have been beaten down in the rush of civilization; the country west of the Mississippi has become hopelessly commercialized, shackled in chains of business to its uttermost limits. The cow-boy—the real thing, mark you . . . disappeared with the advent of the wire fence, and as for the Indian, there are so few of him he doesn't count . . ."[7] So Remington painted impressionistic scenes in which the West, now entirely confined to memory, was invested with a mystery and a poetry the present could not efface. The critics saw things his way at last. In 1909 his annual exhibition at opened to strong reviews, and Remington crowed in his diary: "The art critics have all 'come down'—I have received splendid notices from all the papers. They ungrudgingly give me a high place as a 'mere painter.' I have been on their trail a long while and they never surrendered while they had a leg to stand on. The 'Illustrator' phase has become a background."[8]

Within a month Frederic Remington was dead—December 26, 1909—the victim of appendicitis and his own voracious appetite for food and drink. He had clambered on and off the water wagon so many times over the years that he must have lost count; what did not change was the gradual upward curve of his weight. He was around three hundred pounds near the end and knew that he was tempting fate. "I can't plead age exactly," he had written frankly a few years before, "but I did most d—— faithfully burn the candle at both ends in the days of my youth and I got the high sign to slow down some little time since. Therefore I have cut out the 'boys' . . . I always loose my bridle and when I get going I never know when to stop. If there is anything in the world I love it is to sit 'round the mahogany with a bunch of good fellows and talk through my hat—I like it a lot better than it likes me and I greatly fear it will take more than a year of training to make a calm eyed philosopher out of me."[9] A man of prodigious bulk, Remington had the energies and talent to match.

---

7. Maxwell, "Frederic Remington—Most Typical of American Artists," pp. 396–397.

8. Quoted in Harold McCracken, *A Catalogue of the Frederic Remington Memorial Collection*, p. 31.

9. Frederic Remington to Daniel Beard, undated, in the Daniel Beard Papers, General Correspondence, Box 103, Manuscript Division, Library of Congress, Washington, D.C.

In a career spanning less than twenty-five years he produced a huge body of work—illustration, painting, sculpture, nonfiction, and fiction—the vast majority of it centered on the West. His influence in creating the Wild West of the popular imagination cannot be overestimated. Like his sculpture, it is an influence that has survived, "something that burglar won't have, moth eat, or time blacken."[10] His was a West without softness or subtlety. It was, instead, a grand theater for the testing of manhood. It was a throwback to pioneering days, the embodiment of the best qualities in the national character. More than anything else, it was the setting for a great drama: the *winning* of the West. It was soldier against Indian, civilization against savagery. It was, quite simply, the story of America, and a year or so before he died Remington confidently predicted that "we fellows who are doing the 'old America' which is so fast passing will have an audiance in posterity whether we do at present or not."[11]

Like Remington, Charles Marion Russell was born to moderate wealth and would receive his first exposure to the West in Montana. His first western job would also be as a lowly sheepherder rather than a lordly cowboy. But there the similarities end. For Russell, born in the St. Louis area on March 19, 1864, was so captivated by Montana when he visited in 1880 that he chose to stay, becoming in fact the westerner that both men as boys had dreamed of being. Indeed, it was the persistence of that dream that originally persuaded Russell's parents to let him go west as a sixteenth birthday present. He was to earn his keep tending sheep for a family acquaintance, but his carelessness cost him his job and instead earned him a reputation as being ornery and irresponsible. Ignoring advice to go home and grow up, he stayed in Montana, assisting a professional meat hunter who taught him "nature's secrets," and eventually landing a position in 1882 wrangling horses on a cattle drive. He was still wrangling for a living eleven years later, and while he never claimed to be "a good roper nor rider" he was a genuine cowboy, proud of his profession and in love with Montana's wide open spaces.[12] But change was all about him. The bitter winter of 1886–87 checked what had been a booming, speculative business and marked the end of the cattleman's dominion on the northern plains. Railroads and settlers were altering the face of the land. The days of free grass and the unfenced range were ending, and for Russell the cowboy life was over after 1893.

Even while working as a wrangler, Russell established a local reputation as the affable cowboy who loved to draw. His sketches were crude, but the earliest of them showed an observant eye, a feeling for animal and human anatomy, and a flair for portraying action—all hallmarks of Russell's mature art. Russell captured attention with a little watercolor depicting the devastation brought by the winter of 1886–87—*Waiting for a Chinook*—and had a few works reproduced nationally before he quit cowboying to take up art full time. But fame and fortune did not prove synonymous,

10. William A. Coffin, "Remington's 'Bronco Buster,'" *Century Magazine* 52 (June 1896): 319.

11. Frederic Remington to Carl Rungius, [1908], in the Carl Rungius Papers, Glenbow-Alberta Institute, Calgary, Alberta.

12. Charles M. Russell, "A Few Words about Myself," in *Trails Plowed Under*, p. xix.

and it was not at all clear that he would be able to make a living from his painting when in 1896 he married a young woman named Nancy Cooper. She saw something in the rough-hewn Cowboy Artist that many of his contemporaries did not: the talent and vision to be great.

Nancy Russell provided the business sense and drive that eventually made her unambitious husband one of the highest-paid American artists of his day. This meant exerting control over his financial affairs, of course; but it also meant managing his time, limiting the hours he spent drinking and socializing with his old range cronies, keeping him at his easel, and then marketing what he produced. It is the reason that Nancy looms so large in the Russell story, while Remington's wife, Eva, remains discreetly obscure, completely overshadowed by the exclusively masculine concerns celebrated in her husband's art. Success did not come easily for Nancy. Montana offered few opportunities for sales, and beginning late in 1903 the Russells began branching out. They visited New York most years, established contacts with other artists interested in western themes, secured illustrating assignments (at the very time Remington was getting out of illustration in order to concentrate on his painting), and gained exposure through exhibitions and press coverage. While critics may not have taken Russell's art too seriously in this period, there is no denying they found the artist fascinating. Russell stoutly insisted upon his right to be himself. He dressed as he pleased—in cowboy boots and Stetson, with a woven sash to hold up his pants. His talk, which was guarded and laconic in the best Gary Cooper fashion when he was around strangers, flowed among friends, who regarded him as a master

storyteller and delighted in his dry wit just as readers of his illustrated letters still do. Russell won people over without trying and made the idea of a Cowboy Artist as popular as the paintings from his brush. Finally, a one-man show at New York's Folsom Galleries in 1911, followed three years later by an exhibition at the Doré Galleries in London, marked Russell's emergence as a figure to be reckoned with in the big-time art world. Throughout his rise to eminence Nancy made certain that his prices kept pace, and her efforts paid off with a jackpot of $10,000 for a single oil in 1921.

Russell never took his success too seriously. Pomposity was foreign to him, and he always felt most at home with his Great Falls "bunch." He no longer drank after 1908, but he still mixed with his friends whenever he could and downtown Great Falls' cigar stores and bars—notably the Mint and the Silver Dollar—were favorite haunts. He needed these contacts. Old friends were the links to the past that kept his art young and vital, for Russell really only had one theme, and as the years rolled by, it became increasingly overt: "The west that has passed." A few lines expressed his sentiments:

The West is dead!
You may lose a sweetheart,
But you won't forget her.[13]

The same refrain runs through his art. As much as Remington, Russell could "do" the wild, wild West; but there was in his work a constant, larger vision suggested by the omnipresent buffalo skulls that were in his paintings from the beginning and later formed a part of his signature.

13. Charles M. Russell, *Good Medicine: The Illustrated Letters of Charles M. Russell*, p. vii.

He *felt* the passing of the West. Remington *knew* that his West, too, had vanished, and he took to lamenting it in prose and paint and clay. But Russell's sense of loss touched him with an emotional immediacy. He was haunted not just by the youthful fantasies that first kindled both men's artistry, but by memories of what once was and by the evidence of change that surrounded him as an everyday reality. Thus his art speaks with an almost mystical passion of lost love, while Remington's tells with some detachment of boyhood dreams betrayed by the imperatives of advancing age.

Their separate visions are at the heart of their separate achievements. Remington knew the Southwest best and through the 1890s was more interested in the West as a minimalist stage for action—yellow ochre sands, powder blue skies—than in the land itself. Russell always elaborated setting in his paintings. Montana was home to him, and he loved the landmarks that identified specific locales—the Judith Basin, the Great Falls area, the mountains of Glacier Park. A glance at the paintings in the Richardson collection confirms this obvious distinction. In their time, and especially after Remington's death in 1909, the two artists were often compared. In the eastern press Russell was regularly described as Remington's successor; it was a way of establishing his subject matter but was not especially helpful in getting at the differences between the two. The western press, in turn, was more strident than analytical. "The effete east has her Remington," a Butte, Montana, paper observed in 1903, "but the glorious west has her Russell."[14] A state official was more reasonable the next year in an address delivered at the World's Fair Grounds in St. Louis when he characterized the Russells on exhibit there as "some of the most captivating artistic work of the age," and their creator, "an ordinary cowboy from the City of Great Falls," as "the peer of Remington, and one of the artists destined to live in the history of art within the lines he has made his own."[15] Pride mixed with pugnacity in such assessments, and from them it becomes clear that the case for Russell's superiority rested on the fact that he lived in the West. "Some of Frederic Remington's illustrations are magnificent," a Texas cattleman explained in 1908, "but in certain of his pictures, in not a few of them, in fact, Mr. Remington has not been accurate. This is probably due to the fact that he doesn't know the men and the life with that thorough knowledge an artist who paints it should have. One must live among them to acquire it."[16]

That was the rub: "Remington never lived in the west, notwithstanding statements to the contrary," and thus "the knowledge of the western types he gained was superficial."[17] Those who champion Russell continue to refer to his authenticity rather than his artistry—a

14. "Charles Russell, Cowboy Artist," *Butte Miner*, October 11, 1903, p. 5.

15. "Address by Hon. Thos. H. Carter, Helena, Mont., at the Dedication Exercises, Montana State Building, Louisiana Purchase Exposition, World's Fair Grounds, St. Louis, Mo., June 14, 1904," in *Contributions to the Historical Society of Montana* 5 (1904): 103.

16. "Artists and Western Life," *Great Falls Daily Tribune*, January 21, 1904, p. 8, quoting Erwin E. Smith.

17. "Russell and Remington," ibid., January 6, 1910, p. 6.

position qualified by J. Frank Dobie, who also admired Russell's warm humanism with its concern for the individual rather than the typical and its fondness for what he called "speaking details dear to any lover of Western life."[18] Russell rarely went on record about Remington, though he obviously grew tired of being likened to him and, when pushed, remarked informally on inaccuracies in his art.[19] It should be added that Remington also adhered to the canon of accuracy and was quick to cut down upstarts who challenged his supremacy in the field of western art by declaring them uninformed. "The youngster that attempted to portray the early West must get his material from older artists," he stated at the ripe old age of almost forty-three, "since the typical figures of the plains are as much gone as the Civil War or the Paleozoic period."[20]

The problem is that such comments, by Remington or about Russell, have misled too many students over the years. A conventional distinction, drawn up in 1901 by a St. Louis journalist, went: "Remington is the idealist of the new western art culture. Russell is its realist."[21] Yet just a few years later a more perceptive critic said of Russell: "He is not a painter of stern realism, but rather a delineator of the poetical."[22] Russell would have agreed. He worked hard to make certain that his paintings satisfied the demand for authenticity, but he recognized that the soul of his art was romance.[23] However, even a casual acquaintance with the work of Remington and Russell is adequate to demonstrate that realism is too restrictive a standard for evaluating their respective achievements. After all, both men had to rely on their imaginations in re-creating historical events on canvas, and both moved away from the documentary realism of their early years even as they became more technically proficient. Relying on visual evidence alone, it would be difficult to prove that an 1889 and a 1909 Remington were by the same artist since his technique underwent such a profound transformation as he self-consciously sloughed off the marks of the illustrator. We are told that Remington—who was outspoken in his Americanism and, like Russell, thoroughly parochial when it came to venturing abroad and learning from the Old World masters—responded to his first encounter with Impressionist paintings by blurting, "Say, I've got two maiden aunts up-state who can *knit* better pictures than those."[24] But before long he was sitting at the knees of Claude

18. J. Frank Dobie, "The Conservatism of Charles M. Russell," *Montana, the Magazine of Western History* 8 (Autumn 1958): 63, and his provocative introduction to Frederic Remington, *Pony Tracks*, pp. xix–xxi.

19. See, for example, James W. Bollinger, *Old Montana and Her Cowboy Artist: A Paper Read before The Contemporary Club, Davenport, Iowa, January Thirtieth, Nineteen Hundred Fifty*, pp. 20–22.

20. Maxwell, "Frederic Remington—Most Typical of American Artists," p. 399.

21. "Cowboy Artist St. Louis' Lion," *Daily Independent* (Helena), May 13, 1901, p. 5, reprinting remarks from the *St. Louis Post Dispatch.*

22. Marian A. White, "A Group of Clever and Original Painters in Montana," *Fine Arts Journal* 16 (February 1905): 87.

23. See especially Charles M. Russell to Frank Bird Linderman, January 18, 1919, in Brian W. Dippie, ed., *"Paper Talk": Charlie Russell's American West*, p. 143.

24. Harold McCracken, *Frederic Remington: Artist of the Old West*, p. 106.

Monet.[25] Russell professed no interest whatever in "teck neque," mocked highfaluting artsy talk, and doubted that an Impressionist had any higher motive than to obscure "bum drawin'."[26] But his own painting in the 1920s exhibits a more dramatic use of color and a looseness of style that cannot be equated with Remington's purposeful impressionism but do indicate a similar evolution away from the linear and the literal toward an appreciation of light and the way we feel what we see.

Since their contemporaries so often compared Remington and Russell, the current reticence on the subject is surprising. Few things are more desperately needed in western art studies today than critical comparisons artist to artist, certainly, and within each artist's oeuvre. Fifteen years ago John C. Ewers complained that "far too much" of the writing on western art "consists of biography interlarded with laudatory comments on the artist's work which are more akin to the unrestrained prose of the press agent than to the carefully weighed words of the serious scholar and critic. Too often writers have applied generalized slogans to the western artists—slogans such as 'he knew the horse,' or 'he knew the Indian,' or 'the Mountain Man,' or 'cowboy,' and such gross judgments have been offered in place of the much more difficult, scholarly criticisms of the individual works of the artists under consideration."[27] Some excellent books in recent years, particularly on the earlier documentarians, the landscapists, and Frederic Remington, partially answer Ewers' concerns. But the study of western art continues to suffer from a surfeit of indiscriminate praise (and offhand dismissals by critics too self-absorbed to bother seeing and too insular to ever understand) as well as a general reluctance to engage in controversy. What is needed is criticism that accepts what the artist has set out to do and that offers specific judgments on specific works.

It is an obvious point, but not all Remingtons and Russells are equally good. Dates aside, and the work of both artists changed markedly over the years, neither functioned at a consistent level at any given time. Remington consigned several paintings to the flames during his drive for critical acceptance, and Russell, during one of his last interviews, published a few months before his death on October 24, 1926, claimed to have painted many great pictures in his mind but not yet one on canvas.[28] Both men recognized their shortcomings, and so should we. Consequently, in my commentaries on the individual works in the Richardson collection I have attempted to be critical as well as descriptive, elucidating artistic achievement and content by examining the paintings on their own terms, in comparison with others by the same artist, and in light of works by different artists represented in the collection.

25. Giles Edgerton, "Frederic Remington, Painter and Sculptor: A Pioneer in Distinctive American Art," *Craftsman* 15 (March 1909): 669.

26. Charles M. Russell to Joe De Yong, March 30, 1920, in *Good Medicine*, p. 126; Frank Bird Linderman, *Recollections of Charley Russell*, ed. H. G. Meriam, p. 92.

27. John C. Ewers, "Fact and Fiction in the Documentary Art of the American West," in *The Frontier Re-examined*, ed. John Francis McDermott, p. 82.

28. Frank M. Chapman, Jr., "The Man behind the Brush," *Country Life* 50 (August 1926): 37.

I wish to acknowledge the assistance of the following in the preparation of this book: Doris Fletcher, The Warner Collection of Gulf States Paper Corporation, Tuscaloosa, Alabama; Edward T. LeBlanc, Fall River, Massachusetts; Mary B. Palmer, National Geographic Society, Washington, D.C.; Bertram M. Newhouse and Clyde M. Newhouse of the Newhouse Galleries, New York City; and Carol Clark and Ron Tyler of the Amon Carter Museum of Western Art, Fort Worth, Texas. I also want to thank the following institutions: the Glenbow-Alberta Institute, Calgary, Alberta; the Great Falls Public Library, Montana Collection, Great Falls, Montana; the Huntington Library, San Marino, California; and the Manuscript Division, Library of Congress, Washington, D.C. The Interlibrary Loan Service at the University of Victoria, Victoria, British Columbia, has been as efficient as ever, for which I am most grateful. And, as always, I want to thank Donna, Blake, and Scott for encouragement, patience, and understanding.

Frederic S. Remington (1861–1909)

The Way Post

c. 1881   Gouache on paper
7 x 9½ in. (17.8 x 24.1 cm.)

Signed lower right: F. R.

Frederic Remington's first trip west is veiled in mystery. Boyhood sketchbooks reveal his obsession with military subjects—Civil War scenes reflecting the experiences of his father and, beginning in 1876 with the news of Custer's Last Stand, Indian fighting.[1] His brief stint at the Yale School of Fine Arts (1878–1880) did not wean him from his youthful preoccupations, and when the opportunity presented itself he headed west in August 1881, returning home by mid-October. Where he went and how he passed his time are unknown, though he intended to visit Montana, scene of Custer's defeat five years before, and likely did.[2] He was singularly uninformative on the matter. "Remington has no gift of reminiscence," a journalist noted in 1907. "His stories are best told with the brush."[3] But Remington did set down a few recollections in 1905 that placed him in Montana at the age of nineteen sharing bacon and coffee with "an old wagon freighter" who told him that the West, so new and exciting to the boy, was already a thing of the past. "The old man had closed my very entrancing book almost at the first chapter," Remington remembered.[4]

It is possible, however, that we have one memento of that initial western excursion. *The Way Post*, a simple watercolor study of a pioneer resting his horses at what appears to be a stage stop, may be a product of Remington's two months in Montana. Because the style is so unformed, the painting cannot be attributed to Remington, let alone dated, with any certainty. But it has the documentary ring of his earliest known western scenes, while the signature—the initials "F. R."—is one he used around 1881 but rarely thereafter.[5]

NOTES

1. McCracken, *A Catalogue of the Frederic Remington Memorial Collection*, p. 10; *Frederic Remington (1861–1909): Paintings, Drawings, and Sculpture in the Collection of The R.W. Norton Art Gallery, Shreveport, Louisiana*, pp. 48–50.

2. Atwood Manley, *Some of Frederic Remington's North Country Associations*, pp. 22–23; Hassrick, *Frederic Remington*, pp. 18–20.

3. Maxwell, "Frederic Remington—Most Typical of American Artists," *Pearson's Magazine* 18 (October 1907): 404.

4. "A Few Words from Mr. Remington," *Collier's Weekly*, March 18, 1905, in Peggy and Harold Samuels, *The Collected Writings of Frederic Remington*, p. 551 (hereafter cited as *Collected Writings*).

5. See *Two Men on a Beach* in the R. W. Norton Art Gallery catalogue *Frederic Remington (1861–1909)*, p. 53.

EX COLLECTION

Provenance unknown.

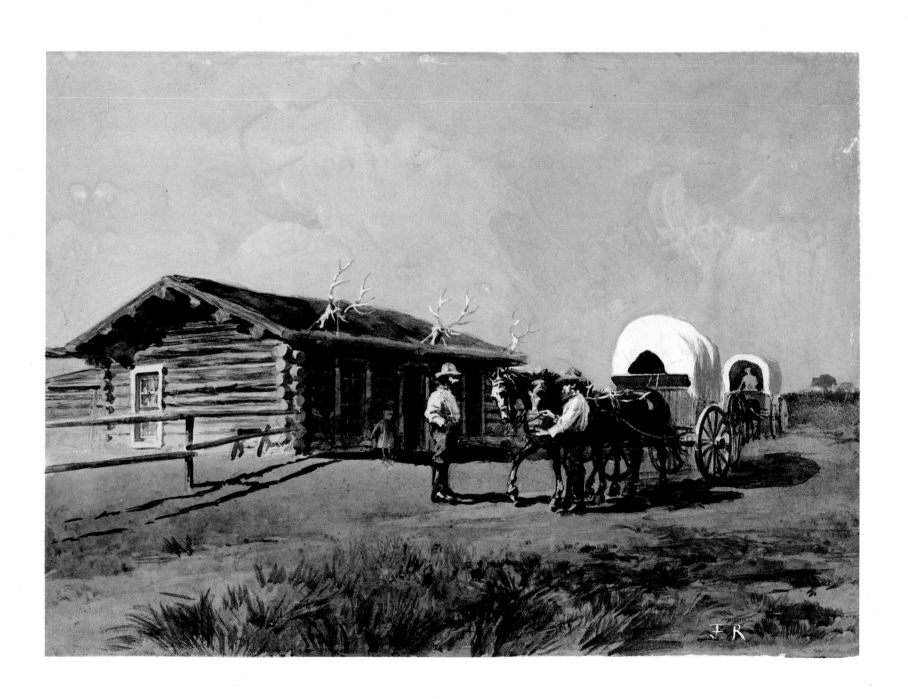

The Riderless Horse

1886   Pencil, pen and ink, and watercolor
on paper
8⅞ x 11⅞ in. (22.5 x 30.2 cm.)

Signed lower left: Frederic Remington.—del.;
inscription upper left: No. 1.; *lower left
(below signature):* sketch with K. Troop 10th
Cav. / mesa near Santa Catilenas [Catalinas]

Arizona 1886.—; *below:*—sand and dust.—;
at left:—brown and sorrele [*sic*] horse.—;
and titled lower right: "The riderless
horse."—

Because Frederic Remington was responsible
for so many vivid pictures of battles between
Indians and soldiers, the impression persists
that he drew on personal experience. In fact,
he was in Arizona in 1886 as a correspondent
for *Harper's Weekly* covering the Geronimo
campaign and did patrol with Company K of
the Tenth Cavalry, a black regiment, in the
Santa Catalinas Mountains north of Tucson
that June.[1] But he saw no action, and such
subjects as *The Riderless Horse* and the
sketch that follows, *The Ambushed Picket*,
were based upon imagination. A few years
later, Remington was on assignment in the
Dakotas during the Sioux campaign of 1890–
91, and he was near Wounded Knee Creek
when the fighting broke out on December 29,
1890, but he missed both the battle *and* the
burial of the dead there two days later. Since
Wounded Knee proved to be the curtain ringer
on almost three centuries of Indian warfare, it
is astonishing that Remington, who was so
keen on the subject, did not avail himself of
the opportunity to witness the denouement of
that sad affair. He was sensitive enough about
his absence to offer a string of limp excuses:

*Two days after [the battle at Wounded Knee]
I rode into the Pine Ridge agency, very hun-
gry and nearly frozen to death having ridden
. . . all night long. I had to look after a poor
horse, and see that he was groomed and fed
. . . Then came my breakfast. That struck me
as a serious matter at the time. There were
wagons and soldiers—the burial party going
to the Wounded Knee to do its solemn duty. I
wanted to go very much. I stopped to think;
in short, I hesitated, and of course was "lost,"
for after breakfast they had gone. Why did I
not follow them? Well, my natural prudence
had been considerably strengthened a few
days previously by a half-hour's interview
with six painted Brulé Sioux who seemed to
be in command of the situation. To briefly
end the matter, the burial party was fired on,
and my confidence in my own good judgment was vindicated . . .*

Instead, Remington rode over to the camp of
the Seventh Cavalry and listened to the of-

ficers and men tell their stories "in that
inimitable way which is studied art with warriors."[2] This close brush with reality did
nothing to dampen Remington's martial ar-
dor. Through the 1890s he continued to han-
ker after a *real* war—in Europe, if need be, or
in Cuba, where he hoped for "a big murder-
ing" until it actually came and he was on
hand to see it.[3] Sickened, he returned home
aware of the distance between his heroic
dreams and war's reality and content thereafter to let armies do their clashing on the field
of his imagination.

The Riderless Horse appeared as one of
thirteen pen drawings collectively titled
Types from Arizona and published in *Harper's Weekly*, August 21, 1886. In it, the cavalryman's head is slightly ducked, suggesting
that he is escaping under fire.

NOTES

1. Peter H. Hassrick, *Frederic Remington: Paintings, Drawings, and Sculpture in The Amon Carter
Museum and The Sid W. Richardson Foundation
Collections*, p. 43.
2. Frederic Remington, "The Sioux Outbreak in
South Dakota," *Harper's Weekly*, January 24, 1891,
in *Collected Writings*, p. 67. Remington, it should
be noted, did a wash drawing of the battle of
Wounded Knee that some have mistaken for an eye-
witness sketch.
3. Frederic Remington to Owen Wister, [June
1898], in Vorpahl, *My Dear Wister*—, p. 233.

EX COLLECTION

Newhouse Galleries, New York City; Samuel H.
Rosenthal, Jr., Los Angeles.

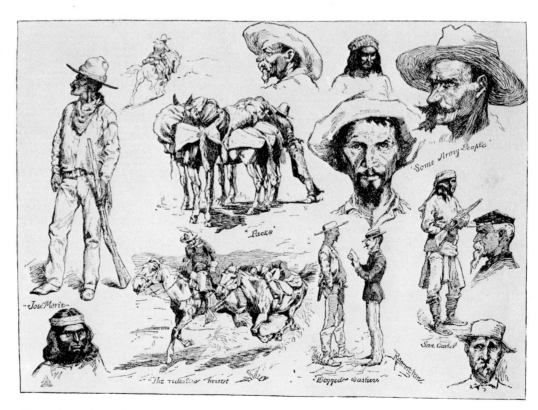

Types from Arizona
Harper's Weekly, August 21, 1886

No. 1.

Frederic Remington - del.

Sketch with K. Troop 10th Cav.
mesa near Santa Catilinas. Arizona 1886.
— brown and sorrel horse. —
— sand and dust. —

"The riderless horse."

The Ambushed Picket

1886 Pencil, pen and ink, and watercolor
on paper
9 x 11⅞ in. (22.8 x 30.2 cm.)

Signed lower left: Frederic Remington del—; *inscription upper left:* No. 2; *lower left (below signature):* "The ambushed picket" / Arizona 1886—; *and lower right:* —please return the sketches—; *below:* dust—mesquit[e]:—foot caught in stir[r]up—horse reins caught in saddle gear / carbine draggin[g] from sling.—

The Ambushed Picket, like *The Riderless Horse*, illustrates the potential danger in Indian fighting, not an actual incident witnessed by Remington. In a note accompanying a related painting published in 1893, *The Advance-Guard, or the Military Sacrifice*, Remington wrote: ". . . when the vidette ranges out in front and flank he is at the mercy of his pot-hunting foe. . . . I remember to have seen two young negroes of the Ninth Cavalry go down a nasty defile commanded by a thousand points, when they had no more chance to escape than poor shooting would afford. The Sixth Cavalry did lots of 'Bad Land scouting' in the last Sioux outbreak, and from an impression I received there I got my picture, though I did not see a man killed."[1] This statement suggests the kind of liberties that Remington, as an illustrator, routinely took with fact. He probably submitted several drawings to *Harper's Weekly* in 1886 similar to *The Riderless Horse* and *The Ambushed Picket* representing dramatic moments in the Geronimo campaign. The *Weekly* for May 29 that year carried a major composition by T. de Thulstrup based on a Remington sketch. Titled *Shot on Picket*, it showed a party of cavalrymen and scouts galloping past the body of a trooper as his horse stands forlornly by. *The Ambushed Picket* was reworked—especially the fallen soldier—and published in the June 8, 1889 *Weekly*. Subjects such as these, full of violent, pounding action, captivated the public and established Remington as the premier western illustrator of his day.

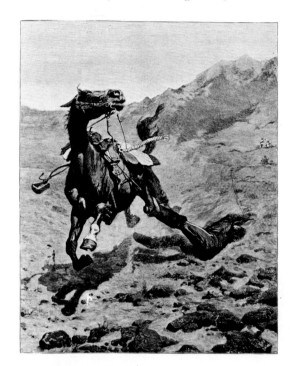

The Ambushed Picket
Harper's Weekly, June 8, 1889

NOTES

1. Frederic Remington, "The Advance-Guard, or the Military Sacrifice," *Harper's Weekly*, September 16, 1893, in *Collected Writings*, p. 109. In a letter of December 1, 1899, to the publisher of *Harper's Weekly*, Remington noted that he *"faked"* one of his Cuban war illustrations, "having lost my sketch book & having no photograph at the time"—a statement that raises not only the issue of invention in his illustrative work but also the whole, thorny question of his use of photographs. We are brought back to the simple reality that only a portion—and perhaps a small portion at that—of Remington's entire artistic output was based on firsthand observation. See Jussim, *Visual Communication and the Graphic Arts*, chap. 7, for the Remington letter to *Harper's Weekly* and the argument that "Remington's career was essentially that of an intermediary between photography from Nature and the printed page."

EX COLLECTION

Newhouse Galleries, New York City; Samuel H. Rosenthal, Jr., Los Angeles.

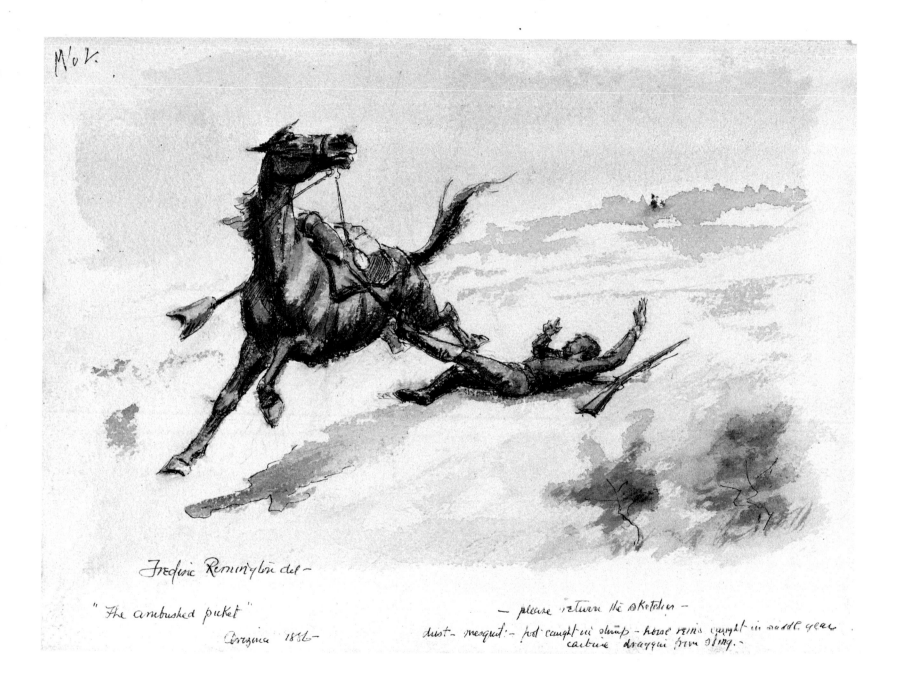

Ms 2.

Fredric Remington del —

"The ambushed picket"
      Arizona 1886 —

— please return the sketches —

dust — mesquit — foot caught in stirrup — horse reins caught in saddle gear
          carbine dragging from sling. —

The Sentinel

1889   Oil on canvas
34 x 49 in. (86.3 x 124.4 cm.)

Signed lower right: FREDERIC REMINGTON. / '89

In several of his major oil paintings, Remington pulled together elements from his field sketches. His early works were as literal and linear as the drawings themselves, though he occasionally made dramatic compositions out of fairly mundane materials. Some routine camp scenes recorded while on patrol with the cavalry, for example, are charged with interest when Remington adds a scout delivering his report to the officers over breakfast. The viewer is left to conclude that a day which has begun like so many others for the cavalrymen in the picture will not end without some dramatic development: there is action in the offing.[1]

The Sentinel was painted in 1889, a year in which Remington made one of his periodic forays into Mexico on assignment for *Harper's Weekly*. But its inspiration was a trip to the Southwest three years earlier that took him through Colorado, Arizona, and New Mexico into Mexico.[2] In the deserts of southern Arizona, Remington sketched the Papagos, a peaceful people long under the sway of the Spaniards and Mexicans. They had no enemies apart from the Apaches, who were a constant menace, and outside the mission at San Xavier a mounted Papago kept vigil. Remington published a sheet of twelve drawings, *Sketches among the Papagos of San Xavier*, in *Harper's Weekly* for April 2, 1887, and combined three of them—a Papago home, the mission proper, and the Apache guard—in this striking oil.

NOTES

1. The painting referred to is *A Cavalryman's Breakfast on the Plains* (c. 1890; Amon Carter Museum of Western Art, Fort Worth); one of its sources is discussed and illustrated in "Remington Metamorphosis," *American Heritage* 26 (October 1975): 103.
2. Hassrick, *Frederic Remington*, pp. 72, 22.

EX COLLECTION

Newhouse Galleries, New York City; John Levy, New York City.

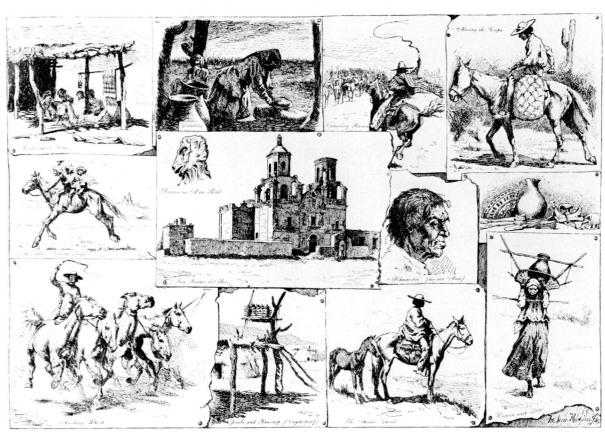

Sketches among the Papagos of San Xavier
Harper's Weekly, April 2, 1887

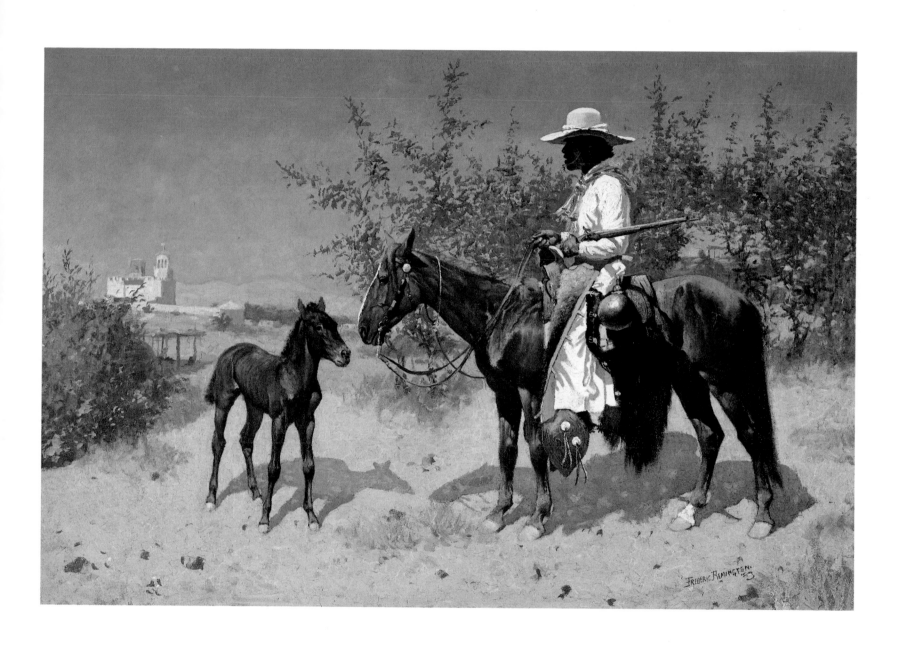

Self-Portrait on a Horse

c. 1890   Oil on canvas
29³⁄₁₆ x 19³⁄₈ in. (74.0 x 48.8 cm.)

Signed lower left: FREDERIC REMINGTON—

In paint and prose Remington paid enduring tribute to his ideal, the wasp-waisted officers and men of the United States Army. He "loved the soldiers," a friend recalled, but was respectful of the distinction between a civilian like himself and the professional fighting man.[1] While he rode with the cavalry, reported on military exercises, equipment, and trivia, and was proud to be an honorary member of several officers' messes—and while he noisily clamored for the sight and smell of real combat throughout the 1890s—he never forgot that soldiers wore uniforms and he did not. Thus, when he came to paint himself into the West he was immortalizing, it was as a cowboy that he showed himself. He never worked as one, though some of his contemporaries assumed that he had. He did, however, claim to know "that gentleman to his characters end."[2] Cowboys "possess a quality of sturdy, sterling manhood which would be to the credit of men in any walk of life," he wrote in 1899, adding, "I wish that the manhood of the cow-boy might come more into fashion further East."[3] This feeling helps to explain the cowboy garb: his self-portrait is a study in self-fulfillment, the easterner become hardy westerner. Asked about the audience for his art, Remington replied in 1903: "Boys—boys between twelve and seventy . . ."[4] Here, in his only full-fledged self-portrait, we have a boy of nearly thirty, dressed up as a cowboy on a white horse under one of those skies that are not cloudy all day. Youthful fantasies, that smug face tells us, *can* be realized.

NOTES

1. Augustus Thomas, "Recollections of Frederic Remington," *Century Magazine* 86 (July 1913): 354.
2. Frederic Remington to Francis Parkman, January 9, 1892, in Wilbur R. Jacobs, ed., *Letters of Francis Parkman*, II, 254.
3. Frederic Remington, "Life in the Cattle Country," *Collier's Weekly*, August 26, 1899, in *Collected Writings*, p. 388. Earlier, in "A Rodeo at Los Ojos," *Harper's New Monthly Magazine*, March 1894, he wrote of cowboys: ". . . these natural men possess minds which, though lacking all embellishment, are chaste and simple, and utterly devoid of a certain flippancy which passes for smartness in situations where life is not so real. . . . They are not complicated, these children of nature, and they never think one thing and say another" (*Collected Writings*, pp. 136–137).
4. Edwin Wildman, "Frederic Remington, the Man," *Outing* 41 (March 1903): 716.

EX COLLECTION

E. L. Dempsey, New York City.

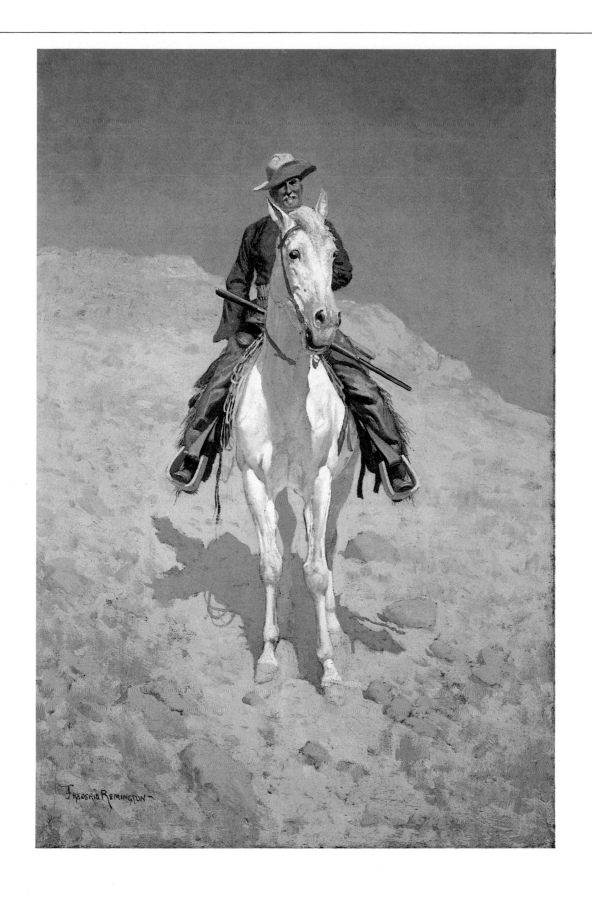

His Last Stand

c. 1890   Oil on canvas
25 ¼ x 29 ¼ in. (64.1 x 74.3 cm.)

Signed lower right: FREDERIC REMINGTON—

In a letter to Owen Wister, Remington confessed to some difficulty with an illustrating assignment involving a musk-ox. "I'm d——if you can imagine how little I know about musk-ox when you get down to brass tacks," he quipped.[1] He might have added that bears also remained a mystery to him. He sketched and painted his share of them over the years but never quite got the hang of bear anatomy. He was of the opinion that "a grizzly can run downhill quicker than a horse," and his bruins were always built to gallop, with legs as long as a thoroughbred's.[2]

His Last Stand shows the climax to a bear hunt on the range. The swarming, yelping dogs have brought their exhausted quarry to bay, and the cowboys, with all due respect for the bear's fearsome reputation, are moving in for the kill. The foreground rider, his rifle at ready, his horse registering the tension of the moment, was distinctive enough to be singled out and repainted by John Scott for use in the Marlin Fire Arms Company's 1900 catalogue. Known as *Danger Ahead*, Scott's copy still serves as Marlin's logo.[3]

NOTES

1. Frederic Remington to Owen Wister, [late October 1895], in Vorpahl, *My Dear Wister*—, p. 168. For those who would care to examine his effort, Remington's *Musk-Ox at Bay* appeared in *Harper's New Monthly Magazine* 92 (April 1896): 730.

2. Frederic Remington, "Bear-Chasing in the Rocky Mountains," *Harper's New Monthly Magazine*, July 1895, in *Collected Writings*, p. 202.

3. *Marlin Guns for 1963*, p. 19; Hassrick, *Frederic Remington*, p. 117, which illustrates the Scott copy.

EX COLLECTION

Newhouse Galleries, New York City; John Douthitt, New York City.

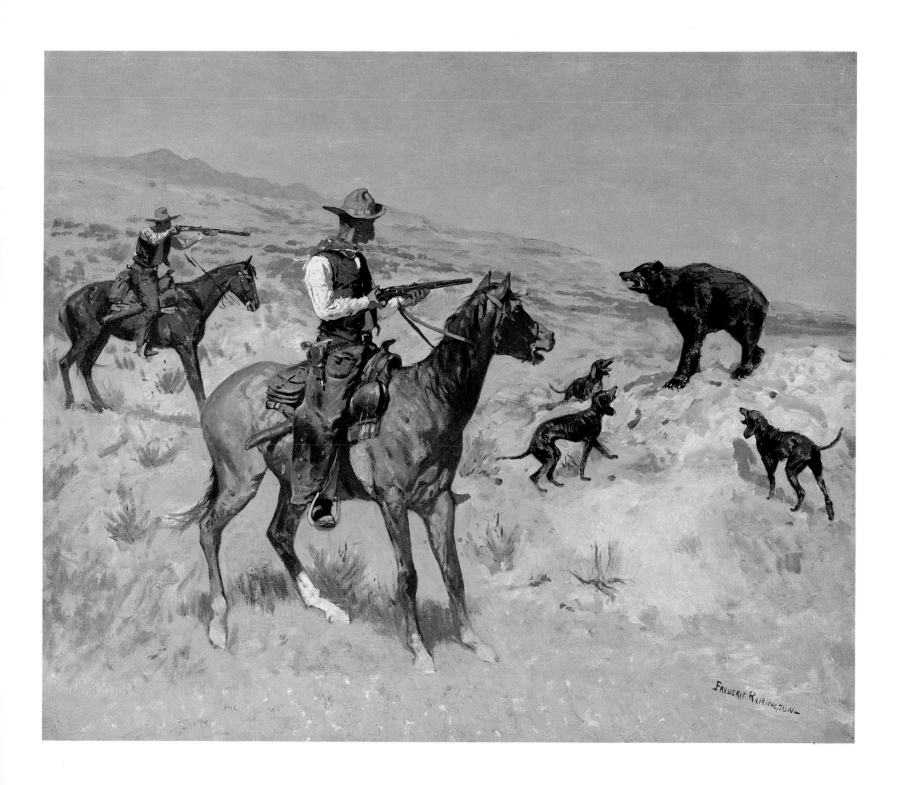

The Courrier [*sic*] du Bois and the Savage

1891   Oil (black and white) on canvas
23⅞ x 35¾ in. (60.6 x 90.8 cm.)

Signed lower right: FREDERIC REMINGTON

The fur trade was a business proposition. It involved Indian and white in what both considered a mutually beneficial partnership, symbolized by the handshake that spans racial and cultural barriers in Remington's *The Courrier* [sic] *du Bois and the Savage.* This black-and-white oil illustrated an article by Julian Ralph narrating the early history of the Hudson's Bay Company in the Canadian Northwest. Before the Bay men, Ralph wrote, were "the French, from the Canadas": "They were of hardy, adventurous stock, and they loved the free-roving life of the trapper and hunter. Fitted out by the merchants of Canada, they would pursue the waterways which there cut up the wilderness in every direction, their canoes laden with goods to tempt the savages, and their guns or traps forming part of their burden. They would be gone the greater part of a year, and always returned with a store of furs to be converted into money, which was, in turn, dissipated in the cities with devil-may-care jollity. These were the *courriers du bois* [*coureurs de bois*] . . ."[1] There was no delicacy to Remington's touch in his illustration, just a thoroughly professional job of depicting something that antedated his personal western experience (here by two centuries) but always fascinated him, the fur trade.

Remington was known for his unsparing realism. It led to mixed results in his first major book assignment, a new edition of Henry Wadsworth Longfellow's beloved epic *Hiawatha,* in 1890. Remington was not in entire sympathy with the poem's spirit, though contemporaries thought his illustrations a cut above the usual noble savage claptrap since

they were a compound of observation and imagination that *appeared* authentic. It was this same aura of knowing realism—nicely suggested in the details of costume and armament in *The Courrier* [sic] *du Bois and the Savage*—that first brought Remington's work to the attention of Francis Parkman and resulted in another, more satisfying commission to illustrate the 1892 edition of Parkman's classic account of western life in 1846, *The Oregon Trail.* A letter that Remington wrote Parkman at the time not only defined the approach he would take but also concisely summed up his credo as an illustrator: "I desire to symbolize the period of the Oregon Trail and I do not hope for your approval since it is impossible but if the men you made do not corospond [*sic*] with the men I make, it [is] their fault, not mine."[2]

NOTES

1. Julian Ralph, "A Skin for a Skin," *Harper's New Monthly Magazine* 84 (February 1892): 374–375. *The Courrier* [sic] *du Bois and the Savage* was reproduced full-page on p. 393.

2. Frederic Remington to Francis Parkman, January 9, 1892, in Jacobs, ed., *Letters of Francis Parkman,* II, 254–255.

EX COLLECTION

Newhouse Galleries, New York City; Arnold Seligman Ray & Company, New York City.

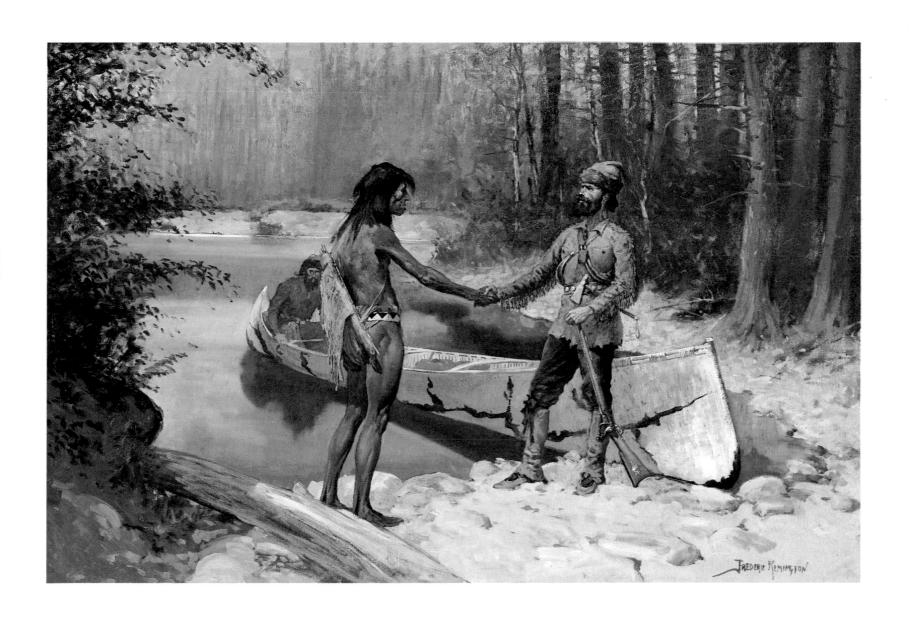

In a Stiff Current

1892   Oil (black and white) on canvas
24 x 36 in. (61.0 x 91.4 cm.)

Signed lower right: REMINGTON.

Canoeing, Remington wrote in 1896, "is my religion."[1] It was a passion that never lost its tang for him. Late in life, when his "elephantine bulk" ruled out horseback riding and made even a long hike taxing, Remington could still be found paddling his canoe near his summer home and studio, Ingleneuk, on Chippewa Bay in the St. Lawrence. The years and his excess poundage slipped away as he headed into the wind to tame the river's "white horses."[2] Canoeing was one of his last concessions to the "strenuous life" ethic, that masculine credo to which he had subscribed so noisily over the years. "Fie on this thing called contentment! . . . it properly only belongs to Florida negroes and house-dogs," he had asserted in 1895.[3] Challenge was everything. "A real sportsman, of the nature-loving type, must go tramping or paddling or riding about over the waste places of the earth, with his dinner in his pocket. He is alive to the terrible strain of the 'carry' [portage], and to the quiet pipe when the day is done. . . . He is fighting a game battle with the elements, and they are remorseless. He may break his leg or lose his life in the tip-over which is imminent, but the fool is happy—let him die."[4]

Julian Ralph, a regular contributor to *Harper's*, was one of those who filled Remington's requirements for "a real sportsman," and their work frequently appeared together.[5] *In a Stiff Current* is an excellent example of Remington's mature technique as an illustrator. A fluent black-and-white oil, it accompanied an article by Ralph on life in the Canadian north woods where the Hudson's Bay Company was into its third century in the fur trade, and "the countless lakes of all sizes, the innumerable small streams, and the many great rivers . . . make waterways the roads, as canoes are the wagons, of the region."[6] Remington's picture shows a party of *voyageurs*, lineal descendants of the *coureurs de bois* according to Ralph, dressed in flannel shirts, corduroy trousers, and jaunty touques, battling their way upstream. It also illustrates a theme that Remington put into words a year later in an essay of his own on canoeing: "The morning comes too soon, and after you are packed up and the boat loaded, if you are in a bad part of the river you do this: you put away your pipe, and with a grimace and a shudder you step out into the river up to your neck and get wet. The morning is cold, and I, for one, would not allow a man who was perfectly dry to get into my boat, for fear he might have some trepidation about getting out promptly if the boat was 'hung up' on a rock . . ."[7] The professionals in *In a Stiff Current* are showing how it is done.

NOTES

1. Frederic Remington, "The Strange Days That Came to Jimmie Friday," *Harper's New Monthly Magazine*, August 1896, in *Collected Writings*, p. 227.

2. Perriton Maxwell, "Frederic Remington—Most Typical of American Artists," *Pearson's Magazine* 18 (October 1907): 397; Manley, *Some of Frederic Remington's North Country Associations*, p. 31. A journalist in 1903 wrote: "Remington and his canoe are inseparable. 'Best exercise on earth; feel my arm,' he says to the skeptical inlander" (Edwin Wildman, "Frederic Remington, the Man," *Outing* 41 [March 1903]: 713).

3. Frederic Remington, "Getting Hunters in Horse-Show Form," *Harper's Weekly*, November 16, 1895, in *Collected Writings*, p. 217.

4. Frederic Remington, "Black Water and Shallows," *Harper's New Monthly Magazine*, August 1893, in *Collected Writings*, p. 105.

5. See Remington's tribute "Julian Ralph," *Harper's Weekly*, February 24, 1894, in *Collected Writings*, pp. 130–131.

6. Julian Ralph, "Talking Musquash," *Harper's New Monthly Magazine* 84 (March 1892): 493. *In a Stiff Current* appeared as a full-page illustration, p. 499.

7. Remington, "Black Water and Shallows," in *Collected Writings*, pp. 107–108.

EX COLLECTION

Newhouse Galleries, New York City; Thomas E. Finger, New York City.

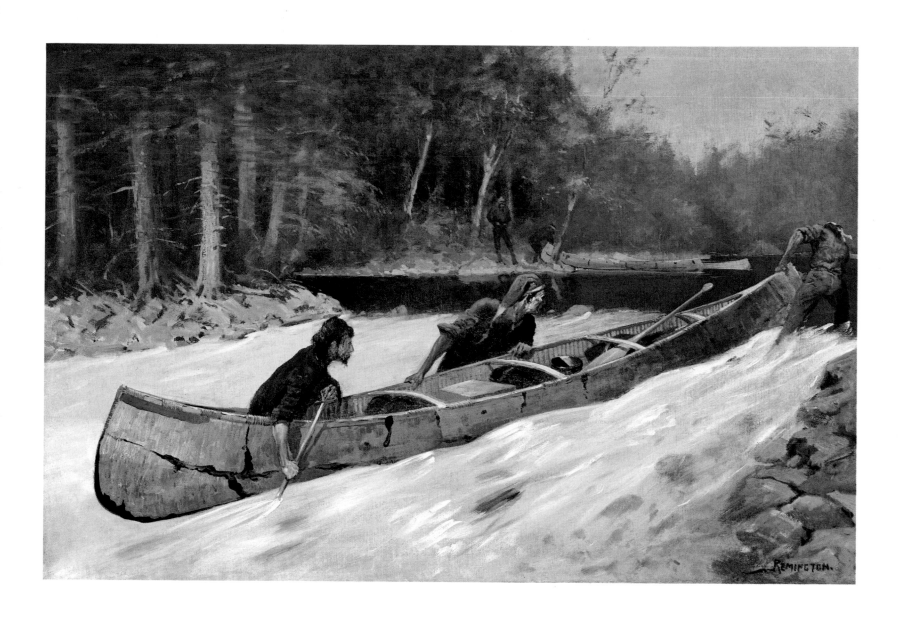

The Puncher

1895   Oil on canvas
24 x 20⅛ in. (60.9 x 51.1 cm.)

Signed lower right: Frederic Remington—;
inscription lower left: To my friend / H. Pyle

This well-painted figure study was executed as a return gift for one of Remington's friends, the celebrated and influential illustrator Howard Pyle (1835–1911). A painting by Pyle titled *Pirates Used to Do That to Their Captains Now and Then* had appeared in the November 1894 issue of *Harper's New Monthly Magazine* where it caught Remington's eye.[1] He ignored Pyle's other illustrations, including one showing Captain Kidd's men burying a treasure chest, in his excitement over the somber depiction of a dead pirate chief sprawled on a beach, his sightless eyes staring at the sky. "If I get that I will worship you, it, and once more take stock in humanity," he wrote Pyle. "As for what you will get—anything I have. I have nothing which is good in oil . . . I shall probably not paint until spring, but whatever you see of mine which suits your fancy, is yours." They eventually agreed on a different exchange—Pyle's dead pirate for a Remington cowboy to be done at some future date. "That's fair trade if I paint it well enough," Remington remarked, and *The Puncher* attests to the fact that he was sufficiently conscious of his own stature as a major American illustrator to be sure that he was represented by one of his best efforts.[2]

The trade seems a satisfying one: if cowboys were "gems" to Remington, pirates were pearls to Pyle.[3] Both men had lifted illustration in their chosen areas to the level of art, and both had indelibly impressed their personalities on the themes they made their own.

NOTES

1. In the same year, 1894, Remington illustrated a minimum of one article in every number of *Harper's New Monthly Magazine*, suggesting just how pre-eminent he was among the illustrators of the day. Only Pyle and a select few others ranked with him.

2. Frederic Remington to Howard Pyle, January 15 and undated, 1895, in Hassrick, *Frederic Remington*, p. 108.

3. Frederic Remington, "Cracker Cowboys of Florida," *Harper's New Monthly Magazine*, August 1895, in *Collected Writings*, p. 208.

EX COLLECTION

Newhouse Galleries, New York City; Walter Latendorf, New York City; Howard Pyle, Wilmington, Delaware.

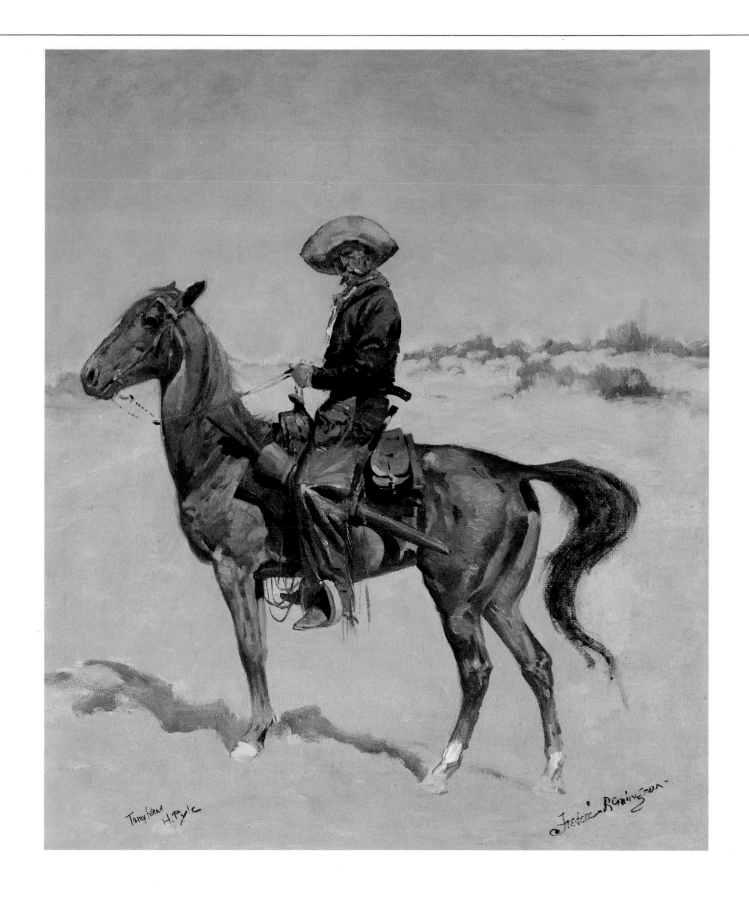

Captured

1899   Oil on canvas
27 x 40⅛ in. (68.6 x 101.9 cm.)

Signed lower left: Frederic Remington / '99

Indian captivity narratives constitute one of America's oldest literary genres. They were harrowing, first-person accounts of capture and sometimes torture, followed by escape (or, as the Puritans would have it, divine deliverance) and return to civil society. Artists were also captivated by the theme, and Remington was working in a venerable tradition when he painted *Captured* in 1899. It serves as a sequel to another oil done the same year, *Missing*, showing a party of plains Indians leading a soldier by a rope around his neck. His arms are bound behind him, and his captors' callousness is evident in the fact that he is afoot while they are riding. But the point of the picture is the trooper's stoicism. Faced with certain and horrifying death, he is a model of the soldierly qualities that Remington most admired: "grim, no emotion," exhibiting "a perfect mental calm."[1] Similarly, the prisoner in *Captured* appears undaunted by his situation. Stripped to his underwear and seated away from the fire on a cold, blustery day, he knows exactly what to expect from his blanket-wrapped captors. They are pitiless, unfeeling, beyond civilized understanding. Presumably they will torture him, though the lookout on the ledge behind and the still-saddled horses grazing on the slope indicate a close pursuit. If so, the deliberation around the fire and—if he is fortunate—the trooper as well will be short-lived. Remington's image of the Indian as unfathomable savage never found starker expression.[2]

NOTES

1. Frederic Remington, "Chicago under the Mob," *Harper's Weekly*, July 21, 1894, in *Collected Writings*, p. 154.

2. *Captured* is reminiscent of an 1885 painting by Henry F. Farny, *The Captive*, which was reproduced in the February 13, 1886, issue of *Harper's Weekly*. Remington broke into the *Weekly* in a big way that same year and doubtless saw and remembered Farny's striking depiction of a white man, clad only in chaps and boots, staked out on the prairie under the watchful eye of a blanket-draped warrior. See Peter Hassrick, *The Way West: Art of Frontier America*, pp. 194–195, for Farny's painting and the related Remington oil *Missing*, which is in the collection of the Thomas Gilcrease Institute at Tulsa, Oklahoma.

EX COLLECTION

Newhouse Galleries, New York City; Scott & Fowles, New York City; Robert Winthrop, New York City; Beekman Winthrop, Old Westbury, Long Island, New York; Robert Dudley Winthrop, Old Westbury, Long Island, New York.

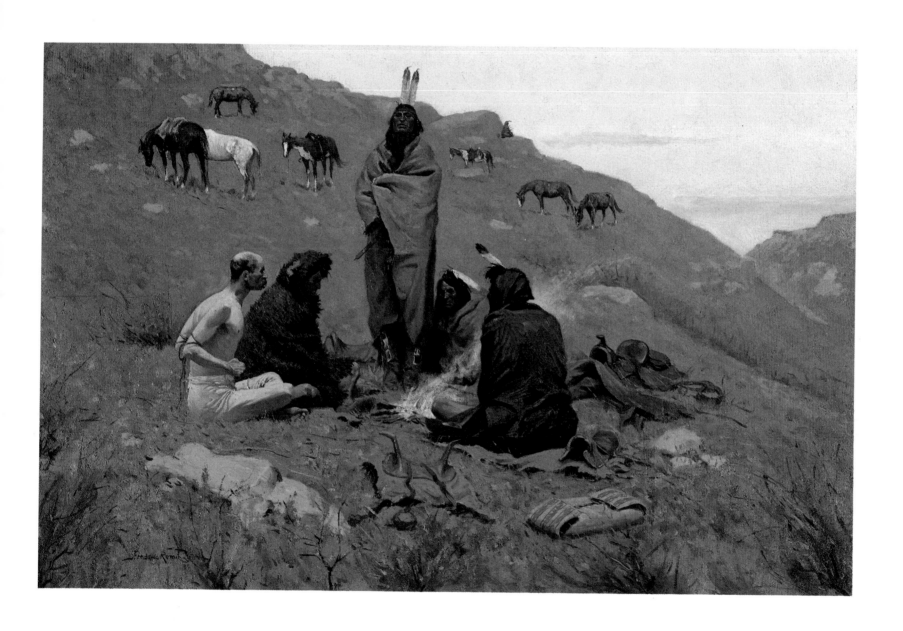

Rounded-Up

1901 Oil on canvas
25 x 48 in. (63.5 x 121.9 cm.)

Signed lower right: Frederic Remington— /
1901

Remington periodically returned to a theme that represented his version of grace under pressure: a group of mountain men, cowboys, or soldiers surrounded by circling Indians and confronting death without a hint of fear. Usually he showed a small party of men—five or six at the outside—facing overwhelming odds. One exception was his 1890 oil *The Last Stand*, which depicts a contingent of troopers and one prominent scout ensconced on a rocky hill. Though not a single Indian is seen, the whole composition melodramatically underlines the point that none of those brave men will escape alive.[1] *Rounded-Up*, painted eleven years later, is even more ambitious but somehow less satisfying. Full of action, it nevertheless seems placid. The colors are disconcertingly bright. Critics regularly complained about Remington's use of color, "a garishness not to be explained alone by the staccato effects of a landscape whelmed in a blaze of sunshine" that resulted in paintings "as hard as nails."[2] In *Rounded-Up* the vibrant hues and grating light might have added poignancy to the scene—men desperately battling for their lives on such a perfect day—were it not for the troopers' unaccountably passive response to their predicament. One can understand the officer standing erect, eyes shaded, his face an emotionless mask, unperturbed by the bullets whizzing by. This was a Remington ideal. But why the scouts would expose themselves in such a fashion is as inexplicable as the action is difficult to comprehend. The breastwork of horses in the foreground does not extend

around the troopers' formation—indeed, the led horses in the center of the ring are just where they should be in a routine dismounted maneuver. Since the officer and buckskin-clad scout are conferring, one can assume that they are pondering their options. But this is precisely where the painting seems least convincing on a purely narrative level. For the Indian foe, despite the numbers implied by the bullets kicking up dirt in the foreground, appears distant and unmenacing. Surely a determined show of force on the part of the soldiers would be more than enough to lift the siege. The plain is flat, the enemy visible—and the path of honor open and obvious. Perhaps the ambivalence in *Rounded-Up* mirrors Remington's own doubts following his first direct exposure to warfare in Cuba.[3]

Rounded-Up does evince the realism for which Remington was known and often reviled. N. C. Wyeth, as a young illustrator aspiring to capture the "sublime and mysterious quality" of the West, was initially appalled by Remington's concentration on "the brutal and gory side of it." But he soon modified his views. "Remington's show was fine," he wrote in 1904. "It was vital and powerful although most of his pictures were too gruesome to allow them to become living works of art. He's too insistent on showing mangled bodies, wounds, etc. Nevertheless the exhibition impresses you and convinces you that Remington had lived in that country and was telling something . . ."[4] Over the next few years Remington would almost completely abandon the literalism that offended his critics, and set himself the task of capturing the West's "sublime and mysterious quality" in paint.

NOTES

1. Originally reproduced as a double-page spread in *Harper's Weekly*, January 10, 1891, pp. 24–25, *The Last Stand* is now in the collection of the Woolaroc Museum at Bartlesville, Oklahoma.

2. Royal Cortissoz, "Frederic Remington: A Painter of American Life," *Scribner's Magazine* 47 (February 1910): 186.

3. Remington may have had misgivings himself about *Rounded-Up*. Before year's end he painted another last stand, *Caught in the Circle*, that was published as a two-page, full-color spread (his first) in *Collier's Weekly* for December 7, 1901. Sold separately as a print, it proved immensely popular. Its power resides in its simplicity: three troopers and a scout make a stand against circling Indians. This time there is no question of options. They are badly outnumbered and their horses are all down, precluding escape. All they can do is sell their lives dearly. The drama is clearcut and convincing.

4. N. C. Wyeth to his mother, November 29, 1903, and March 25, 1904, in Betsy James Wyeth, ed., *The Wyeths: The Letters of N. C. Wyeth, 1901–1945*, pp. 65, 79.

EX COLLECTION

Newhouse Galleries, New York City; Scott & Fowles, New York City; Robert Winthrop, New York City; Beekman Winthrop, Old Westbury, Long Island, New York; Robert Dudley Winthrop, Old Westbury, Long Island, New York.

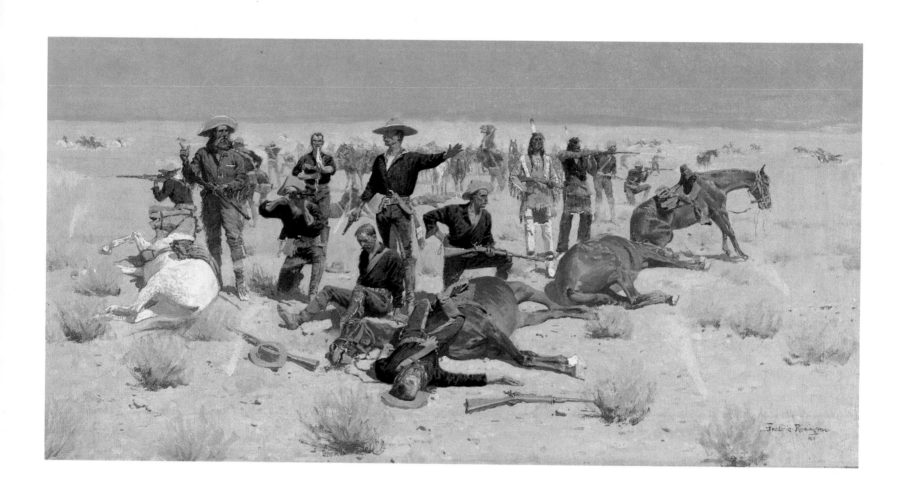

The Cow Puncher

1901   Oil (black and white) on canvas
28⅞ x 19 in. (73.3 x 48.3 cm.)

Signed lower right: Frederic Remington.

By 1900 Remington was given to mourning the passing of *his* West. A trip to Colorado late that autumn brought only disappointment. "Shall never come west again," he wrote his wife. "It is all brick buildings—derby hats and blue overhauls—it spoils my early illusions—and they are *my* capital."[1] It was in just such an elegiac mood that Remington painted his stirring black-and-white study *The Cow Puncher*. Horse and rider make a blatant bid for the viewer's attention as they come to a sliding halt in a cloud of dust before him. The cowboy, lean and unsmiling, is a figure of myth, and when *Collier's Weekly* for September 14, 1901, reproduced the painting it was with an accompanying poem by Owen Wister:

No more he rides, yon waif of might,
  His was the song the eagle sings,
Strong as the eagle's his delight,
  For like his rope, his heart had wings.

Subsequently, Wister modified his verse to bring it into line with Remington's intentions. Instead of a eulogy, it becomes a tribute to the cowboy's enduring appeal:

He rides the earth with hoofs of might,
  His is the song the eagle sings;
Strong as the eagle's, his delight,
  For like his rope, his heart hath wings.

And so the cowpuncher, a mythic figure from America's past, lingers on in the present.[2]

Peter Hassrick has commented on some of the flaws in this authentic-looking but fanciful portrayal of the cowboy: the floppy hat that has all but obscured his vision, the dragging loop, the awkward position of his left hand which ensures that his throwing hand will get tangled in the coil.[3] This might seem like nitpicking. But Remington had always prided himself on his accuracy, and it must have annoyed him to read in the same *Collier's Weekly* in 1908 Charlie Russell's laconic observation: "That fellow may be able to handle a rope with his quirt hanging on his right wrist while he's roping; but I never saw it done in real cow work myself."[4]

NOTES

  1. Frederic Remington to his wife, undated [November 18, 1900], in Hassrick, *Frederic Remington*, p. 39.
  2. Vorpahl, *My Dear Wister—*, p. 326.
  3. Hassrick, *Frederic Remington*, p. 128.
  4. "Pays Tribute to Russell," *Great Falls Daily Tribune*, December 26, 1908, p. 6, quoting an Emerson Hough article in *Collier's Weekly.*

EX COLLECTION

Newhouse Galleries, New York City.

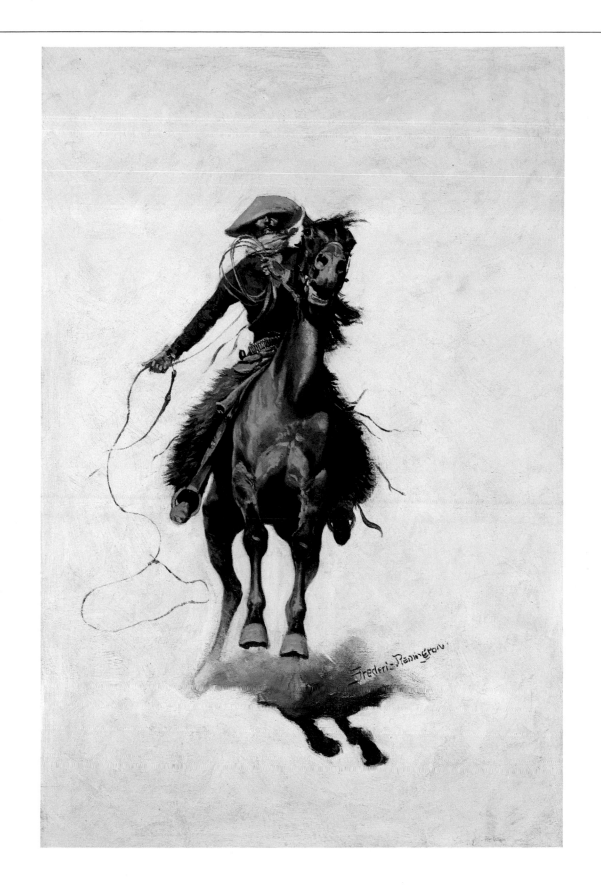

A Sioux Chief

1901   Pencil and pastel on composition
board
31⅞ x 22⅞ in. (81 x 58.1 cm.)

Signed lower right: Frederic Remington

While covering the Sioux campaign of
1890–91 for *Harper's*, Remington recorded a
few observations typical of his attitude at the
time: "I sat near the fire and looked intently
at one human brute [a Brulé Sioux] opposite, a
perfect animal, so far as I could see. Never
was there a face so replete with human de-
pravity, stolid, ferocious, arrogant, and all the
rest—ghost shirt, war-paint, feathers, and
arms. As a picture, perfect; as a reality, hor-
rible."[1] But the soldiers that Remington idol-
ized in turn expressed a "decided respect"[2] for
their plains Indian adversaries, and conventional army wisdom, which he eagerly absorbed, held that they were "naturally the
finest irregular cavalry on the face of this
globe."[3] The passage of time only confirmed
him in the view that plains warriors were
born to fight, not farm, and as the 1890s came
to an end he was prepared to give them their
due: "They were fighting for their land—they
fought to the death—they never gave quarter,
and they never asked it. There was a nobility
of purpose about their resistance which com-
mends itself now that it is passed."[4]

A Sioux Chief, one in a series of eight pas-
tels of western types that Remington published in 1901 as *A Bunch of Buckskins*, is
his tribute to the fighting Sioux. He essayed
the same pose in other single-figure studies—

notably *An Indian Trapper* (1889; Amon Carter Museum of Western Art, Fort Worth)—
though here the twist of the torso and un-
gainly angle of neck and head create a rather
awkward impression compounded by the
wind, which has flattened one side of his warbonnet. But the haughty arrogance that Remington detected a decade earlier is preserved
intact.

NOTES

1. Frederic Remington, "Lieutenant Casey's Last
Scout," *Harper's Weekly*, January 31, 1891, in *Collected Writings*, p. 75.
2. Frederic Remington, "Indians as Irregular Cavalry," *Harper's Weekly*, December 27, 1890, in *Collected Writings*, p. 59.
3. Frederic Remington, "Artist Wanderings
among the Cheyennes," *Century Magazine*, August
1889, in *Collected Writings*, p. 44. Also "Indians as
Irregular Cavalry" and *John Ermine of the Yellowstone* (1902), in *Collected Writings*, pp. 65, 512.
4. Frederic Remington, "How Stilwell Sold Out,"
Collier's Weekly, December 16, 1899, in *Collected
Writings*, p. 397.

EX COLLECTION

Newhouse Galleries, New York City.

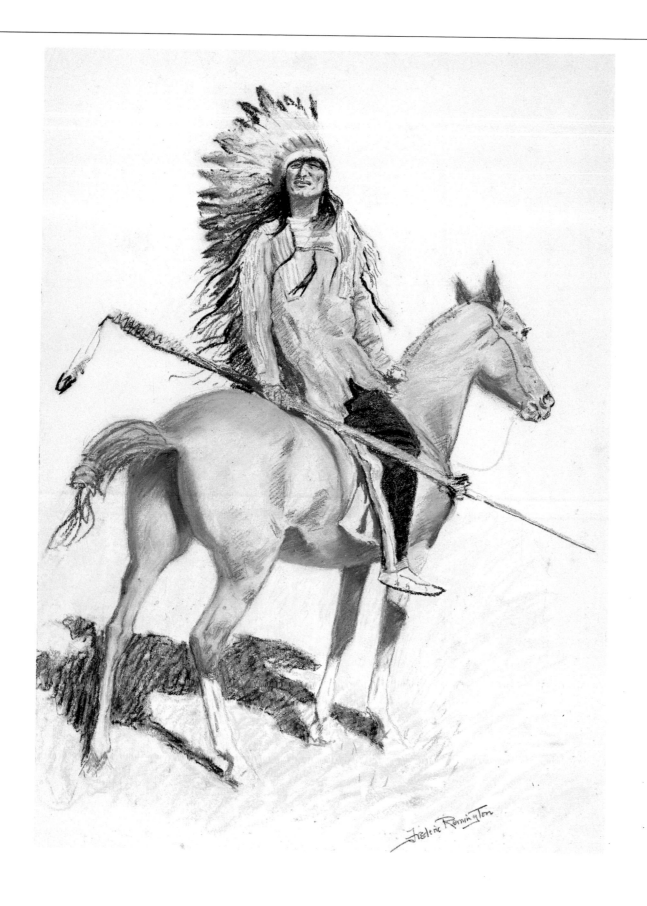

Frederic Remington

A Taint in the Wind

1906   Oil on canvas
27⅛ x 40 in. (68.9 x 101.6 cm.)

Signed lower right: Frederic Remington;
and base center: copyright 1906
by Frederic Remington

In dealing with subjects he knew at firsthand, Remington had always been a stickler for accuracy. When his novel *John Ermine of the Yellowstone* was being adapted for the stage in 1903, his voice was ever on the side of authenticity in costume and props.[1] That same year he charged into a public controversy by pronouncing a cavalry scene painted by New Jersey artist Charles Schreyvogel "half baked stuff" and listing his criticisms point by point.[2] Remington "is the most conscientious of historians," a critic wrote as late as 1907. "He has never 'faked' an action, a costume or an episode."[3] Of course this claim is absurd—even such early field sketches as *The Riderless Horse* and *The Ambushed Picket* were imaginary—but there is no doubt that Remington had always aimed at verisimilitude. However, as his artistry ripened in the twentieth century he abandoned the illustrator's concern with form, precision of line, and accuracy of detail to concentrate on light and color in his painting. His goals had changed, in short, and his later work cannot be judged by the same criteria as his earlier illustrations. The Schreyvogel controversy was a last hurrah; thereafter, Remington, who had always made pictures that conformed to his personal vision of the West, broke away from the literal and gave his imagination free rein. He particularly loved night scenes. Darkness concealed the mundane, while moonlight and shadow created instant drama.

A Taint in the Wind is redolent with tension as the spooked horses turn their heads toward some unseen peril lurking in the shadowy sagebrush outside the picture's borders. One could ask of Remington the illustrator why a coach traveling through dangerous country at night would have two lanterns lit, but Remington the artist had his reasons: he needed to build light sources into his night scenes—white horses, white hats, moonlight on dirt or snow. Here, without the lanterns, one could not see the startled reactions of the men on the coach or, for that matter, the coach itself. Thus accuracy is sacrificed to aesthetic considerations, and the result is a carefully integrated work of art.

Remington enjoyed such success with his nocturnals that they made up perhaps half of his output during his later years.[4] A friend noted that they were "keyed to the mute though not inglorious poet in him."[5] His study of nighttime light convinced him that the appropriate color range was browns and black on a field of greens—jades, mints, no tone was too daring. When a patron inquired about a nocturnal she had purchased in 1908, Remington briefly told its history, described the painting as an attempt "at that very elusive thing moonlight," and grandly concluded that he hoped she would "never be able quite to penetrate the mysteries of the technique which is the greatest charm of all painting."[6] While a friendly critic thought that Remington's stars looked stuck on,[7] and while the lanterns are thick blobs of white pigment suggesting some difficulty in making them stand out naturally, *A Taint in the Wind*, along with the other three nocturnals in the Richardson collection, represents Remington at his painterly best.

NOTES

1. See Remington's four undated (1903) letters to Louis Shipman, reproduced in *Frederic Remington (1861–1909)*, pp. 97–101.

2. See James D. Horan, *The Life and Art of Charles Schreyvogel: Painter-Historian of the Indian-Fighting Army of the American West*, pp. 31–40.

3. Perriton Maxwell, "Frederic Remington—Most Typical of American Artists," *Pearson's Magazine* 18 (October 1907): 399. Also Augustus Thomas, "Recollections of Frederic Remington," *Century Magazine* 86 (July 1913): 358: "Accuracy . . . was his religion. In his chosen field he abhorred anachronisms."

4. Hassrick, *Frederic Remington*, p. 41.

5. Thomas, "Recollections of Frederic Remington," p. 361.

6. Frederic Remington to Mrs. Greenway, December 11, 1908, in *"How the West Was Won": Paintings, Watercolors, Bronzes by Frederic Remington and Charles M. Russell, for the Benefit of the Hospital for Special Surgery*, no. 16. Remington was describing his oil *Scare in a Pack Train*.

7. Childe Hassam to Frederic Remington, December 20, 1906, in Hassrick, *Frederic Remington*, p. 159.

EX COLLECTION

Newhouse Galleries, New York City; Scott & Fowles, New York City; Robert Winthrop, New York City; Beekman Winthrop, Old Westbury, Long Island, New York; Robert Dudley Winthrop, Old Westbury, Long Island, New York; Grant B. Schley, New York City.

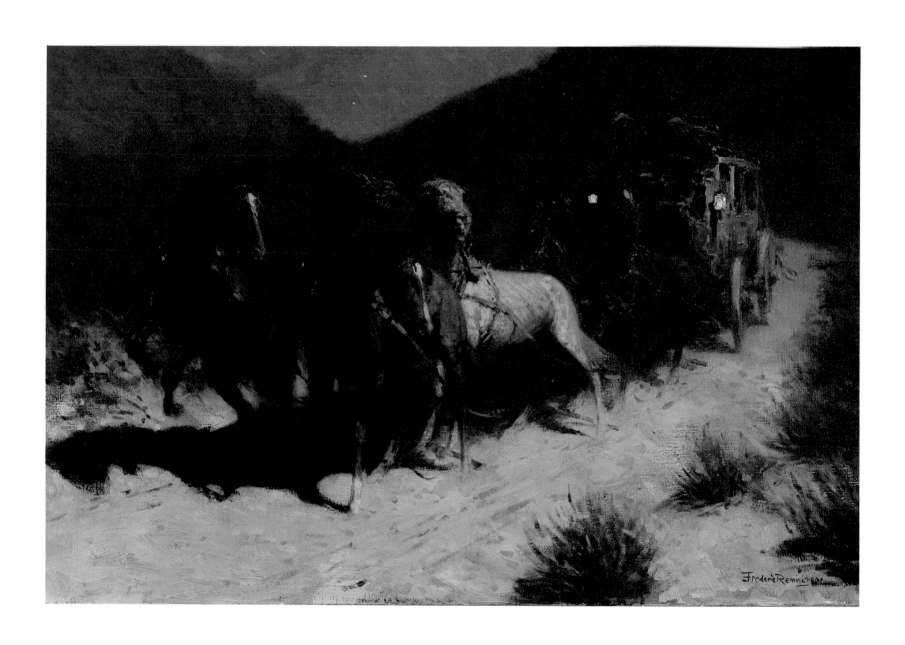

Apache Medicine Song

1908 Oil on canvas
27⅛ x 29⅞ in. (68.9 x 75.9 cm.)

Signed lower right: Frederic Remington / 1908

In *Apache Medicine Song* the campfire's glow provides orange highlights in a sea of greens and browns, while deep shadows fringe the picture. The flickering light plays over the faces of the chanting warriors, distorting their features. The effect is demonlike and chilling, as though the men are congregated about the fire to cast an evil spell. Back in 1888, on a journalistic assignment for *Century Magazine*, Remington had witnessed this scene on the San Carlos Reservation:

It grew dark . . . Presently, as though to complete the strangeness of the situation, the measured "thump, thump, thump" of the tom-tom came from the vicinity of a fire some short distance away. One wild voice raised itself in strange discordant sounds, dropped low, and then rose again, swelling into shrill yelps, in which others joined. . . . We drew nearer, and by the little flickering light of the fire discerned half-naked forms huddled with uplifted faces in a small circle around the tom-tom. The fire cut queer lights on their rugged outlines, the waves of sound rose and fell, and the "thump, thump, thump, thump" of the tom-tom kept a binding time.

We grew in sympathy with the strange concert, and sat down some distance off and listened for hours. . . .

The performers were engaged in making medicine for the growing crops, and the concert was a religious rite, which, however crude to us, was entered into with a faith that was attested by the vigor of the performance.[1]

As an illustrator, Remington had always been attracted to campfire scenes. (The compositional precedent for *Apache Medicine Song*, oddly enough, was a sketch he made during the 1890–91 Sioux campaign, *Troopers Singing the Indian Medicine Song*, which appeared in the December 6, 1890, issue of *Harper's Weekly*.) But it was in his late, impressionistic phase that he fully realized the dramatic potential of firelight. A critic who was struck by the "extraordinary variation

. . . of light flooding canvas after canvas" in Remington's 1908 show at M. Knoedler and Company in New York, singled out for praise an oil "in which the flaunting wind-blown camp fire breaks the blackness of night and opens spaces in the dark for fear, or sorrow, or revenge to show on the faces of the men about the fire."[2] This effect was only one of several that Remington perfected in the burst of creative energy that marked the last years of his life.

NOTES

1. Frederic Remington, "On the Indian Reservations," *Century Magazine*, July 1889, in *Collected Writings*, pp. 34–35. Interestingly, Remington did not illustrate this vivid passage in his *Century* essay but instead showed a group of Apaches playing monte by the light of a lantern! However, he did do a sketch a few years later, *Apache Signal Fire* (*Century Magazine* 41 [March 1891]: 655), that includes a squatting figure much like the warrior seated second from the right in *Apache Medicine Song*.

2. Giles Edgerton, "Frederic Remington, Painter and Sculptor: A Pioneer in Distinctive American Art," *Craftsman* 15 (March 1909): 669.

EX COLLECTION

Newhouse Galleries, New York City; Scott & Fowles, New York City; Robert Winthrop, New York City; Beekman Winthrop, Old Westbury, Long Island, New York; Robert Dudley Winthrop, Old Westbury, Long Island, New York.

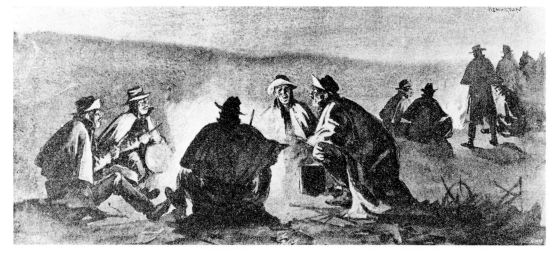

Troopers Singing the Indian Medicine Song
Harper's Weekly, December 6, 1890

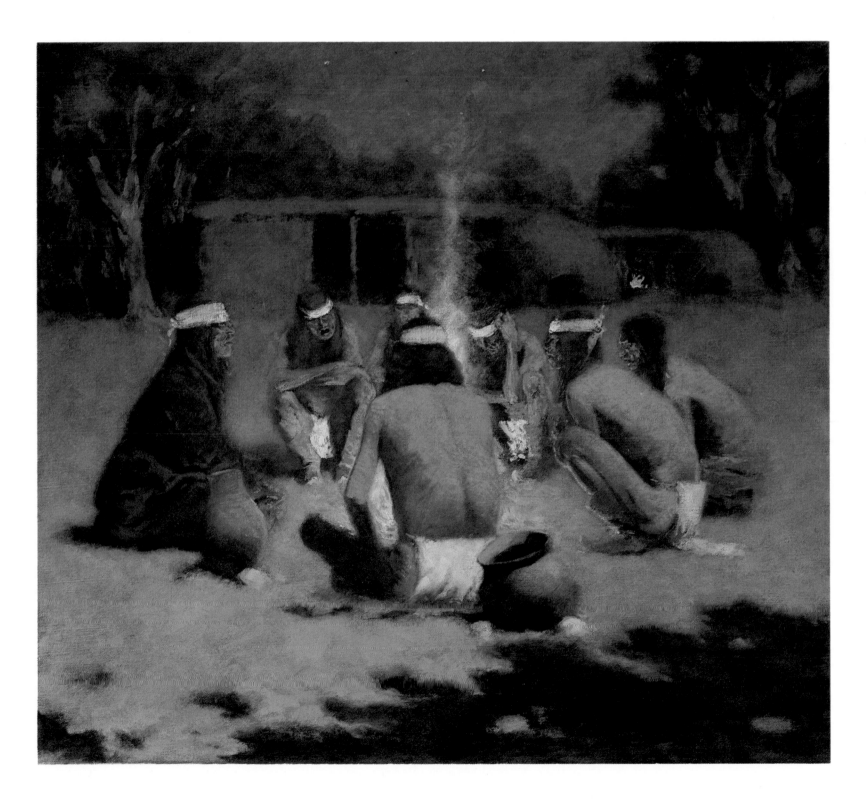

The Unknown Explorers

1908   Oil on canvas
30 x 27¼ in. (76.2 x 69.2 cm.)

Signed lower right:
Frederic Remington / 1908—

Because mountain men carried such a burden of the West's romantic tradition for Remington, he always thought of them as grey-bearded old-timers. But trapping was a young man's occupation, a high-risk first career for those who survived. (The violent mortality rate among one sample of 446 mountain men active between 1805 and 1845 was 40 percent!)[1] Jedediah Smith was a retired veteran who had survived two major Indian fights, explored routes from Salt Lake to Los Angeles and from the Sacramento to the Columbia, and been in business himself when he was killed by Comanches in 1831 while guiding a wagon train to Santa Fe. Smith was only thirty-two years old.[2] So much living crammed into so few years—then, like the frontier, the mountain men had vanished in a twinkling. Remington confessed that they were *passé* before he ever went west, but he was sure they all looked much alike.[3] A photograph of Jim Bridger elicited this response: "I had thought there could be no such thing in existence. He was the real old mountain type however by his picture. Those fellows all had a strong family resemblance—didnt they."[4] When Francis Parkman disappointed his expectations by sending him a photograph of a young, smooth-faced mountain man of his acquaintance in 1846, Henry Chatillon, to aid in preparing the illustrations for *The Oregon Trail*, Remington replied: "H.C.—does not look at all as he should according to my mind—people never do. He looks like a Boston fisherman and not like a wild horseman of the American desert—I take it he did not shave in the mountains. I shall take liberties with H.C. which the good soul would resent were he alive."[5] Remington was given to painting "types" anyway—a standard army officer, a standard cowboy—so it was natural that in dealing with one he had never seen he would draw upon his own imagination. This tendency did not escape notice. "I don't like him or his illustrations," Hamlin Garland wrote. "His red men and trappers are all drawn from one model. All his trappers have close-set eyes and bushy beards, and his red men are savages without being graceful. He does not see the Western men and Indians as I see them."[6]

But in *The Unknown Explorers* Remington rose above stereotyping. A few years before he had painted an oil of identical title. The figures were similar, but the lighting was not, and therein lay the difference.[7] A critic who attended Remington's 1908 exhibition observed that "above and beyond all his extraordinary presentation of the people and their picturesque existence is the absolute quality of the West itself,—the bronze of the day, the green of the twilight, the wind that stifles, the sun that blinds, the prairies that glisten and quiver with thirst, water that is a mockery, and storms that are born and vanish in the sky. And each phase of this marvelous country expressed through a medium so fluid, so flexible, so finally sympathetic that you become unconscious of it as was the artist himself when he painted."[8] *The Unknown Explorers* is itself an exploration in sunlight and shadow. During the 1890–91 winter expedition against the Sioux in Dakota, Remington described "the tangled masses of the famous Bad Lands—seamed and serrated, gray here, the golden sunset flashing there, with dark recesses giving back a frightful gloom—a place for stratagem and murder . . ."[9] In this painting, the point of view is reversed: the men emerge from a shadowy defile into dazzling sunlight. But the emotion of riding into the unknown is effectively conveyed by the very glare of the sun, so harsh that it temporarily blinds the mountain men. A world of unseen perils is opening up before them. In an 1897 letter to a pioneer who, unlike him, "dated back," Remington made some relevant comments: "I read your passage of the desert with gusto and have often wondered in riding New Mex. & Arizona how the devil the pioneers ever got over that country having no knowledge of the water. I suppose lots of them didn't as a matter of fact."[10] From the alert posture and self-assured expressions on the faces of his "unknown explorers," one can conclude that locating the next waterhole will be the least of their worries.

NOTES

1. William H. Goetzmann, "The Mountain Man as Jacksonian Man," *American Quarterly* 15 (Fall 1963): 408–409.

2. Remington did an oil painting titled *Jedediah Smith*, which appeared in *Collier's Weekly* for July 14, 1906. It showed Smith as one of his typical bearded mountain men of indeterminate but presumably advanced age.

3. Frederic Remington to Francis Parkman, January 9, 1892, in Jacobs, ed., *Letters of Francis Parkman*, II, 254.

4. Frederic Remington to John B. Colton, December 11, 1899, in the Huntington Library, San Marino, California (JA 806). Colton also supplied Remington with photographs of Kit Carson and Jim Baker ("He was a great type—wasn't he?" Remington replied on December 26, 1899 [JA 807]). When Remington sketched Bridger (*Outing*, November 1887), he showed him as the usual buckskin-clad, white-bearded old mountain type; it is unlikely that any photograph would change his impression.

5. Remington to Parkman, January 13, 1892, in Jacobs, ed., *Letters of Francis Parkman*, II, 255. Parkman, it should be noted, approved the liberties that Remington took, writing him on February 23, 1892: "The pictures are admirable. You have rendered the 'Mountain Man' type perfectly. . . . H. Chatillon, if he were alive, would have every reason to be pleased with his image" (p. 256).

6. Hamlin Garland, *Roadside Meetings*, p. 394.

7. See Hassrick, *Frederic Remington*, pp. 160–161, for discussion and illustration of the two versions.

8. Giles Edgerton, "Frederic Remington, Painter and Sculptor: A Pioneer in Distinctive American Art," *Craftsman* 15 (March 1909): 669.

9. Frederic Remington, "Lieutenant Casey's Last Scout," *Harper's Weekly*, January 31, 1891, in *Collected Writings*, p. 71.

10. Remington to Colton, April 22, 1897, Huntington Library (JA 804).

EX COLLECTION

Newhouse Galleries, New York City; Scott & Fowles, New York City; Robert Winthrop, New York City; Beekman Winthrop, Old Westbury, Long Island, New York; Robert Dudley Winthrop, Old Westbury, Long Island, New York.

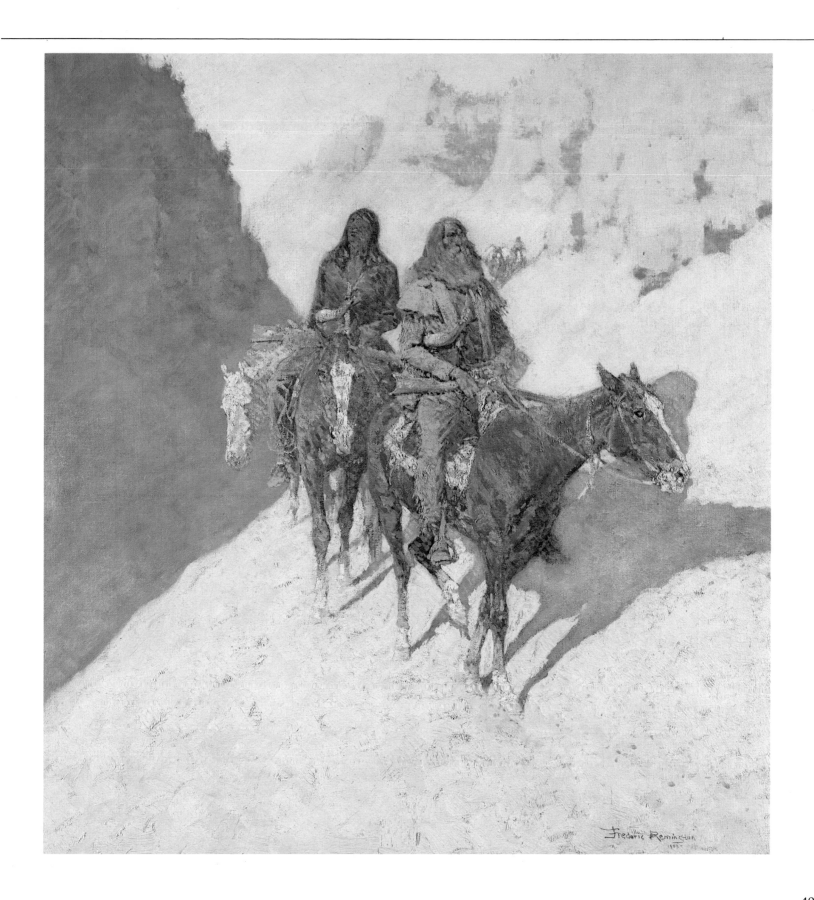

The Sentinel

1908   Oil on canvas
30 x 21⅛ in. (76.2 x 53.6 cm.)

Signed lower right: Frederic Remington /
1908—; *and base center:* copyright 1908
by Frederic Remington—

"Big art is a process of elimination," Remington explained to a friend in 1902. "Cut down and out—do your hardest work outside the picture, and let your audience take away something to think about—to imagine. . . . What you want to do is to just create the thought—materialize the spirit of a thing, and the small bronze—or the impressionist's picture—does that; then your audience discovers the thing you held back, and that's skill."[1] It was a long statement for a man not usually given to overt analysis of his craft, but it reflected the self-conscious direction that Remington's art had taken after 1900. At one time it had seemed to him enough to "observe the things in nature which captivate your fancy and above all draw—draw—draw—and always from nature. Do not try to make pictures. When you are studying—do the thing simply and just as you see it—use india ink—crayon or some broad medium at first—then color either water or oil . . ."[2] But as he experimented with his own technique his naturalistic credo faded. Art, instead of being a direct statement, was supposed to be an enticement, actively involving the viewer in the search for its meaning.

The Sentinel is a case in point. Its story line is so cryptic that one can see the solitary rider as a lookout, camouflaged by the trees around him, or as a forerunner to "the luckless hunter" Remington painted the next year, returning home after a wearying day with nothing to show for his efforts. He is no typical Remington warrior. His round, soft face wears a timorous expression. Perhaps he is a boy doing a man's job. The shadows on the snow and the dark woods behind encircle him like the jaws of a giant trap. There is imminent danger here, though from *what* is left to the viewer's imagination. Instead of being a picture in paint, *The Sentinel* is a painting. By 1908 Remington thought that the distinction was everything.

NOTES

1. Edwin Wildman, "Frederic Remington, the Man," *Outing* 41 (March 1903): 715–716.
2. Frederic Remington to Maynard Dixon, September 3, 1891, in Wesley M. Burnside, *Maynard Dixon: Artist of the West*, p. 215.

EX COLLECTION

Newhouse Galleries, New York City; John Douthitt, New York City.

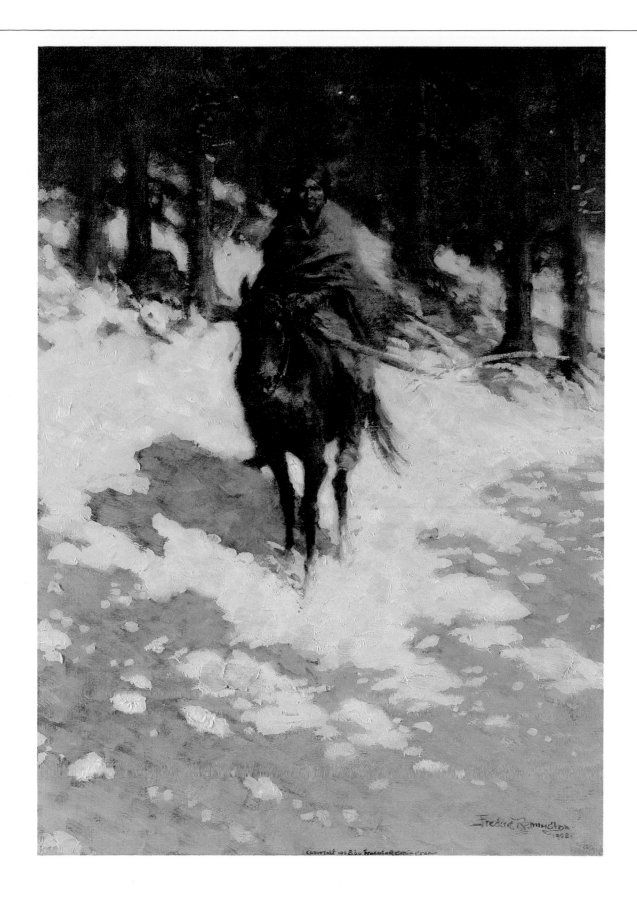

The Buffalo Runners, Big Horn Basin

1909   Oil on canvas
30⅛ x 51⅛ in. (76.5 x 127.3 cm.)

Signed lower left: Frederic Remington / 1909;
with additional inscription: "Bighorn Basin"

This stunning explosion of light, color, and sinewy action seems a flawless reflection of the sunny, boyish side of Remington's nature. Painted in his last year of life, *The Buffalo Runners, Big Horn Basin* is a throwback to his earliest western experiences and the emotions they generated. It is a testament to his abiding love of horses, "men with the bark on," and "the grand silent country."[1] In his first published article (1887) Remington told of a morning's gallop across the Kansas prairie on a horse whose "stride was steel springs under me as she swept along, brushing the dew from the grass of the range and taking the bit smartly in her teeth as though to say, 'Come on, let's have a run' . . ." Other riders joined them in a rabbit chase:

On over the smiling reach of grass, grown dry and sere in the August suns and hot winds, we galloped four abreast. . . . The rise and fall of the perfect lope peculiar to the American broncho was observable in all its ease and beauty. . . .

The horses tore along, blowing great lungfulls of fresh morning air out in snorts. Our sombreros blew up in front from the rush of air, and our blood leaped with excitement.[2]

The contagious enthusiasm of such prose remained a challenge for the artist. "I have always wanted to be able to paint running horses so you could feel the details instead of seeing them," Remington confided to his diary in 1908,[3] and in *The Buffalo Runners* he achieved all he could have wished and more. It is a highpoint in his hard-earned transformation into an American impressionist.

Remington (and most of his critics) had always doubted his color sense. In 1895, in the throes of his newly discovered abilities at sculpting, he renounced painting as "fooling my time away—I can't tell a red blanket from a grey overcoat for color."[4] But in the process of making himself over into an artist after

1900 he also discovered the joys of applying paint freely, stroking boldly, and allowing his own sense of light and shadow to dictate his range of colors. In 1898 he wrote that "a fine green" came over the sky from the east just before dawn, but "no one of the painter guild would have admitted it was green, even on the rack . . ."[5] At the time, he was as stodgy as his peers. But when he did acknowledge his perception and use green in his own work, he did it with a vengeance in his celebrated succession of nocturnals. Similarly, he had despaired of ever capturing the intense, dazzling glare of western sunlight.[6] *The Buffalo Runners* is a riot of sunstruck hues—yellow ochres, warm browns, rusts, and reds—sweeping across the canvas with an abandon to match that of the racing riders. It was Renoir who said, "I want a red to ring clearly like a bell. If it doesn't turn out that way, I add more reds until I get it. . . . I have no rules and no methods."[7] And it was Remington who, according to a contemporary critic, "under a burning sun . . . has worked out an impressionism of his own."[8] Around the time he painted *The Buffalo Runners* he imparted one secret of his new-found success to a fellow artist: "If you will allow me to observe, I will say I think the lighting in your studio is too cold. I have found the same trouble and two years ago I painted or stained both my studio here and my summer one a rich red which had the effect of warming up my paint immediately. Why dont you try it. In most galleries your paintings go against hot backgrounds and one should try to get the same environment."[9] The results of his experimentation speak for themselves.

In an oft-quoted personal statement written in 1905, Remington said: "I knew the wild riders and the vacant land were about to vanish forever, and the more I considered the subject the bigger the Forever loomed."[10] *The Buffalo Runners, Big Horn Basin* is one encounter with the Forever in which the artist emerged clear victor.

NOTES

1. "A Few Words from Mr. Remington," *Collier's Weekly*, March 18, 1905, in *Collected Writings*, p. 551.

2. Frederic Remington, "Coursing Rabbits on the Plains," *Outing*, May 1887, in *Collected Writings*, pp. 3–5.

3. "Remington Diary," entry for October 3, 1908, quoted in Hassrick, *Frederic Remington*, p. 48.

4. Frederic Remington to Owen Wister, [January 1895] in Vorpahl, *My Dear Wister—*, p. 158. In a revealing letter to Wister—possibly written before his sketching trip to southern Colorado and New Mexico in the fall of 1900—Remington expressed a renewed determination to establish himself as a pure painter: "The thing to which I am going to devote two months is *color*. I have studied *form* so much that I never had a chance to 'let go' and find if I can see with *the wide open eyes of a child*. What I know has been pounded into me—I *had* to know it—now I am going to see . . ." (quoted in N. Orwin Rush, "Frederic Remington and Owen Wister: The Story of a Friendship, 1893–1909," in *The Diversions of a Westerner*, pp. 136–137).

5. Frederic Remington, "The Essentials at Fort Adobe," *Harper's New Monthly Magazine*, April 1898, in *Collected Writings*, p. 288.

6. Hassrick, *Frederic Remington*, p. 53 n. 67.

7. Hereward Lester Cooke, Jr., "Great Masters of a Brave Era in Art," *National Geographic* 119 (May 1961): 686.

8. Royal Cortissoz, "Frederic Remington: A Painter of American Life," *Scribner's Magazine* 47 (February 1910): 192.

9. Frederic Remington to Carl Rungius, [1908–09], in the Carl Rungius Papers, Glenbow-Alberta Institute, Calgary, Alberta.

10. "A Few Words from Mr. Remington," in *Collected Writings*, p. 551.

EX COLLECTION

Newhouse Galleries, New York City; Mary Mc-Clennen Hospital, Cambridge, New York.

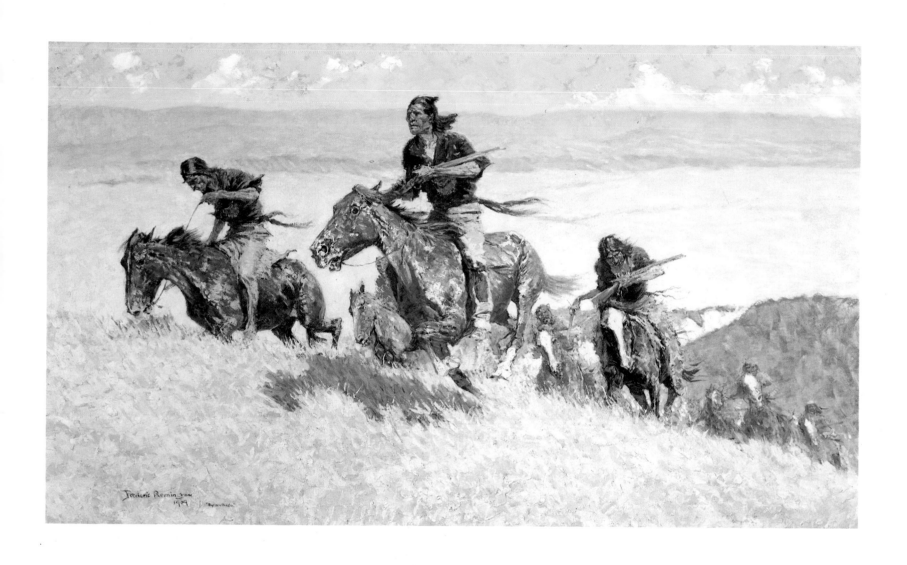

The Luckless Hunter

1909   Oil on canvas
26⅞ x 28⅞ in. (68.3 x 73.3 cm.)

Signed lower right:
Frederic Remington / 1909

For all his boyishness, there was a darker side to Remington as well. Late in life he frequently painted pictures without clear victories, and scholars recently have taken to probing the sobered, even chastened man who, back from his long-awaited confrontation with real war in Cuba in 1898–99, could no longer glamorize combat as he had been wont to do in the past.[1] Much of his youthful exuberance had vanished, replaced by an uneasy recognition of his physical decline as he passed his fortieth birthday and a growing sense of loss over the Wild West that had once nurtured his artistry and was now a fading memory. Even as he turned away from the kind of illustrating that had made his reputation and disavowed the contemporary West and modern soldiering as lacking in pictorial interest, he embraced the old West with renewed passion. An artist who had been a master of action, a storyteller in line and paint, became a student of mood, and some of his paintings were infused with a brooding intensity.

Contemporaries recognized this new direction in oils like *The Luckless Hunter* with its almost palpable aura of despair. Instead of being conquered by heroic boys in blue in an equal combat on some sun-drenched battlefield, the Indian is shown reduced to helplessness by hunger. The night air is brittle, the sky speckled with frozen stars, the snow-covered landscape as barren as the moon that washes it in pale light. There is nothing here to sustain the will to resist, or even to go on. Speaking of this "masterpiece of expression," a contemporary wrote: "In all of Remington's pictures, the shadow of death seems not far away. If the actors in the vivid scenes are not threatened by death in terrible combat, they are menaced in the form of famine, thirst or cold. One sees the death's head through the skin of the lean faces of his Indians, cowboys and soldiers. . . . The presence, in Mr. Remington's characteristic work, of a great central motive like this . . . is an indication of power, and the ability to express the motive in a hundred vivid forms, is a proof of genius."[2]

On November 29, 1909, *The Luckless Hunter* went on display with twenty-two other oils at M. Knoedler and Company in New York. Less than a month later Frederic Remington was dead at the age of forty-eight.

NOTES

1. This theme informs two books by Ben Merchant Vorpahl—*My Dear Wister—: The Frederic Remington–Owen Wister Letters* and *Frederic Remington and the West: With the Eye of the Mind*—and is discussed in Hassrick, *Frederic Remington*, pp. 38–40, and in the notes to *Collected Writings*, pp. 604, 617–619.

2. Unidentified review, quoted in McCracken, *Frederic Remington*, p. 121.

EX COLLECTION

Newhouse Galleries, New York City; M. Knoedler & Company, New York City; Robert Woods Bliss, Dumbarton Oaks, Georgetown, Washington, D.C.; William H. Bliss, New York City.

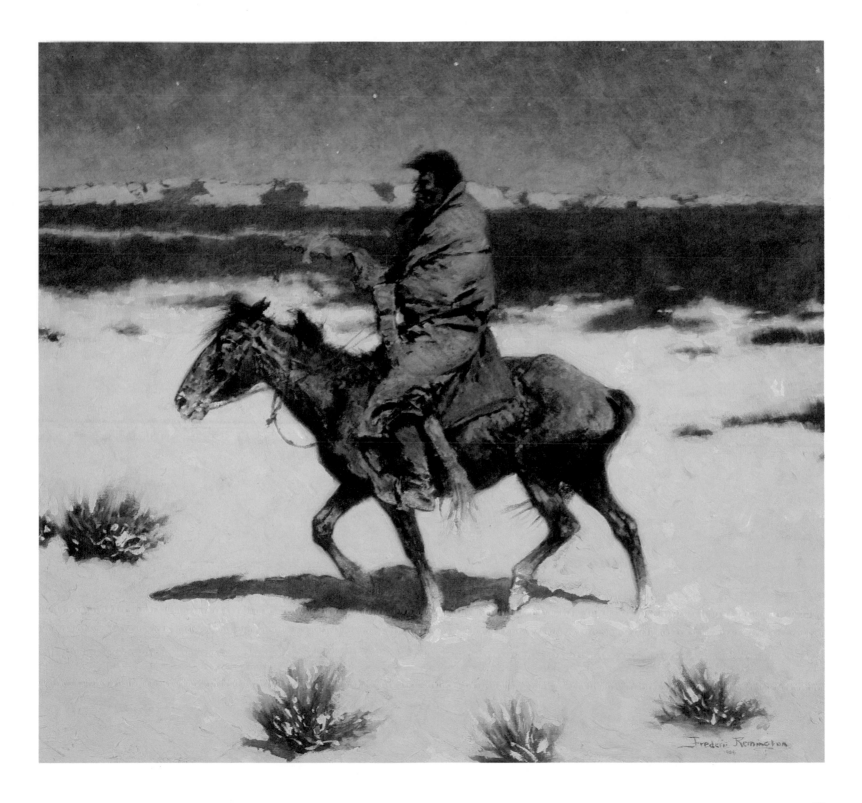

Charles M. Russell (1864–1926)

Roping the Renegade

c. 1883 Pencil, watercolor, and gouache
on paper
12½ x 16⅝ in. (31.7 x 42.2 cm.)

Signed lower right: CMR

This painting was probably done in 1883, at a time when "Kid Russell" was still learning the ropes both as cowboy and as artist. He first worked as a horse wrangler with the Judith roundup in the spring of 1882, and the next year as a cowpuncher on the Shonkin range, in the southern extremity of Choteau County below Fort Benton.[1] With watercolors and brushes that he carried rolled up in a pair of socks, Russell recorded what he saw. Most of his later roping scenes depict moments of high drama and danger—saddles slipping, horses falling, mad cows charging, ropes getting hopelessly tangled, guns being drawn for self-protection. But in 1883 the typical still engrossed Russell because it was still novel to him. *Roping the Renegade* shows an everyday occurrence on the roundup. The cowboy on the left, decked out in California fashion, has lassoed a bolter, taken his dallie-welts (that is, wrapped his rope around his saddle horn), and is shown bracing to hold the steer while his partner rides up to drop a second loop.[2] This second cowboy, I believe, may actually be Russell. Throughout his life the Cowboy Artist liked to include himself in rangeland scenes—witness, for example, *Utica* (p. 134) —and the smooth-faced young man shown here and in another watercolor of the same vintage resembles Russell's known self-depictions from the 1880s.[3] Thus, *Roping the Renegade* is possibly a graphic memento of Charlie Russell's only direct experience as an all-around cowhand; over the next nine years he confined himself to wrangling on the roundups.

NOTES

1. Al. J. Noyes (Ajax), *In the Land of Chinook; or, the Story of Blaine County*, p. 120.

2. See Russell, "The Story of the Cowpuncher," in *Trails Plowed Under*, pp. 2–3, for his distinction between California- and Texas-influenced cowboy styles. Based on circumstantial evidence, the cowboy shown here may be one Jasper McFry; see Frankie M. Taylor, "Russell Watercolors Found!" *True West* 17 (November–December 1969): 17, 62.

3. See Carl S. Dentzel, "The Roots of Russell: The Earliest Known Frontier Sketches of Charles Marion Russell," in *The Westerners Brand Book, Number 14*, pp. 103–121. The other watercolor mentioned, *Roping 'Em*, is in the collection of the Amon Carter Museum of Western Art, Fort Worth.

EX COLLECTION
Newhouse Galleries, New York City.

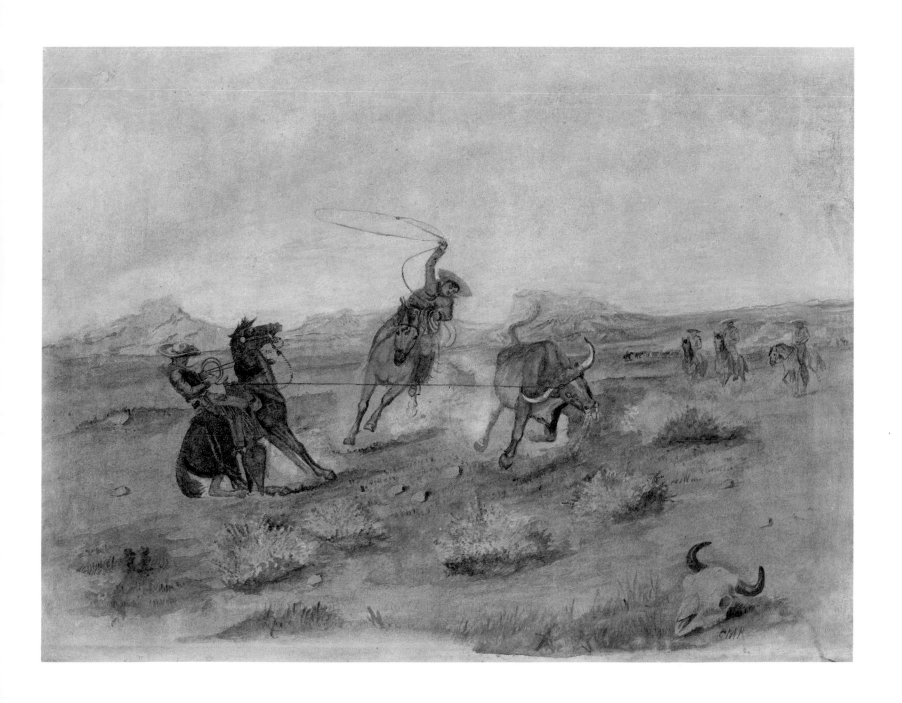

Western Scene [The Shelton Saloon Painting]

c. 1885   Oil on wood panel
17½ x 69 in. (44.5 x 175.3 cm.)

Signed lower left: C M RUSSELL

Frederic G. Renner has described this painting as Russell's "first formal commission."[1] His patron was James R. Shelton, proprietor of the original saloon-hotel in Utica, the little town founded in 1881 in Montana's Judith Basin.[2] A saloon without some artwork was a sorry spectacle indeed, and Shelton turned to the Cowboy Artist for a mural-sized painting to hang above his bar. Russell had neither oil paints nor artist's canvas so he settled for house paints and a pine board one and one-half feet wide and nearly six feet long. *Western Scene* is an obviously amateurish effort. Its crudeness and raw color can be accounted for in part by the circumstances, but mostly by the fact that in 1885 Russell was still more cowboy than artist.

The three subjects included in the mural are all ones that Russell returned to: the wagon train drawn up in a protective circle and the attacking Indians keeping a respectful though inadequate distance, judging from the dead horse and dying warrior; the herd of elk, presaging his superb 1912 oil *The Exalted Ruler* (B.P.O.E., Great Falls); and the curious pronghorn antelope being flagged by the hunters on the ridge to the right, a theme he subsequently handled from the viewpoint of the hunters. Russell did introduce an interesting twist into his mural by presenting reverse perspectives in the side paintings. In the one, the attackers fire at distant targets; in the other, the targets—that is, the antelope—occupy the foreground. There is another point of interest as well. At a date when Russell had not even worked out a signature, he included a buffalo skull in the composition (as he did in *Roping the Renegade*). The skull became such a fixture in his work that a Helena paper in 1887 described it as his "trade mark."[3] He chose it as his personal insignia and eventually incorporated a stylized version of it in his signature because, on a literal level, buffalo bones were omnipresent in the Montana of his youth. Moreover, they symbolized the theme that would be his lifelong preoccupation, the West that has passed. They gain a particular poignancy in his cowboy scenes showing the "white man's buffalo" grazing over the remnants of "nature's cattle," unaware that they too will soon be replaced by the newer order represented by the farmer.

NOTES

1. Frederic G. Renner, *Charles M. Russell: Paintings, Drawings, and Sculpture in the Amon G. Carter Collection,* p. 6.
2. Mildred Taurman et al., *Utica, Montana,* p. 9. A photograph of Shelton's saloon appears in Ramon F. Adams and Homer E. Britzman, *Charles M. Russell, the Cowboy Artist: A Biography,* p. 83, where it is described as Russell's "first studio."
3. *Helena Weekly Independent,* July 7, 1887; quoted in Harold McCracken, *The Charles M. Russell Book: The Life and Work of the Cowboy Artist,* p. 108.

EX COLLECTION

James R. Shelton, Utica, Montana.

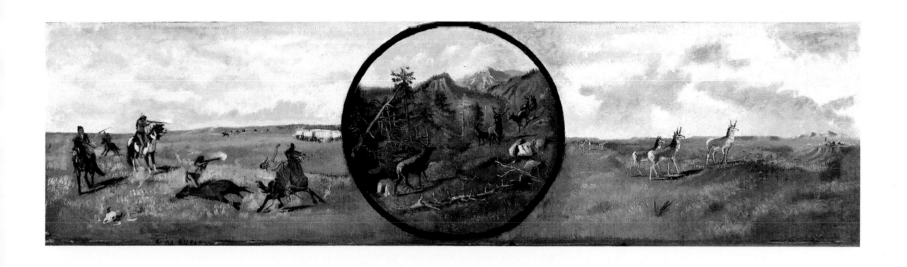

Cowpunching Sometimes Spells Trouble

1889   Oil on canvas
26 x 41 in. (66.1 x 104.1 cm.)

Signed lower right: C M Russell / 1889

Everyone pretty well agrees that Russell was no great shakes as a cowpuncher himself. His range pals said as much and he was quick to concur, noting: "Although I worked for many years on the range, I am not what the people think a cowboy should be. I was neither a good roper nor rider. I was a night wrangler."[1] But Russell admired the work of the top hands he associated with, and he watched them during the day as they matter-of-factly went about their business and demonstrated their skills. Riding and roping scenes became staples for him. Bronc busting was an individual activity, and Russell's paintings often isolate the cowboy and the horse in an elemental contest, man against animal, that was a test of nerve, stamina, and will. Roping scenes, in contrast, were usually more complicated, story-telling pictures with several figures involved in the action unfolding before the viewer.

In *Cowpunching Sometimes Spells Trouble* the roper on the right has heeled the cow but has been unable to prevent its charging the other riders. One horse has bolted out of the way; the other, less fortunate, has been sent to the ground, pinning its rider and likely breaking his leg. Amidst the tangle of his rope

he desperately claws for his revolver. There are still signs of awkwardness in this early oil. The horse on the right appears to have given Russell trouble, and the pigment is applied in such a way that it resembles coloring with paint. But the red bandanas, yellow slickers, and clear blue sky lend brightness to the scene in a period when Russell's tones were frequently muddy. The action is convincingly rendered. And Russell was pleased enough with the composition to repeat much of it in his popular 1901 oil *The Strenuous Life* (Thomas Gilcrease Institute, Tulsa).

NOTES

1. Charles M. Russell, "A Few Words about Myself," in *Trails Plowed Under*, p. xix.

EX COLLECTION

Newhouse Galleries, New York City.

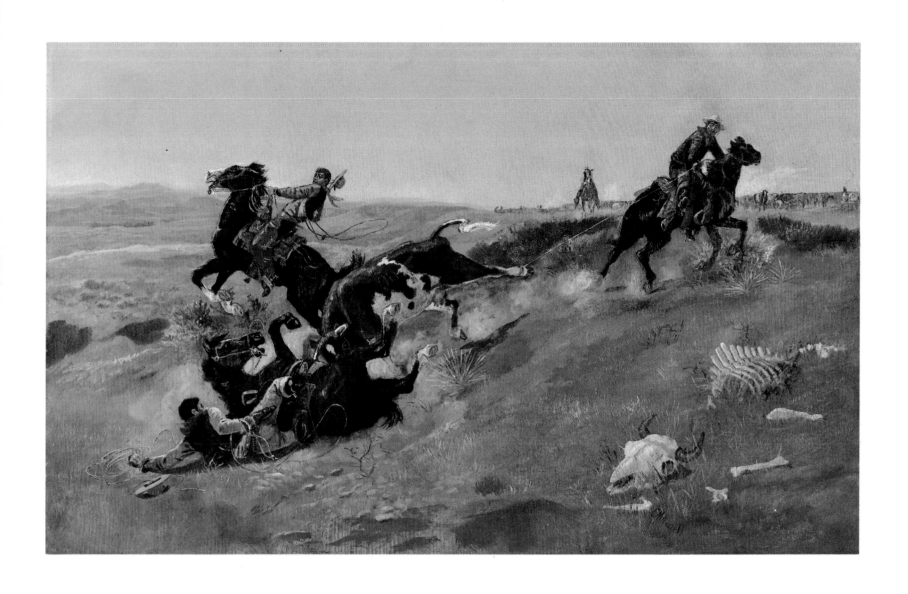

Cowboy Sport—Roping a Wolf

1890   Oil on canvas
20 x 35¾ in. (50.8 x 90.8 cm.)

Signed lower left: (skull) / C M Russell / 1890

Wolves were a nuisance on the range during Russell's cowboy days. Deprived of game to eat, they preyed on the cattle. Ranchers fought back against this cunning, fleet-footed menace as best they could. Bacon rind poisoned with strychnine was a common bait.[1] Cowboys also did their bit and had a little fun in the bargain. Whenever they startled a wolf during their chores, they gave chase "at headlong speed, utterly regardless of the broken dangerous ground," Granville Stuart wrote about the time Russell painted *Cowboy Sport—Roping a Wolf.* "Loosing their lariats from their saddles as they run, the deadly noose is soon swinging swiftly around their heads as they close in on the frightened animal, who strains every nerve to escape. Often several misthrows are made, till some lucky fling catches it around the neck or body and it is dragged some distance till so exhausted that it cannot bite the rawhide lariat in two . . . Its career is then ended by a pistol shot . . ."[2]

Russell painted similar scenes many times over the years, but *Cowboy Sport—Roping a Wolf,* an early version, has remained the popular favorite. It is a crude effort in some respects and murky in color (browns, blacks, and grays predominate). But it is bursting with energy and shows great care for detail.

The faces of the riders are distinctive, no doubt because Russell, still a working cowboy in 1890, was portraying two friends. The lead rider appears a little grim, but his companion is evidently enjoying himself while the wolf, with its sneaky, backward-glancing expression, is also clearly in the spirit of things.

NOTES

1. Paul C. Phillips, ed., *Forty Years on the Frontier: The Reminiscences and Journals of Granville Stuart,* II, 171–172.
2. Granville Stuart, commentary for *Cowboy Sport (Roping a Wolf),* in Charles M. Russell, *Studies of Western Life.*

EX COLLECTION

Newhouse Galleries, New York City; Homer E. Britzman, Pasadena, California.

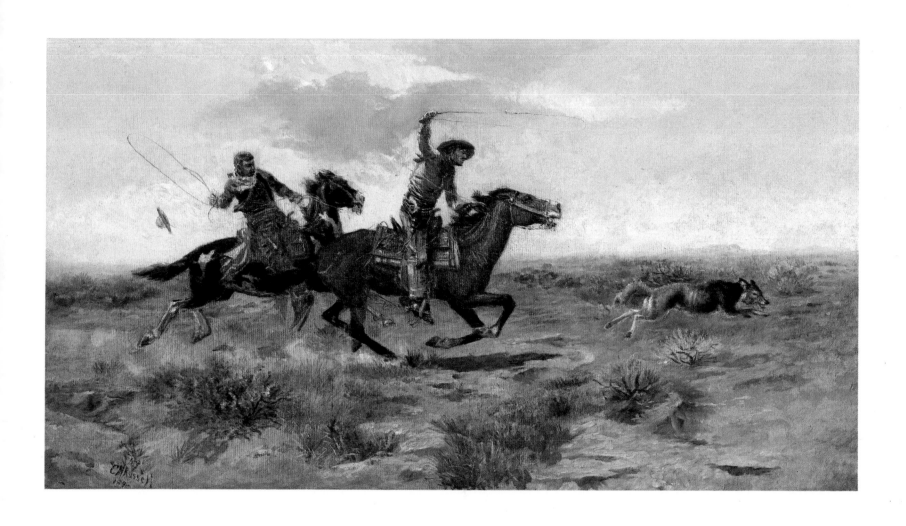

The Buffalo Runners

c. 1890   Oil on canvas
27⅝ x 39⅜ in. (70.2 x 100.0 cm.)

Signed lower left: C M Russell

If the buffalo hunt is one of the supreme tests of a western artist's abilities, few met it more successfully or more often than Russell, whose love of the old West found expression in dozens of paintings on this single theme. When he first tackled it he tended to isolate one mounted hunter and one buffalo, ordinarily shown broadside to minimize difficulties of perspective and to keep a complicated subject as simple as possible.

The Buffalo Runners, done about 1890, is unusually ambitious. It exhibits a fine feel for the terrain, especially the steep drop to the river where the herd is crossing in the distance. But the central action is less effective. The foreground bull is poorly articulated and seems much too long—a failure of foreshortening readily apparent when *The Buffalo Runners* is compared to a later painting like *Redman's Meat* (p. 110). The arrow in the bull also seems inappropriate. Normally the hunter would single out a cow, as he is shown doing, or would at least finish off the bull he has wounded. Similarly, the buffalo dropping to its knees behind the hunter is wounded on the left side, while a right-handed bowman almost always approached his target from the right. Finally, if the one hunter is responsible for all three wounded animals, as represented,

then he is a phenomenal marksman, since the average Blackfoot required three or more arrows for a kill,[1] and considered himself fortunate to down two buffalo during a prolonged chase.[2]

Russell did a close variation on the horse and rider in *The Buffalo Runners* in another undated oil executed in the same period, *Meat for the Tribe* (Amon Carter Museum of Western Art, Fort Worth). In it, he armed the hunter with a rifle instead of a bow.

NOTES

1. John C. Ewers, *The Horse in Blackfoot Indian Culture, with Comparative Material from Other Western Tribes*, p. 155.
2. John C. Ewers, *The Blackfeet: Raiders on the Northwestern Plains*, p. 80. Michael S. Kennedy, ed., *The Assiniboines: From the Accounts of the Old Ones Told to First Boy (James Larpenteur Long)*, p. 109, notes that during the chase each Assiniboine hunter killed one or two buffalo "according to his needs."

EX COLLECTION
Newhouse Galleries, New York City.

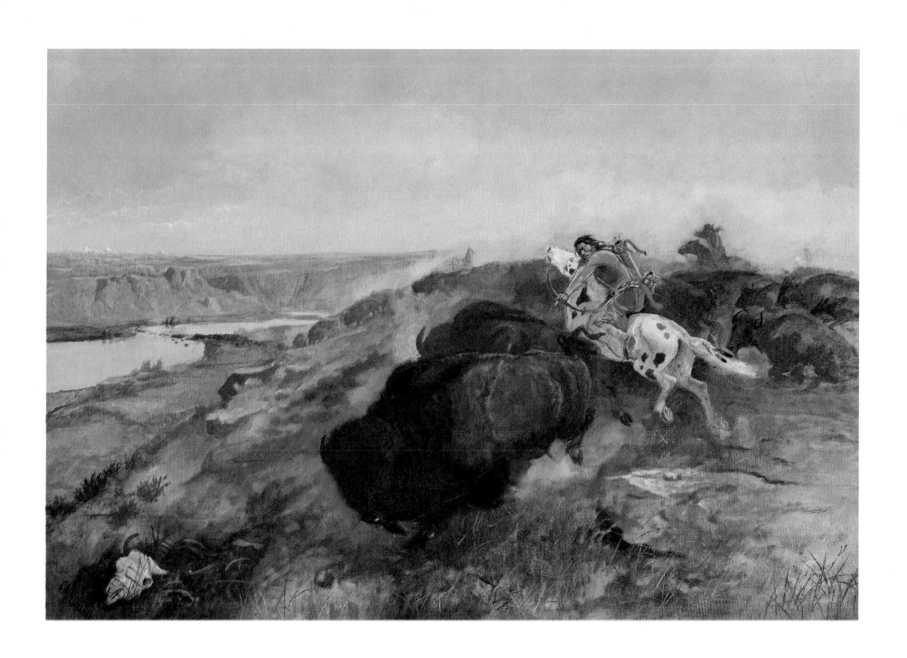

Seeking New Hunting Grounds [Indian Women and Children on the Trail]

c. 1891   Oil on canvas
23¾ x 35⅞ in. (60.3 x 91.1 cm.)

Signed lower left: C M Russell / (skull)

Russell's earliest studies of Indian and cowboy life compensate for their artistic deficiencies with a freshness of observation that gives them a documentary quality lacking in his mature, more polished work. His later Indian paintings are populated with heroic clusters of lean, muscular warriors astride splendid horses, clearly masters of their own domain. His paintings done in the 1880s and early 1890s, in contrast, show Indian raiding parties costumed in a crazy-quilt mixture of native and white fashions, riding tough, scrawny ponies. They are at once wary, dangerous, and utterly realistic. This excellent early oil, *Seeking New Hunting Grounds*, is another case in point. It is almost photographic in its precise detail. Moving camp, while not a theme as stirring as the buffalo hunt and one that Russell returned to less often, nevertheless was one of his favorites in the 1890s. While the men rode ahead and guarded the flanks, the women and children moved the band's worldly wealth in a long, straggling procession. The mother, with her baby wrapped in her blanket on her back and her next youngest mounted in front of her, also drags a travois. Apparently made from the lodge poles not pulled by the packhorse behind, it is secured to her saddle, which is held in place by the martingale and crupper. Ideally, a Blackfoot family on the move used three packhorses in transporting their tipi, two to pull the lodge poles and the third to carry the lodge cover.[1] But reality was something else, and Russell here shows one horse doing double duty.

Seeking New Hunting Grounds could just as well be titled "Families" in recognition of the mare and its gangly colt, the wolflike dog and its puppies peeping out of the camp kettle on the travois, and the Indian mother and her children.

NOTES

1. Ewers, *The Horse in Blackfoot Indian Culture*, pp. 95–99, 103–105, 107–110, 132–139.

EX COLLECTION

Newhouse Galleries, New York City.

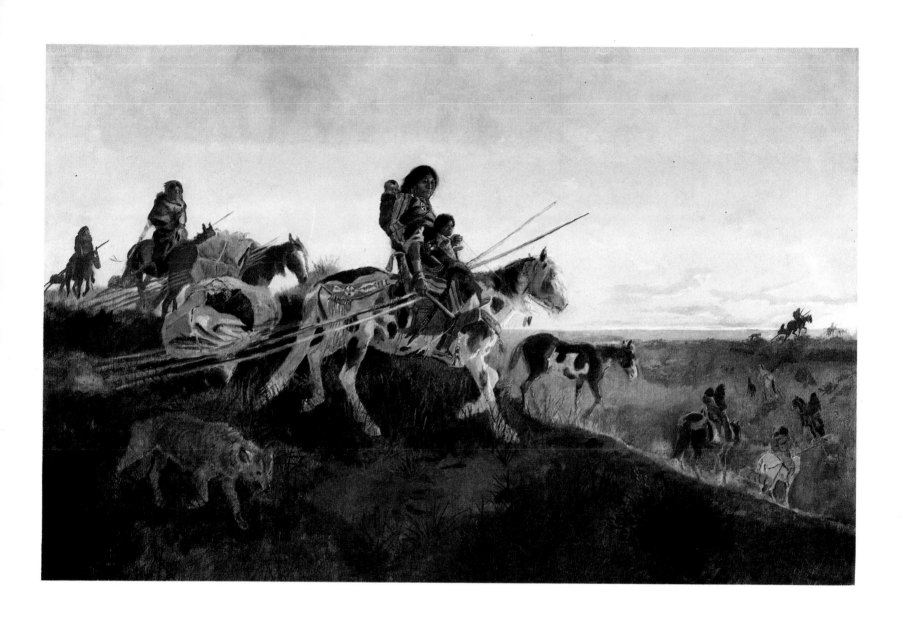

The Evening Pipe

c. 1891   Oil on canvas
9⅝ x 16⅜ in. (24.4 x 41.6 cm.)

Signed lower left: C M Russell / (skull)

Day's end. A quiet time, a time for reflection, even brooding over an evening pipe. Europeans acquired the tobacco habit from America's natives and created a whole lore based on it. Smoking was a solace, a heart's balm, a source of individual contentment. With each puff on the pipe, one's worries were said to lift like the smoke and dissipate in the air. Indians made smoking into a ritual. In some cultures it was a part of religious practice as well as of ordinary social intercourse. Smoking the pipe could be an invocation to the gods, a test of integrity, or a sign of friendship.

The pensive Cree in *The Evening Pipe* appears oblivious to the activity behind him as a party of hunters wend their way home. The camp seems still. The pale moon, the pink glow on the distant bluffs, and the blanket-wrapped figure squatting beside his temporary shelter, tobacco pouch and drum at hand, all convey a hushed, twilight mood. Russell was known as a painter of action, but in many of his Indian pictures he exhibited a contemplative side.

EX COLLECTION
Newhouse Galleries, New York City.

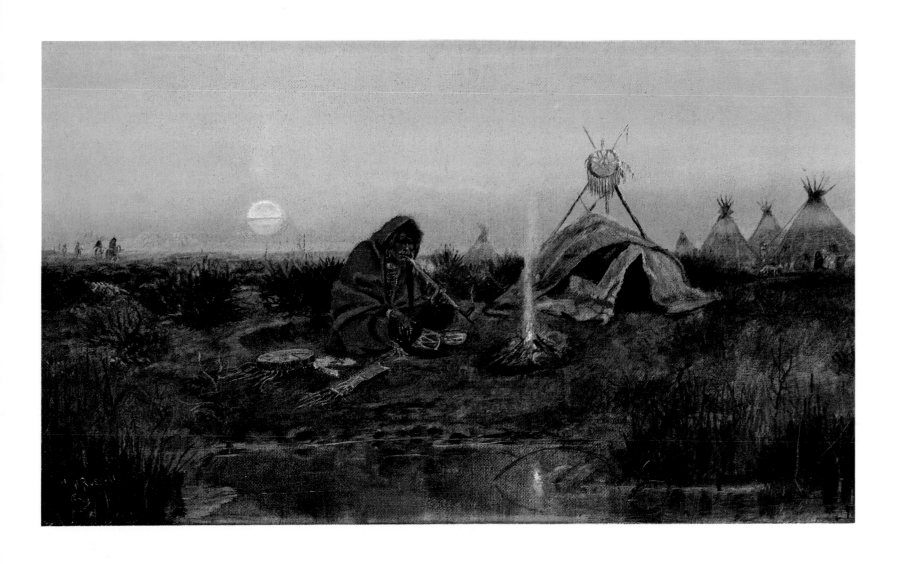

The Brave's Return

c. 1891   Pencil, watercolor, and gouache
on paper
21¼ x 31⅞ in. (54.0 x 81.0 cm.)

Signed lower left: C M Russell / (skull)

In the 1890s, in particular, Russell gave free expression to his fondness for domestic scenes from Indian life. *The Brave's Return* records a tender moment as two women gaze up from their chores to find their warrior-husband returned safely from a raiding expedition that may have kept him away for several weeks. There is no indication of what he has accomplished—no stolen horses, no scalps dangling from his belt, just a tired man about to dismount from an equally tired horse. Through Russell's eyes we see the fierce plains Indian in his family setting, a fully rounded individual; the wife's shy reaction in drawing her blanket around her bespeaks her affection and possibly the length of her husband's absence. The returned warrior will receive a properly respectful reception. "Men were the undisputed lords of their households," John Ewers has written of the Blackfeet. "They expected their wives to wait upon them hand and foot, to bring them food when they wanted it, to light their pipes and remove their moccasins."[1] Among the Assiniboines, a successful hunter could anticipate an especially warm welcome: "He slid off his mount, and his wife led him into their lodge, where he lay down. She unpacked the horses, picketed them where the grass was good, . . . then devoted all her time to him; first taking off his moccasins, washing his feet, and powdering them with dry vermillion-colored earth paint. Then she removed all his clothing, and, while he wrapped himself in a robe and rested, she prepared hot food for him. As she waited on him, she carried on a pleasant conversation and talked of things agreeable to him. There was peace and contentment in the lodge."[2] Russell's returned brave will receive similar attention, his wives gladly abandoning the task of scraping the buffalo hide in order to accommodate his wishes and make his homecoming a celebration.

NOTES

1. Ewers, *The Blackfeet*, p. 100.
2. Kennedy, ed., *The Assiniboines*, pp. 112–113.

EX COLLECTION

Newhouse Galleries, New York City.

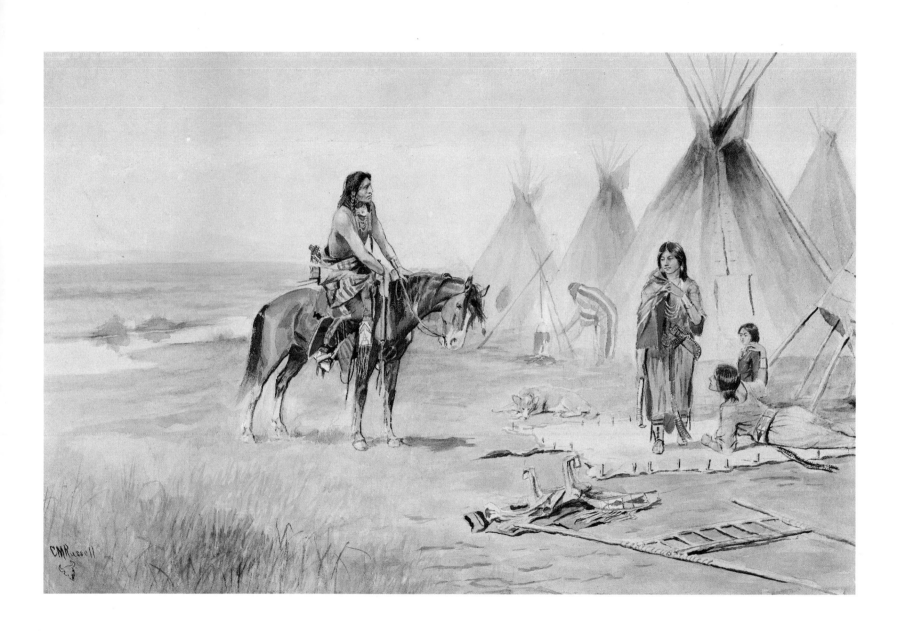

Caught in the Circle

c. 1892   Oil on canvas
26⅛ x 35⅞ in. (66.4 x 91.1 cm.)

Signed lower left: C M Russell / (skull)

Frederic Remington frequently depicted what has become a stock-in-trade for western artists: the desperate stand of a small band of men—trappers, soldiers, or cowboys—surrounded by circling Indians (often implied rather than shown) and resolved to sell their lives dearly. Russell did his share of such scenes in the 1890s, including one heroic-sized oil, before abandoning the subject for good after painting an obligatory Custer's Last Stand on commission in 1903.[1] In his pictures of men under siege Russell resorted to standard types—the boy, the grizzled old-timer, the intrepid, buckskin-clad frontiersman. The subject matter did not derive from his personal experience, and the resulting works, overblown and gory as they were, came as close to saloon art as anything he ever painted.

Caught in the Circle is one of the earliest Russell surrounds. Less elaborate than those he did near the end of the 1890s, its simplicity, the off-center arrangement of the cluster of men, and the fact that they are keeping their heads down and performing no suicidal heroics behind the barricade of dead horses add up to an effective storytelling picture full of the tension of the moment and the unanswered question: is this group of frontiersmen fated to stand off the foe and survive, or will they all die on the open plains, more nameless martyrs to the cause of westering?

NOTES

1. The oil referred to is *The Trappers' Last Stand*, now in the collection of the R. W. Norton Art Gallery, Shreveport; 4 x 6 ft. in size, it was painted in 1899. *Custer's Last Battle*, a black-and-white watercolor, illustrated William A. Allen, *Adventures with Indians and Game; or, Twenty Years in the Rocky Mountains*, p. 63, and is now in the collection of the Thomas Gilcrease Institute at Tulsa.

EX COLLECTION
Newhouse Galleries, New York City.

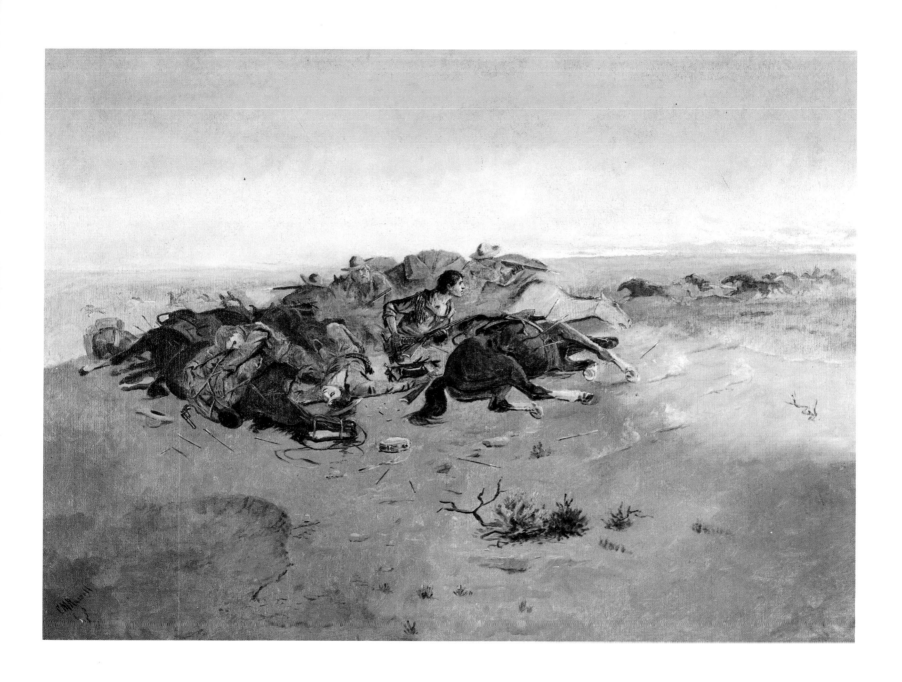

There May Be Danger Ahead [Hunting Party on Mountain Trail]

1893   Oil on canvas
36¼ x 22 in. (92.1 x 55.9 cm.)

Signed lower left: C M Russell / (skull) '93

Most plains Indian men aspired to be two things above all else in life: good hunters, and thus good providers, and bold warriors, thus enjoying both the material wealth acquired through horse raids and the social prestige that followed on war honors. No single subject engaged Russell more consistently than that of a small party of Indians on the prowl for game, horses, or scalps. He painted them in the 1880s and was still painting them the year he died.

This early oil bears the title *There May Be Danger Ahead* and appears to show a group of warriors descending a steep mountain trail en route to enemy country. Their purpose would be horse theft, by far the most common activity of such raiding parties, though it should be noted that horse-stealing expeditions usually set out on foot in order to travel inconspicuously and in the expectation there would be horses aplenty to ride on the return journey.[1] It is possible that the men in this painting (which has also been called *Hunting Party on Mountain Trail*) were merely looking for game, though naturally they would not pass up the chance to kill and butcher a stray cow or steal a few horses. Garbed in a mixture of white and traditional costume, armed with rifles, and riding scrub ponies, they are the very sort Russell encountered in Montana in the 1880s.

The colors used in *There May Be Danger Ahead*—drab browns and flat blues—are typical of Russell's work in this period, and there does appear to be too much foreground in the picture. But Russell wanted to indicate the precipitous nature of the incline, and so he showed the steep rocky ledge, the white horse gingerly picking its way down the trail, the tense expression on its rider's face, and the thread of river running through the valley below.

NOTES

1. See George Bird Grinnell, *Blackfoot Lodge Tales: The Story of a Prairie People*, p. 251; Kennedy, ed., *The Assiniboines*, p. 48; and David G. Mandelbaum, *The Plains Cree: An Ethnographic, Historical, and Comparative Study*, p. 241. However, Ewers, *The Horse in Blackfoot Indian Culture*, pp. 184–185, notes that "in the last decade of horse raiding the mounted party gained in popularity, especially in expeditions directed against the Crow. The mounted party could travel much faster and could more easily evade white authorities who at that time were seeking to put an end to intertribal horse raiding."

EX COLLECTION

Newhouse Galleries, New York City; Elizabeth V. Sprague, Great Falls, Montana; Robert Vaughn, Great Falls, Montana.

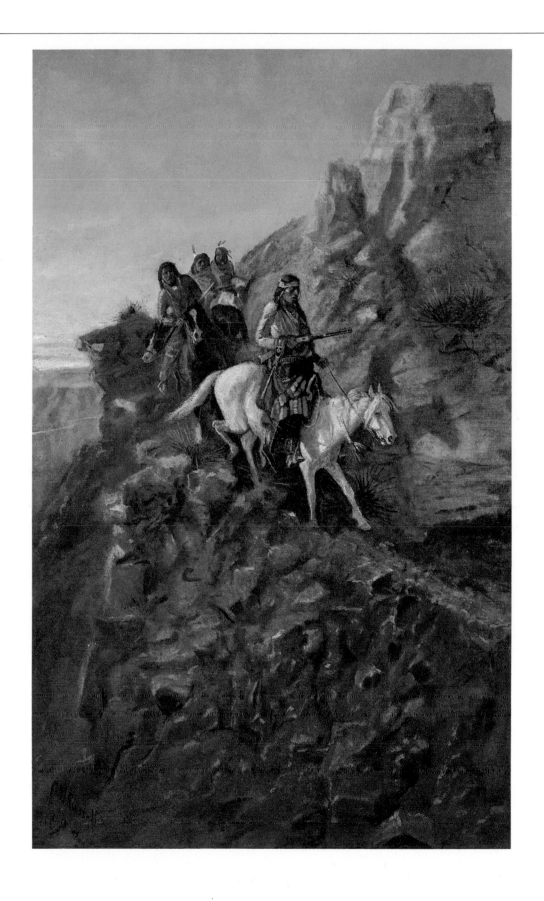

Plunder on the Horizon [Indians Discover Prospectors]

1893   Oil on canvas
24 x 36 in. (61.0 x 91.4 cm.)

Signed lower left: C M Russell / (skull) '93

Russell occasionally painted companion pieces, even story sequences. *Plunder on the Horizon* and the following oil, *Trouble on the Horizon*, are a matched set. In the first, Indians emerge from a tangle of trees to spy on three prospectors panning for gold in the stream below; in the second, two prospectors on a mountain slope survey an Indian village nestled in a piney valley. Badly outnumbered, they will give the camp a wide berth; in contrast, the Indians are clearly calculating the odds and planning a surprise attack on the unwary prospectors, who are about to relax over a meal. While both oils are well painted, especially *Plunder on the Horizon*, their viewpoint is surprisingly ethnocentric. The Indians are stealthy, skulking savages, pure products of the raw wilderness they inhabit.

The whites, on the other hand, are open, upright, and calm, with nothing to hide and interested only in self-preservation. A possible explanation is that Russell's patron, Montana pioneer Robert Vaughn, suggested the subject matter and Russell responded accordingly. The two paintings involve a reversal in perspective, as Russell neatly emphasizes by reversing the viewer's perspective as well.

EX COLLECTION

Newhouse Galleries, New York City; Elizabeth V. Sprague, Great Falls, Montana; Robert Vaughn, Great Falls, Montana.

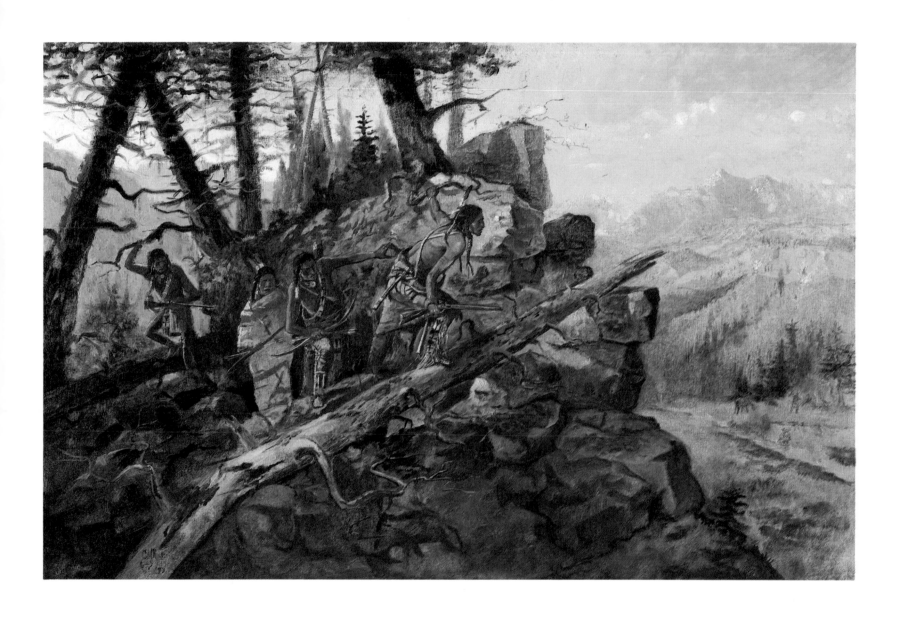

Trouble on the Horizon [Prospectors Discover an Indian Camp]

1893   Oil on canvas
26⅛ x 34 in. (66.4 x 86.4 cm.)

Signed lower left: C M Russell / (skull) '93

In both *Plunder on the Horizon* and *Trouble on the Horizon*, Russell employed a device that often appeared in his early paintings, a fallen tree separating foreground from background. Its use suggests a lack of confidence in his ability to convey the sensation of height and depth without some artificial line of demarcation. Fallen trees also serve as aids to perspective in *Attack on the Mule Train* (p. 84), *Big Nose George and the Road Agents* (p. 92), and *The Ambush* (p. 94). In *Plunder on the Horizon* and *Trouble on the Horizon*, the gnarled broken trunks carry an added symbolic import, running across the canvases like slash marks signifying the cultural barrier forever dividing red and white.

EX COLLECTION

Newhouse Galleries, New York City; Elizabeth V. Sprague, Great Falls, Montana; Robert Vaughn, Great Falls, Montana.

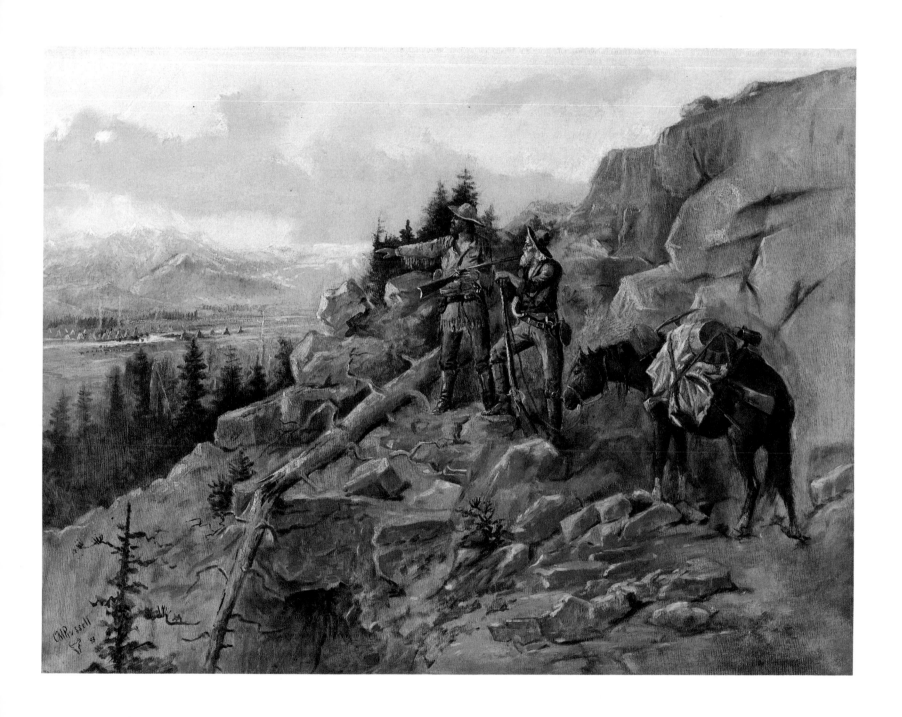

Indians Hunting Buffalo [Wild Men's Meat]

1894   Oil on canvas
24⅛ x 36⅛ in. (61.3 x 91.8 cm.)

Signed lower left: C M Russell / (skull) 1894

Those familiar with Russell's work will immediately recognize this buffalo hunt as peculiar. Simply put, it is more a flight of fancy than the kind of realistic observation expected of Russell. The hunter's position is all wrong. His leaping steed has carried him past the buffalo, yet he remains intent on making the kill from an impossible angle. A right-handed hunter rode alongside the buffalo on its right and directed his arrows at the vital spot immediately behind the forelegs.[1] The bow, rarely more than three feet in length, ordinarily was held slightly off vertical, or even horizontally.[2] The buffalo here, huge as a locomotive and improbably long, is the incar-

nation of awesome, mindless power as it lowers its head and, mysteriously wounded on the side opposite the hunter, makes a last, convulsive charge. The Indian's horse, in turn, hardly resembles the average buffalo runner. These were all details Russell rendered accurately elsewhere. Why the discrepancies here? *Indians Hunting Buffalo* was long in the collection of Robert Vaughn. In his memoirs of life in early-day Montana it illustrated his recollections of his first buffalo hunt, in 1872, during which "a fat young cow," twice shot, whirled around "as quick as lightning," caught Vaughn's foot "with her crooked horn and came very near throwing

me out of the saddle and as near goring the horse."[3] Perhaps this experience gave Vaughn the idea for a buffalo-hunt picture and he instructed Russell accordingly. Certainly someone suggested Titian Ramsay Peale's 1832 lithograph *American Buffaloe* as a model.[4] The composition of *Indians Hunting Buffalo*, especially the conventionalized white steed (admired by some as the best ever "off the Russell brush"),[5] indicates that the Cowboy Artist worked directly from Peale's print, though he managed to include a few realistic touches of his own. The hunter is carefully modeled and convincing. He wears a wrist-guard as protection against the snap of his bow string and uses a pad saddle with stirrups for a firmer seat while guiding his buffalo horse with his knees and allowing the long bridle rope to trail behind.[6] Nevertheless, no other Russell buffalo hunt ever looked more like the product of an eastern studio.

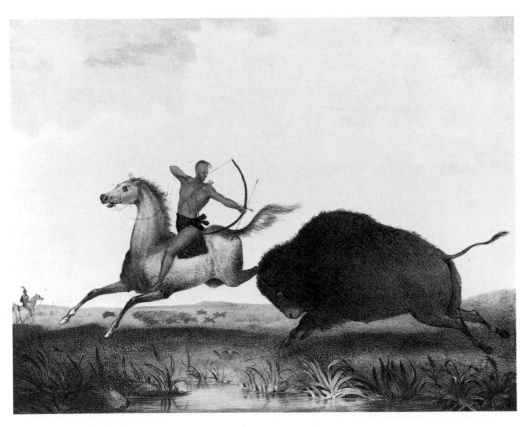

American Buffaloe by Titian Ramsay Peale,
1832, Lithograph
Amon Carter Museum of Western Art,
Fort Worth

NOTES

1. Ewers, *The Horse in Blackfoot Indian Culture*, p. 158; and *The Blackfeet*, p. 79.

2. Ewers, *The Horse in Blackfoot Indian Culture*, p. 158; Mandelbaum, *the Plains Cree*, pp. 94–95.

3. Robert Vaughn, *Then and Now; or, Thirty-Six Years in the Rockies*, pp. 124–126.

4. See Jessie Poesch, *Titian Ramsay Peale and His Journals of the Wilkes Expedition, 1799–1885*, pp. 30–31, 45, 58–60.

5. "Vaughn Collection of Russell Paintings Sold to Newhouse Galleries of New York," *Great Falls Daily Tribune*, undated clipping (c. June 1946) in the C. M. Russell scrapbook, Amon Carter Museum of Western Art, Fort Worth. In this article, *Indians Hunting Buffalo* is simply titled *Buffalo Hunt*.

6. Ewers, *The Blackfeet*, p. 78, and *The Horse in Blackfoot Indian Culture*, pp. 76–77, 158; Edward Ahenakew, *Voices of the Plains Cree*, ed. Ruth M. Buck, p. 59.

EX COLLECTION

Newhouse Galleries, New York City; Elizabeth V. Sprague, Great Falls, Montana; Robert Vaughn, Great Falls, Montana.

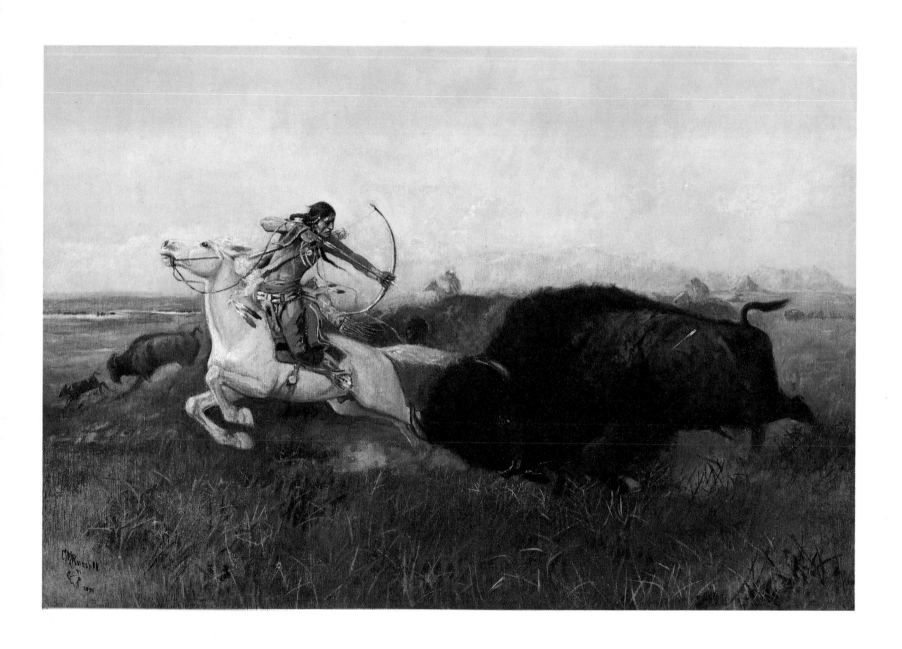

Attack on the Mule Train [Mule Pack Train]

1894   Oil on canvas
23⅛ x 35⅛ in. (58.8 x 89.2 cm.)

Signed lower left: C M Russell / (skull) 1894

Mules were not Russell's favorite animals, judging from their infrequent appearance in his work. In fact, he made mule pack trains the subject of only three major oils. *Bell Mare* (1910; Thomas Gilcrease Institute, Tulsa) and *When Mules Wear Diamonds* (1921; National Cowboy Hall of Fame and Western Heritage Center, Oklahoma City) are similar, uneventful scenes of mule trains moving through spectacular mountain scenery; *Attack on the Mule Train*, painted in 1894, is something else again. It depicts a moment of high drama as Indians fire with telling effect upon a pack train. The mule skinner riding the bell mare has been taken completely by surprise. Hit, he jerks back, reins slipping through his fingers, foot out of his stirrup, his rifle untouched. While his horse rears in panic, the mules respond variously to the gunfire: one plunges forward, another is down and apparently about to topple over the precipice, and the rest in the line of fire mill about frantically. In sharp contrast are the calm procession still winding its way down the narrow trail to the right, the distant mule skinner just beginning to react to the report of firing ahead, and the peaceful mining camp in the valley unaware of the drama being enacted on the heights above. Though its parts do not make a satisfactory artistic whole and the Indian snipers appear to be stuck onto the background, *Attack on the Mule Train* tells a coherent story in which Russell displays dexterity and daring in handling complicated perspectives. The distant mountain range is well painted, and the foreground action carries conviction.

EX COLLECTION

Newhouse Galleries, New York City; Elizabeth V. Sprague, Great Falls, Montana; Robert Vaughn, Great Falls, Montana.

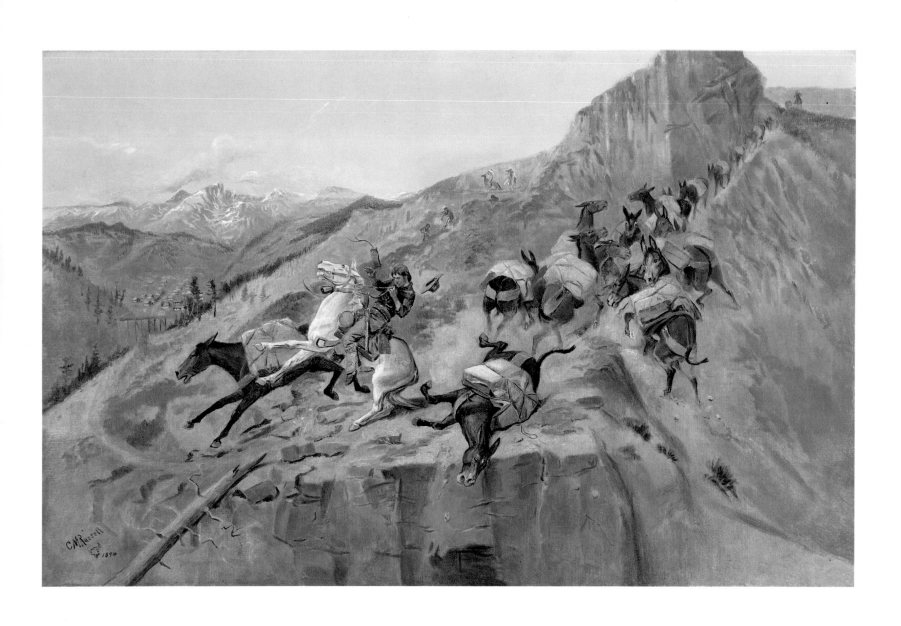

The Marriage Ceremony [Indian Love Call]

1894   Oil on cardboard
18½ x 24⅝ in. (47.0 x 62.5 cm.)

Signed lower right: C M Russell / 94 (skull)

Indian courtship was a theme that especially attracted Russell in the 1890s. It was common practice for an unmarried man to take his horse to water, then loiter by the stream to admire—and be admired by—a young woman who had caught his fancy. In one of his short stories, Russell recounted an old Blackfoot's courting days: ". . . he's 'bout nineteen—the age the Reds begin lookin' for a mate—when he starts ridin' 'round on a painted pony an' puttin' in his time lookin' pretty. When a bunch of young squaws is down gettin' water, he accidentally rides through the creek, givin' them a chance to admire him. He's ablaze with paint an' feathers—to hear him tell it he's rigged out so it hurts your eyes to look at him . . ."[1] A humble lover might cajole and flatter the woman he wanted, wooing her with lines like: "Did you say something? Perhaps I am mistaken. You have been in my thoughts so much and I have imagined many times that you have spoken to me. Now that you are so near, I may seem to hear your voice. If you haven't said anything, it is well and good, for I am like dirt under your feet and why should you waste your kind voice on lowly things. See, I dare not touch you, lest I soil so beautiful a being."[2] Russell's bold suitor has obviously decided on the direct approach. During the day maidens were rigorously chaperoned as they went about their business picking berries, digging roots, gathering wood, and carrying water. For some reason the young woman

in *The Marriage Ceremony* is unaccompanied—her chaperone, if such, is already well up the path back to the village. The startled expression on her face and the dramatic nature of the brave's entry as he swoops down on her like some great bird of prey make this courtship appear more like an abduction. Indeed, among the Plains Cree and the Blackfeet, unescorted maidens were fair game for lurking males and had no recognized right of resistance or retaliation.[3] This would make the title under which *The Marriage Ceremony* is more commonly known, *Indian Love Call*, savagely ironic.

While the painting is bright and colorful, with the reds in the brave's blanket and leggings reflecting in the water, the woman's figure obviously gave Russell problems. Though he moved it about and repainted it, her pose remains overly melodramatic. In 1894, he was still learning his craft.

NOTES

1. Charles M. Russell, "Finger-That-Kills Wins His Squaw," in *Trails Plowed Under*, p. 124.
2. Kennedy, ed., *The Assiniboines*, p. 28.
3. Mandelbaum, *The Plains Cree*, p. 147, Ewers, *The Blackféet*, p. 98.

EX COLLECTION

Newhouse Galleries, New York City.

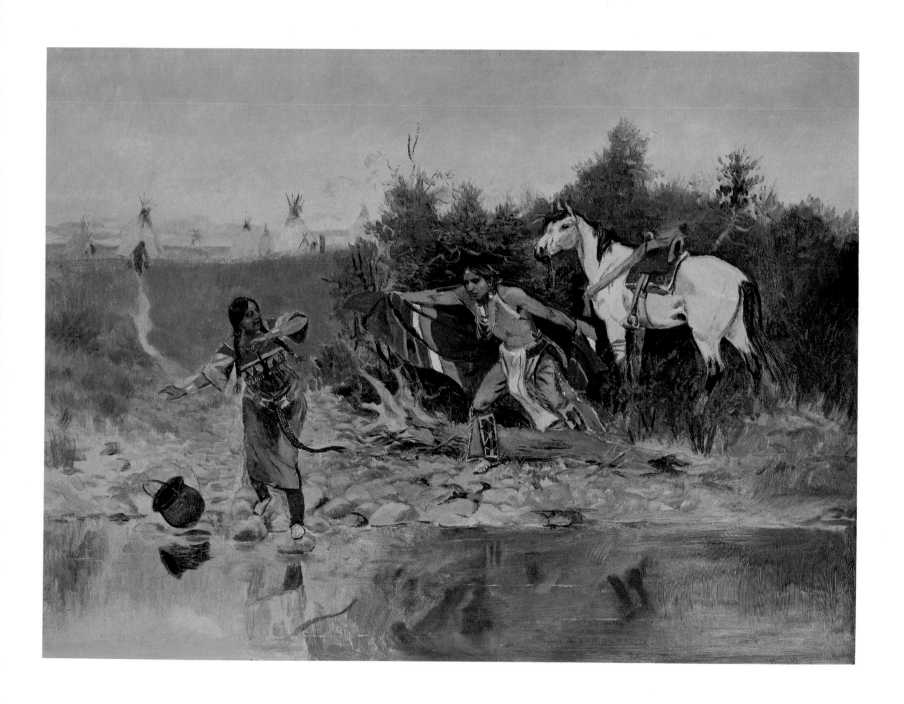

Bringing Up the Trail

1895   Oil on canvas
22⅞ x 35 in. (58.1 x 88.9 cm.)

Signed lower left: C M Russell / (skull) 95

Usually an Indian band on the move would select its campsite by late afternoon to allow the women ample time to erect the lodges in daylight.[1] Here, darkness is falling and the women and children bringing up the rear are anxiously scanning the horizon for sign of the men. Their concern is suggested by the woman shading her eyes against the setting sun, which casts an orange glow over the land, by the posture and expression of the boy watering his horse, and even by the dog's alert stance. The same theme subsequently inspired two fine oils, *In the Wake of the Hunters* (1896; Leon Kelly, Columbiana, Alabama) and *In the Wake of the Buffalo Runners* (1911), but *Bringing Up the Trail* is impressive in its own right. The sense of movement is nicely carried through from the woman topping the rise on the right to the dog poised in the left corner. The strong evening light effects that Russell favored are well handled here, though he did not utilize the whole pictorial space available to him, with the result that the lower-right quarter of *Bringing Up the Trail* is void of interest while the rest of the foreground is too busy with blades of grass.

Russell painted many scenes similar to *Bringing Up the Trail*, but one in particular, *Following the Buffalo Run* (1894; Amon Carter Museum of Western Art, Fort Worth), could be a prelude to this version, so close are they in treatment.

NOTES

1. Ewers, *The Horse in Blackfoot Indian Culture*, p. 146.

EX COLLECTION

Newhouse Galleries, New York City.

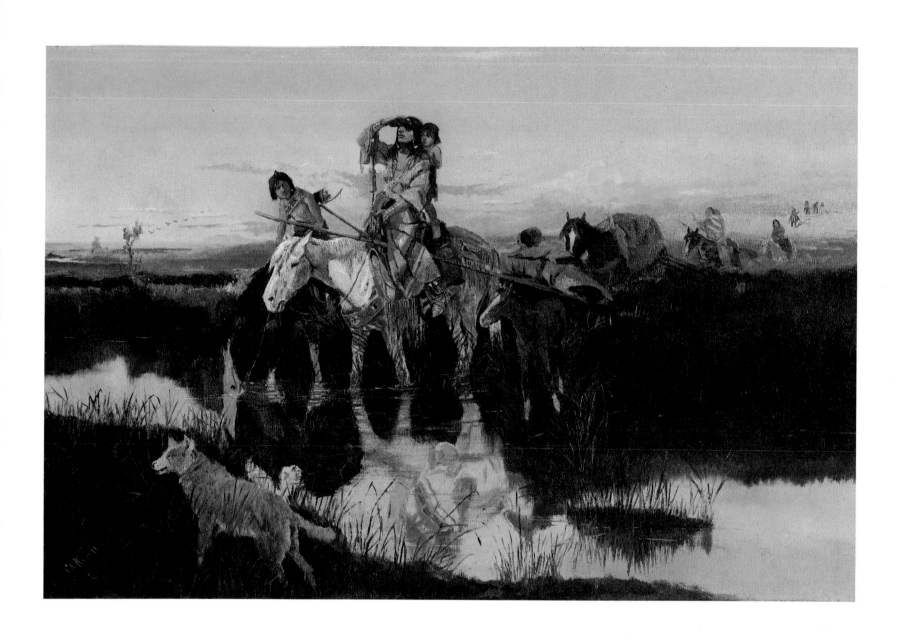

The Defiant Culprit

1895   Oil on masonite panel
18½ x 24⅜ in. (47.0 x 61.9 cm.)

Signed lower left: C M Russell / (skull) 1895

Lacking specific information on the incident depicted here, it is a fair guess that the "defiant culprit" has been captured on a horse raid and is now about to pay the price of his temerity. Russell has underlined the melodramatic nature of the scene by throwing the tipi into deep shadow, allowing the flickering firelight to play over the stern features of the culprit's judges and the stooped figure of the cackling crone, who could have stepped right out of the pages of *Macbeth*. Captor and captive also strike theatrical poses. The long arm of the law literally rests on the culprit's shoulder while he stands with his blanket dropped at his feet, vulnerable in his nakedness but arrogant in his pride. His stance mirrors his contempt as he awaits his fate. "It's their religion to die without a whimper," Russell wrote in one of his stories. "In olden times when a prisoner's took, there's no favors asked or given. He's up agin it. It's a sure case of cash in—skinned alive, cooked over a slow fire, or some such pleasant trail to the huntin'-ground—an' all Mister Prisoner does is to take his medicine without whinin'. If he makes any talk it's to tell ye you're a green hand at the business . . ."[1] It was a trait right out of the noble savage convention that Russell professed to disdain but could not resist, judging from *The Defiant Culprit* and a similar 1897 watercolor more revealingly titled *Sioux Torturing a Blackfoot Brave* (Whitney Gallery of Western Art, Cody). Here, clothing and hair styles suggest that the tables have been turned and a Sioux is facing his Blackfoot captors.

NOTES

1. Charles M. Russell, "Finger-That-Kills Wins His Squaw," in *Trails Plowed Under*, p. 121.

EX COLLECTION

Provenance unknown.

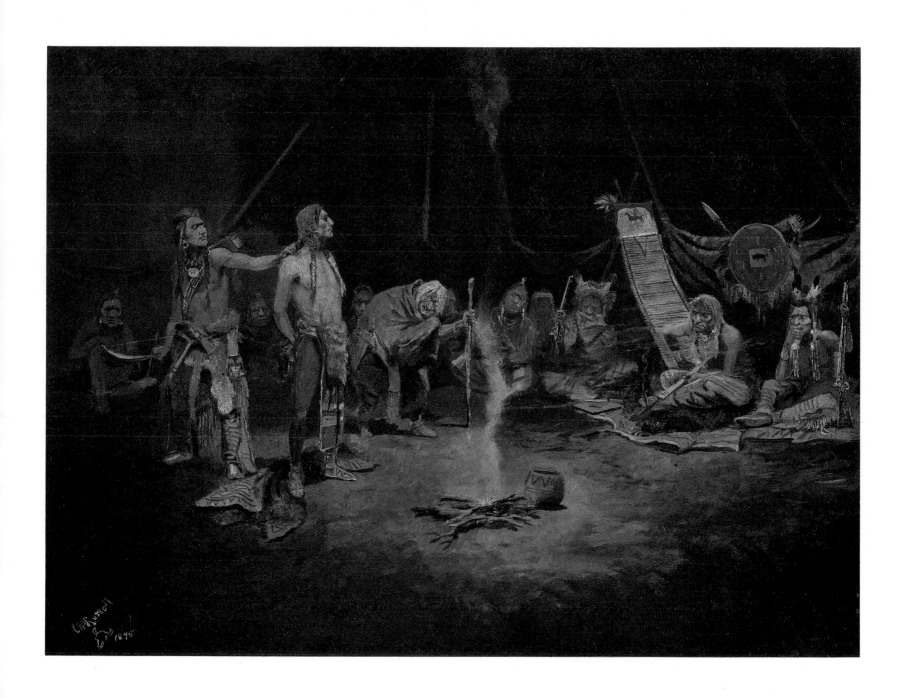

Big Nose George and the Road Agents

1895 Pencil, watercolor, and gouache
on paper
14 x 20 in. (35.6 x 50.8 cm.)

Signed lower left: C M Russell / (skull) 1895

Big Nose George and the Road Agents and the painting that follows, *The Ambush*, done a year apart but almost identical in composition, attest to Russell's continuing fascination with a gang of Black Hills hold-up men active in the late 1870s. Their leader, "Big Nose George" Parrot, was arrested in Miles City, tried in Rawlins, Wyoming, and hung by vigilantes in 1881—only a year after Russell arrived in Montana, an impressionable youth of sixteen.[1] Not surprisingly, Big Nose George captured his imagination. Robert Vaughn, the Montana pioneer and good friend of Russell on whose wall *The Ambush* hung for many years, described the activities of road agents in Montana "during the gold excitement of 1862–63":

The plan of operations of the road agents was to lie in wait at some secluded spot on the road for a coach, a party, or a single individual, of whom information was given by their confederates, and when near enough, [they] would spring from their cover with shotguns with the command, "Halt! throw up your hands!" And while a part of the gang kept their victims covered others would "go through" their effects. A failure to comply with the order or any hesitancy in obeying it, was sure to cause the death of the person so disobeying; and, indeed, if there was probability that any information which a victim might communicate would result in danger to themselves, he was shot, on the principle that "dead men tell no tales."[2]

Despite this dark picture of road agents as cold-blooded murderers, Russell included them in a toast "to all old-timers" that he addressed to Vaughn in 1911:

Here's to the holdup an' hoss thief
  That loved stage roads an' hosses too well,
Who asked the stranglers [vigilantes] to hurry
  Or he'd be late to breakfast in Hell.[3]

And when he went on to paint his popular 1899 oil *The Hold Up* (Amon Carter Museum of Western Art, Fort Worth) showing an actual robbery in progress, Russell still managed to make Big Nose George's activities appear more comic than threatening. Realism simply lost out to his conviction that everything was better in the old days. "Even in my time Montana was a lawless land but seldom dangerous," he told an interviewer in 1921. "We had outlaws, but they were big like the country they lived in."[4] This was a sentiment that, in one shape or another, informed all of Russell's work.

NOTES

1. For Big Nose George and his activities, see Agnes Wright Spring, *The Cheyenne and Black Hills Stage and Express Routes*, pp. 200, 252, 254, 285–287; Mark H. Brown and W. R. Felton, *The Frontier Years: L. A. Huffman, Photographer of the Plains*, pp. 157–158.

2. Vaughn, *Then and Now*, pp. 268–269. Granville Stuart, another pioneer Montanan, also provided a vivid description of the road agent's activities in a caption to an even earlier Russell painting, *"Hands Up,"* in Russell's *Studies of Western Life*.

3. C. M. Russell to Robert Vaughn, 1911, in *Good Medicine*, p. 38.

4. "Four Paintings by the Montana Artist, Charles M. Russell," *Scribner's Magazine* 70 (August 1921): 146.

EX COLLECTION

Newhouse Galleries, New York City.

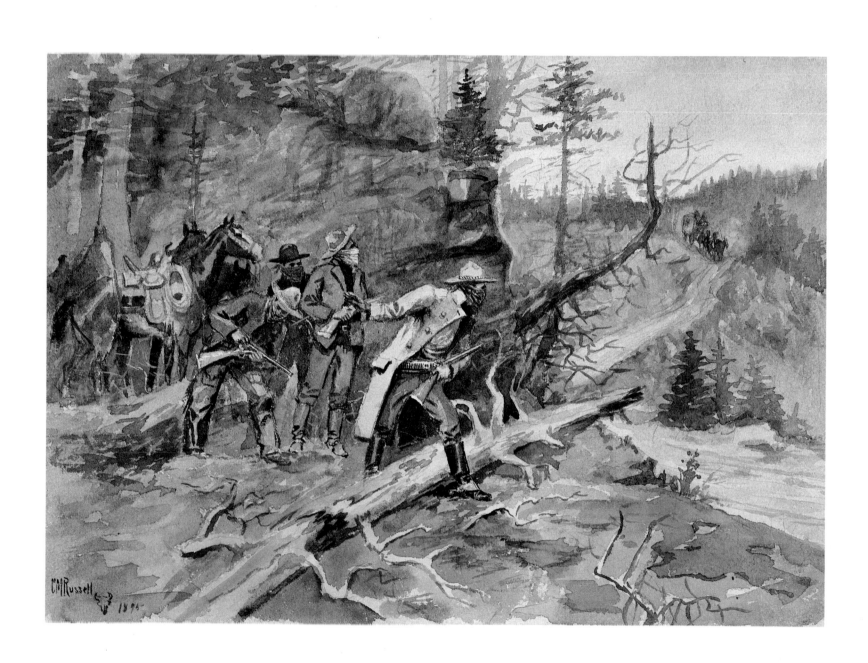

The Ambush

1896   Oil on canvas
26⅛ x 35 in. (66.3 x 88.9 cm.)

Signed lower left: C M Russell / (skull) 1896

What may be an anecdote about *Big Nose George and the Road Agents* or *The Ambush* was told by Russell's cowboy friend Con Price many years later. Con stayed with Charlie in Cascade in the period 1894–95 and "just in fun," he remembered, posed for Russell "in a stage hold-up. I had a sawed-off shot-gun, big hat and my pants legs inside my boots. We found an old Prince Albert coat somewhere that I wore and a big handkerchief around my neck. I surely looked tough." Price went on to say that Russell "painted that picture in a rough way" and was flabbergasted a few years later when it fetched $800 from a foreign nobleman visiting in New York.[1] This part of the story sounds apocryphal, but the part about Con's services as a model was no doubt true.

NOTES

1. Con Price, *Memories of Old Montana*, pp. 141–142.

EX COLLECTION

Newhouse Galleries, New York City; Elizabeth V. Sprague, Great Falls, Montana; Robert Vaughn, Great Falls, Montana.

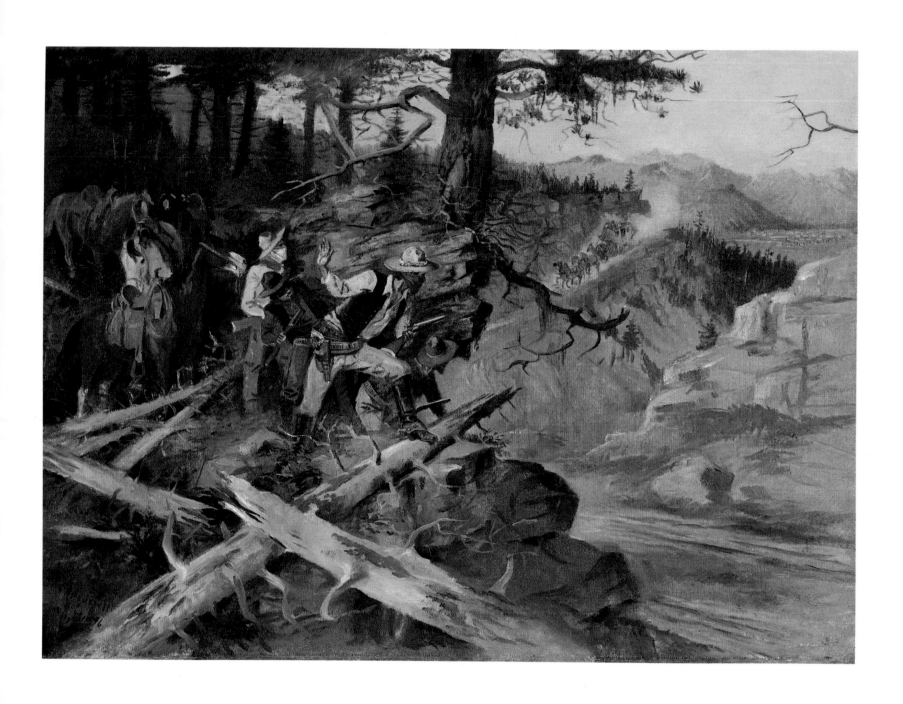

Sighting the Herd [Buffalo Hunt]

1896   Oil on paper mounted on masonite
18 ½ x 24 ⅛ in. (47.0 x 61.3 cm.)

Signed lower left: C M Russell / 1896 (skull)

A small party of hunters approaches a herd of buffalo grazing on the distant plain. Their position is favorable—they are out of view and doubtless downwind from the buffalo and so will have the necessary advantage of surprise when they begin the chase. Russell described the excitement and anticipation of a moment like this in one of his stories:

[The hunters] . . . ain't gone four miles when a scout looms up on a butte an' signs with his robe. This signal causes them all to spread out an' every Injun slides from his pony an' starts backin' out of his cowskin shirt an' skinnin' his leggin's. 'Tain't a minute till they're all stripped to the clout an' moccasins, forkin' their ponies naked like themselves, barrin' two half hitches of rawhide on the lower jaw. That sign means that the herd is in sight an' close. When they're all mounted, the scout on the butte swings his robe a couple of times around his head an' drops it. Before it hits the ground every pony's runnin', with a red rider quirtin' him down the hind leg . . . At the top of the ridge the herd shows—a couple of thousand, all spread out grazin'. But seein' these red hunters pilin' down on 'em, their heads leave the grass. One look's a plenty, an' with tails straightened, they start lumberin' together.[1]

The chase, which Russell portrayed so often elsewhere, was on.

Critics have noted Russell's fluency at spatial composition, evident even in a painting that exhibits as casual a disregard for polish as this one does. Russell virtually ignores a quarter of the canvas—the lower-right portion—but the rest of his composition is tightly structured as the Indian riders funneling up the slope lead the viewer's eyes to the figure on the summit and the buffalo herd spread out far below him.

NOTES

1. Charles M. Russell, "How Lindsay Turned Indian," in *Trails Plowed Under*, p. 143.

EX COLLECTION

Newhouse Galleries, New York City.

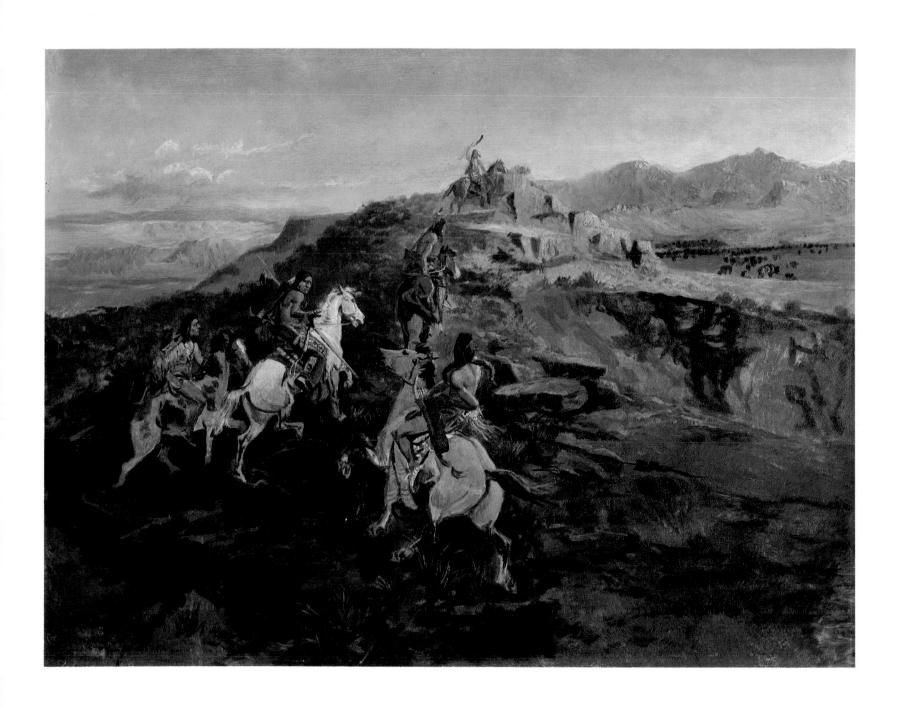

The Snow Trail

1897 Oil on canvas
18 x 25⅜ in. (45.7 x 64.5 cm.)

Signed lower left: C M Russell (skull) 1897

Russell's work did not progress evenly through the 1890s, and he did several oils around 1897–98 that are crudely conceived and executed—melodramatic pictures of hand-to-hand duels, cowboys shooting snakes or being dragged by their horses, buffalo trampling fallen Indians, and the like. Perhaps they were intended to attract buyers at a time when the newly married Russells were struggling to make ends meet. Certainly they indicate haste, an unwillingness to lavish time on careful finishing, and, in some respects, a decline in the standard Russell was attaining by 1896. But the slapdash quality of a surprising number of his paintings from the late 1890s may have represented a necessary transition in his artistic evolution. Russell was moving away from subjects closely based on personal experience as he accepted illustrating assignments that required him to draw as much upon imagination as memory.

The Snow Trail exhibits some of the weaknesses in Russell's oil paintings of this period. Apart from the central figure, the foreground group is indifferently modeled, especially the two horses on the right, and there is an impression of the figures' having been outlined and then painted in. But there are nice touches, too, including the light along the horizon under the leaden sky that casts pink highlights on the men, the white rime on the red blanket drawn up beneath the one brave's mouth, and the strong features of the leader, who resembles the great Blackfoot chief Crowfoot. Russell's careful observation of detail is also evident in the Hudson's Bay Company blanket coats, or capotes, favored by the Blackfeet, the rifles in their cases indicating that no trouble is anticipated, the shaggy winter coats of the horses, and the typical quirting motion of plains Indian riders who rhythmically raised and lowered their whips with "every other jump of the horse."[1] Indian bands preferred to winter in protected river bottoms away from the blizzards sweeping the plains. They moved only when necessity—scarcity of game, exhaustion of wood for fuel or grass for the horses—dictated.[2] Russell passed the winter of 1888–89 with the Bloods in southern Alberta and subsequently did a handful of fine paintings of Indian life during a season when the wolf was never far from the tipi door, nor the hunter's skills at a greater premium.

NOTES

1. Ewers, *The Horse in Blackfoot Indian Culture*, pp. 181–183, 70.
2. Ibid., pp. 124–126.

EX COLLECTION

Newhouse Galleries, New York City.

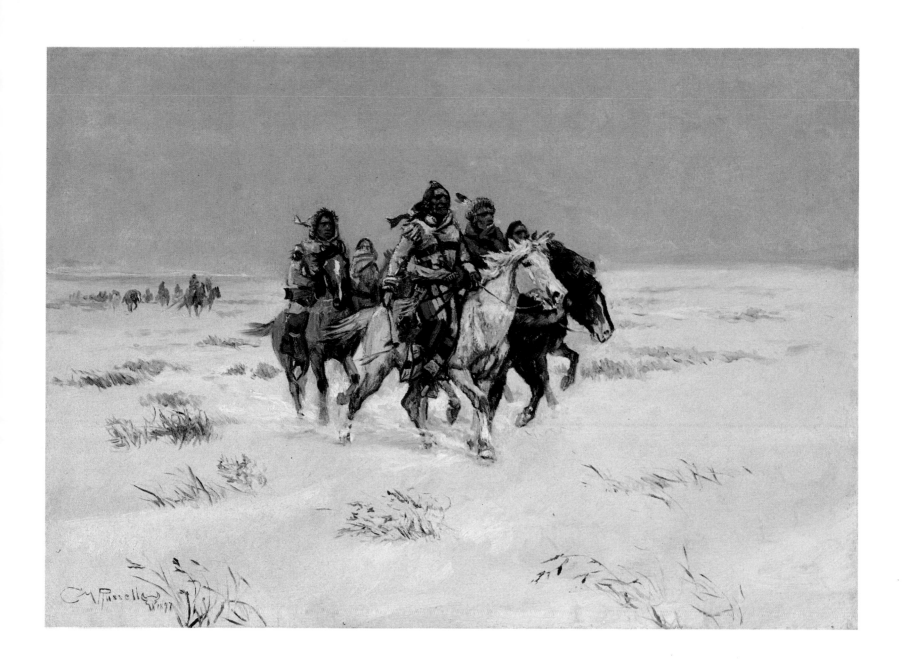

Three Generations

1897   Oil on canvas
17⅛ x 24¼ in. (43.5 x 61.6 cm.)

Signed lower left: C M Russell / (skull) 1897

Though the point has been much mooted, there is good reason to believe that, during his winter with the Bloods in Alberta, Russell seriously considered settling down with a woman and becoming in fact what he often fancied himself, a white Indian. He wrote a humorous letter about the experience to a cowboy friend a few years after his return to Montana, noting:

I went out north a cross the line and lived six month with the Blackfeet . . . I was suprised to here that you were married but think it was the best thing you ever did and hope you will settel down and live like a whit man . . . I expect if I ever get married it will be to this kind [drawing of an Indian woman] as there is a grat many fo [of] them here and I seem to take well among them   I had a chance to marry Young Louses daughter he is black foot Chief   It was the only chance I ever had to marry into good famley but I did not like the way my intended cooked dog and we broke of our engagment.[1]

Though he always treated it lightly, Russell again hinted strongly at the liaison in some of the stories he recorded in print years later. One is particularly revealing. Squaw Owens, a Russell persona, is speaking:

. . . I can talk some Blackfoot . . . I get this talk from a "Live Dictionary" the year before, when I wintered up on Old Man River; that is, I marry a Blood woman. When I say marry, I traded her pa two ponies an' a Winchester, an' in accordance with all Injun's law we're necked all right. . . .

But our married life ain't joyful—I sure kick on that cookin', for there ain't enough Injun in me to like it.

Thinkin' to civilize her a little, I buy her a white woman's rig at [Fort] McLeod, an' when she slips this on I'm damned if you can tell which way she's travelin'.

We ain't been married a week till I've learned enough of the talk to call her all the names known to Blackfeet . . . When grass comes we separate; there's no divorce needed, as we're both willin', so we split the blankets; she pulls for camp, an' I drift south.[2]

Russell's fascination with Indian domestic life is undeniable. Camps on the move, women scraping buffalo hides, courtship, family life in the tipi, and lovely young Indian women were among his favorite subjects in the 1890s. But the conclusion he had reached that he was too white to be an Indian also found expression in works like *Three Generations*. On one level it is a straightforward family portrait. On another, it can be seen as a statement on the toll that time took on the fair Indian maidens he had found so attractive. White observers commonly claimed that ceaseless drudgery quickly stripped Indian women (and, for that matter, pioneer white women) of their charms and made them old well beyond their years. "Their hands are large, coarse, and knotted by hard labor; and they early become wrinkled and careworn," George Bird Grinnell wrote of Blackfoot women in 1892.[3] In this depiction of three generations is one of the fears that may have haunted Russell when he contemplated staying with the Bloods. What would happen when youthful infatuation wore off, and the young mother sitting by the stream had aged into the stooped, toothless grandmother beaming down at her grandchild? The old crone, a ubiquitous presence in Russell's camp scenes, represents his vision of the last stage of Indian womanhood, and it was not an alluring one.[4]

NOTES

1. C. M. Russell to Friend Charly, May 10, 1891, in Dippie, ed., *"Paper Talk,"* p. 20.
2. Charles M. Russell, "Finger-That-Kills Wins His Squaw," in *Trails Plowed Under,* p. 122; also, "How Lindsay Turned Indian," p. 133, and "The War Scars of Medicine-Whip," p. 177. Two of these stories first appeared in *Outing Magazine* in the period 1907–08.
3. Grinnell, *Blackfoot Lodge Tales,* p. 197.
4. For other crones in the Richardson Collection see *The Defiant Culprit* (p. 90), *Captain William Clark of the Lewis and Clark Expedition Meeting with the Indians of the Northwest* (p. 102), and *Returning to Camp* (p. 122).

EX COLLECTION

Newhouse Galleries, New York City.

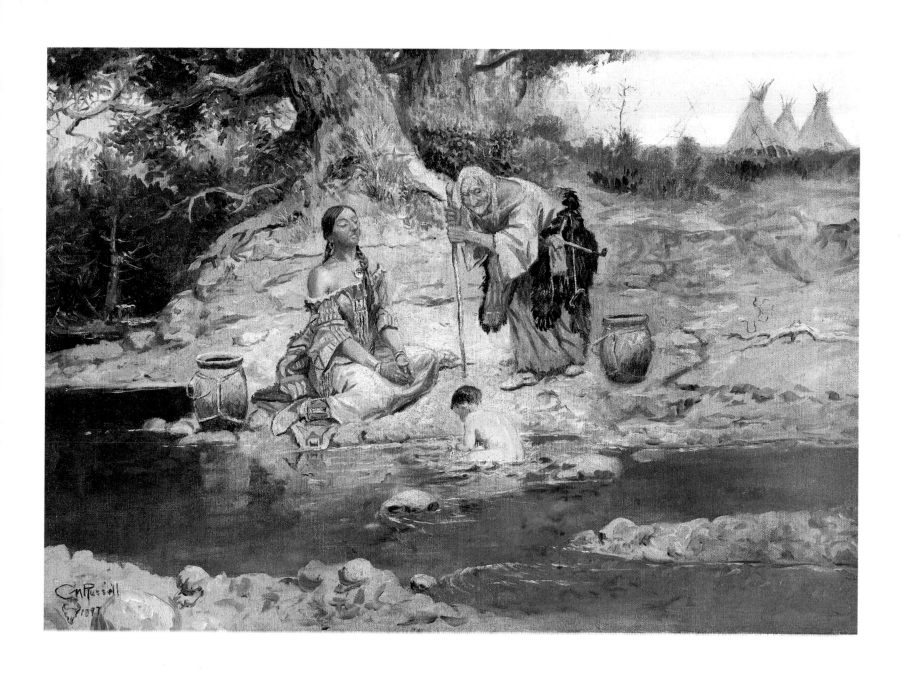

Captain William Clark of the Lewis and Clark Expedition Meeting with the Indians of the Northwest

1897   Oil on canvas
29 ½ x 41 ½ in. (75.0 x 105.4 cm.)

Signed lower left: C M Russell (skull) 1897

The Lewis and Clark Expedition (1804–1806) stirred Russell's imagination as no other event in Montana's past. He returned to it for subject matter throughout his career, and it inspired some of his finest work, including two superb watercolors, *Lewis and Clark on the Lower Columbia* (1905; Amon Carter Museum of Western Art, Fort Worth) and *York* (1908; Montana Historical Society, Helena), and his celebrated mural for the Montana State Capitol in Helena, *Lewis and Clark Meeting Indians at Ross' Hole* (1912). Russell's fascination with Lewis and Clark extended to a boating trip down the Missouri retracing the portion of their route between Fort Benton and Fort Clagett at the mouth of the Judith River. A copy of their journals in hand, Russell responded with boyish enthusiasm to the adventure, occasionally reading "paragraphs aloud, particularly when they were about our surroundings," a companion on the trip recalled.[1]

Despite his personal interest in the subject and the fact that some of his paintings were directly based on passages in the explorers' journals, Russell's reconstructions of the Lewis and Clark Expedition were filled with anachronisms reflecting his tendency to depict western Indians of whatever era in the costumes and with the accoutrements he saw in the 1880s.[2] This large oil is a case in point. The cradle boards, tipi designs, dress styles, and capote shown here all derive from a later period. The specific episode that Russell intended to depict is unclear. The painting was first published as *Lewis and Clark Meeting the Mandan Indians*, but when it was sold by its original owners in 1946 it was known as *Captain William Clark of the Lewis and Clark Expedition Meeting with the Indians of the Northwest* and was supposedly set on the Marias River near the Great Falls of the Missouri in mid-June 1805.[3] Nothing can be proven either way, though the problem is compounded by the painting's similarity to a black-and-white oil executed the same year for *Western Field and Stream* magazine, *Lewis and Clark Meeting the Mandans.*[4]

Common elements include the costumes and hair styles of some of the Indians, a detail that would suggest Russell may have intended this more elaborate painting to depict the same event. It is obvious that he lavished attention on it. The figures are carefully delineated as Clark, with aloof dignity, steps forward to shake hands with the Indians while Charbonneau, husband of Sacajawea, interprets and Clark's black servant, York, looks on. Some of the poses seem conventionalized and stiff, and the colors are, as Russell remarked years later about his work, "kind of stout."[5] But *Captain William Clark of the Lewis and Clark Expedition Meeting with the Indians of the Northwest* is an impressive, large-scale performance at this stage of the Cowboy Artist's career.

NOTES

1. Linderman, *Recollections of Charley Russell*, p. 66.
2. This point is expertly made in John C. Ewers, *Artists of the Old West*, pp. 230–232.
3. "Vaughn Collection of Russell Paintings Sold to Newhouse Galleries of New York," *Great Falls Daily Tribune*, undated clipping (c. June 1946) in the C. M. Russell scrapbook, Amon Carter Museum of Western Art, Fort Worth.
4. Wm. Bleasdell Cameron, "Russell's Oils Eye-Opener to the East," *Canadian Cattlemen* 13 (February 1950): 27. This painting was reproduced in the January 1898 number of *Western Field and Stream.*
5. "Russell Exhibiting Fine Collection of His Western Paintings in the East," unidentified clipping (December 1919) in the C. M. Russell scrapbook, Amon Carter Museum of Western Art.

EX COLLECTION

Newhouse Galleries, New York City; Elizabeth V. Sprague, Great Falls, Montana; Robert Vaughn, Great Falls, Montana.

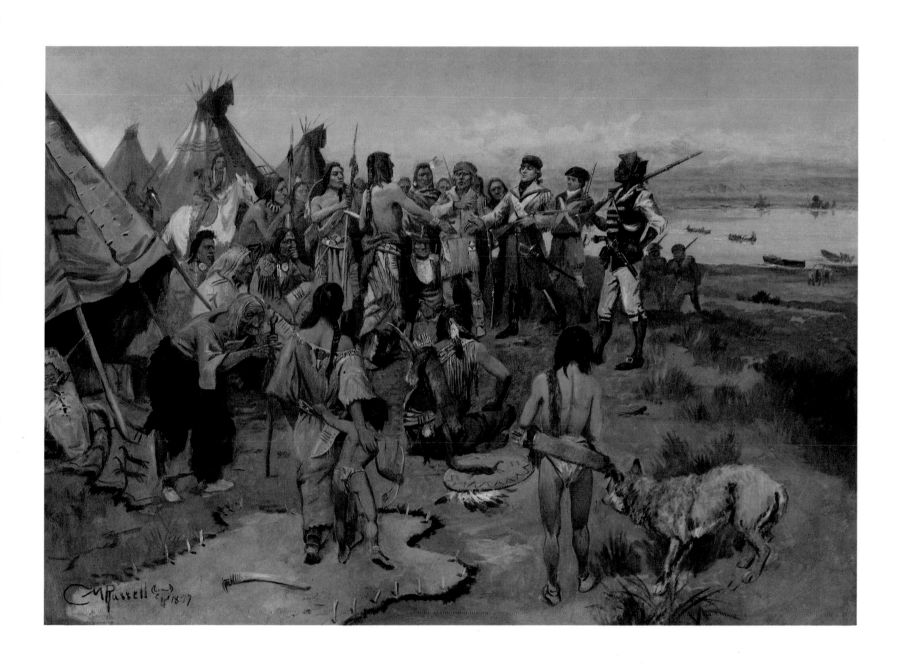

Chief Bear Claw

c. 1898 Pencil, watercolor, and gouache
on paper
10⅝ x 9 in. (27.0 x 22.9 cm.)

Signed lower left: C M R (skull) 1898 [?]

A student of Russell's work would be hard pressed to think of a single portrait he did of a white man, yet he painted many individual Indians. A few of his portraits were of celebrated leaders he had never met, but most were of Indians of his own acquaintance. Russell often went on sketching trips to the Montana reservations, and some of his Cree friends posed for him in his Great Falls studio.

This little watercolor, done basically in brown with the earrings providing a yellow highlight, was possibly intended for use as an illustration and may be a composite portrait rather than an individual likeness. The face bears a family resemblance to Sleeping Thunder, the subject of a bronze, and Deaf Bull, the subject of an 1899 watercolor. But the features are distinct enough to suggest that Russell had someone else in mind.

EX COLLECTION
Provenance unknown.

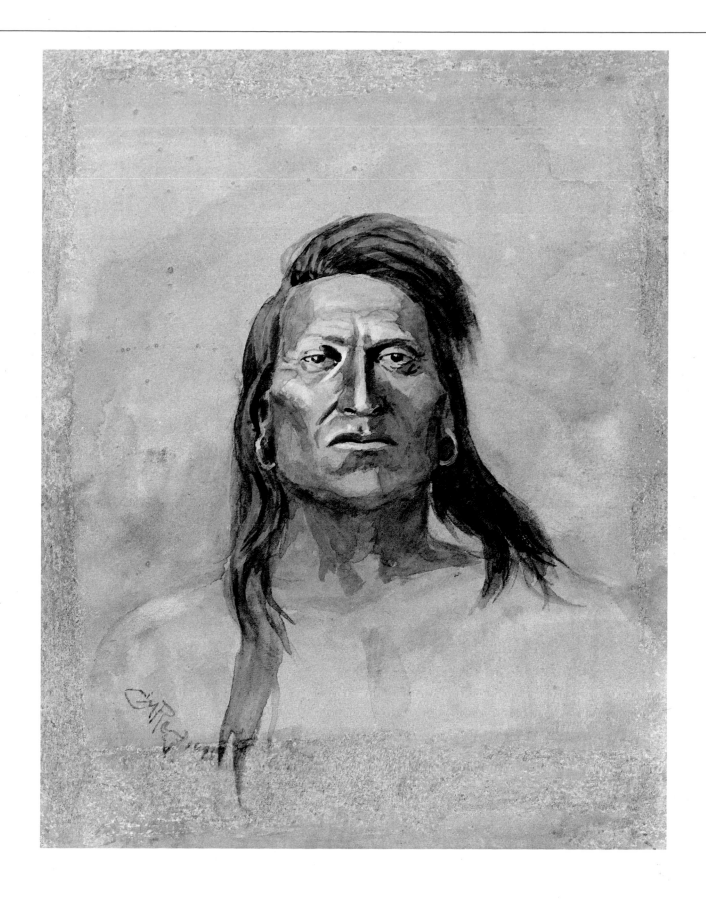

Guardian of the Herd

1899   Pencil, watercolor, and gouache
on paper
20⅝ x 29⅛ in. (52.4 x 74.0 cm.)

Signed lower left: C M Russell (skull) 1899

No one who saw the great herds of buffalo drifting down to the river to drink ever forgot the sight. George Bird Grinnell, who witnessed such scenes in the 1870s, wrote in 1892: "From the high prairie on every side they stream into the valley, stringing along in single file, each band following the deep trail worn in the parched soil by the tireless feet of generations of their kind. At a quick walk they swing along, their heads held low. The long beards of the bulls sweep the ground; the shuffling tread of many hoofs marks their passing, and above each long line rises a cloud of dust that sometimes obscures the westering sun."[1] Russell had arrived in Montana just in time to see the remnants of the awesome multitudes of the recent past still roaming at large. Ten years before, a Montanan recalled, "I rode from Sun River to Milk River, and from there to Fort Benton, about 210 miles, and during the whole journey I was constantly surrounded by the animals, and never for a moment out of sight of them."[2] Russell witnessed no such spectacle in 1880, but had he come even a few years later he would have seen no wild buffalo at all. By 1885 the herds had vanished, leaving tribes like the Blackfeet desolate. "The buffalo were their main dependence," a Canadian anthropologist wrote at the time. "Suddenly, almost without warning, they found themselves stripped of nearly every necessary of life. The change was one of the greatest that could well befall a community."[3]

No wonder Russell made a buffalo skull his personal insignia, for the buffalo's fate was that of the whole West that he knew so briefly and loved so well. On Thanksgiving Day in 1925, a year before he died, he penned a warm tribute to the buffalo:

turkey is the emblem of this day and it should be in the east but the west owes nothing to that bird but it owes much to the humped backed beef . . .

the nickle weares his picture dam small money for so much meat   he was one of natures bigest gift and this country owes him thanks[4]

Russell's own gratitude found expression in paintings, sketches, and sculpture featuring buffalo, and *The Guardian of the Herd* represents one of his favorite themes, the herd on the move. His major achievement along these lines, the splendid oil *When the Land Belonged to God* (1915; The Montana Club, Helena), did not come easily. The lead bull gave him no end of trouble. He painted and repainted it, unable to make the animal "stand still," before he was satisfied.[5] *The Guardian of the Herd*, done sixteen years earlier, does not meet such a high standard. Russell conveys the undulating motion of the herd descending in the distance and topping the rise in the foreground. But his featured bull—the "guardian" of the title—is not so successful. Heavy shadows make his hindquarters appear detached from the rest of his body, while his head is awkward and ill-proportioned.

NOTES

1. George Bird Grinnell, "The Last of the Buffalo," *Scribner's Magazine* 12 (September 1892): 267.
2. Hamlin Russell, "The Story of the Buffalo," *Harper's New Monthly Magazine* 86 (April 1893): 796.
3. Horatio Hale, "Report on the Blackfoot Tribes," in *Report on the North-Western Tribes of Canada*, pp. 3–4.
4. Charles M. Russell to Ralph Budd, November 26, 1925, in *Good Medicine*, p. 37.
5. Linderman, *Recollections of Charley Russell*, p. 95.

EX COLLECTION

Provenance unknown.

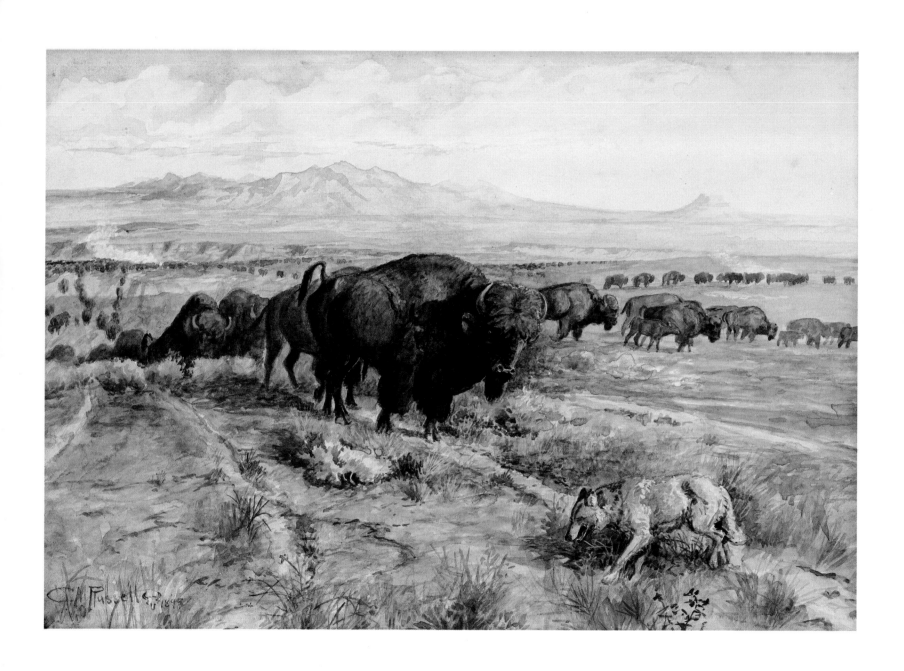

The Buffalo Hunt [Wild Meat for Wild Men]

1899   Oil on canvas
24⅛ x 36⅛ in. (61.3 x 91.7 cm.)

Signed lower left: C M Russell / (skull) 1899

This painting, approximately 2 x 3 ft. in size, shows the remarkable development in Russell's ability to portray Indians hunting buffalo. He was in complete command of the subject by 1899. That same year he painted another major buffalo hunt, 2½ x 4 ft. (Amon Carter Museum of Western Art, Fort Worth), and the next, a similar, even larger (4 x 6 ft.) oil (Thomas Gilcrease Institute, Tulsa). All three paintings were called simply *The Buffalo Hunt*, and in order to differentiate among them and the many other identically titled Russell paintings, Frederic G. Renner has assigned each one a number. This is *The Buffalo Hunt No. 25*. It exhibits Russell's ease not only in handling buffalo on the run but also in seeing the subject from any perspective. No longer did he stick to broadside views; rather, in the paintings he executed in 1899 and 1900 he ran the buffalo and their pursuers toward the viewer. His bowmen are convincing. Here, as in most of his buffalo hunts, one of the background figures sports a headband—a detail that not only serves as a color highlight but also represents the custom of, for example, the Assiniboines who before the chase stripped to their mocassins and breech clouts "and tied their hair with bands on top of their heads."[1] Russell frequently showed one of the hunters carrying an extra

arrow or two in his bow hand or, as here where the rather odd absence of a quiver would make it necessary, in his mouth.[2] The sense of verisimilitude is wonderful. Only the choking cloud of dust that would obscure such a scene from view is lacking. By 1899, no other artist could touch Russell when it came to conveying the wild excitement of a buffalo chase.

NOTES

1. Kennedy, ed., *The Assiniboines*, p. 112.
2. In "How Lindsay Turned Indian," Russell told how an Indian hunter would pull "five or six arrows at a draw, holdin' the extras in his mouth an' bowhand . . ." (*Trails Plowed Under*, p. 143). An 1836 lithograph based on Titian R. Peale's *Buffaloe Hunt on The River Platte* showed one Indian with an arrow in his mouth, a second with a spare arrow in his bow hand. See Poesch, *Titian Ramsay Peale*, p. 59.

EX COLLECTION

Newhouse Galleries, New York City.

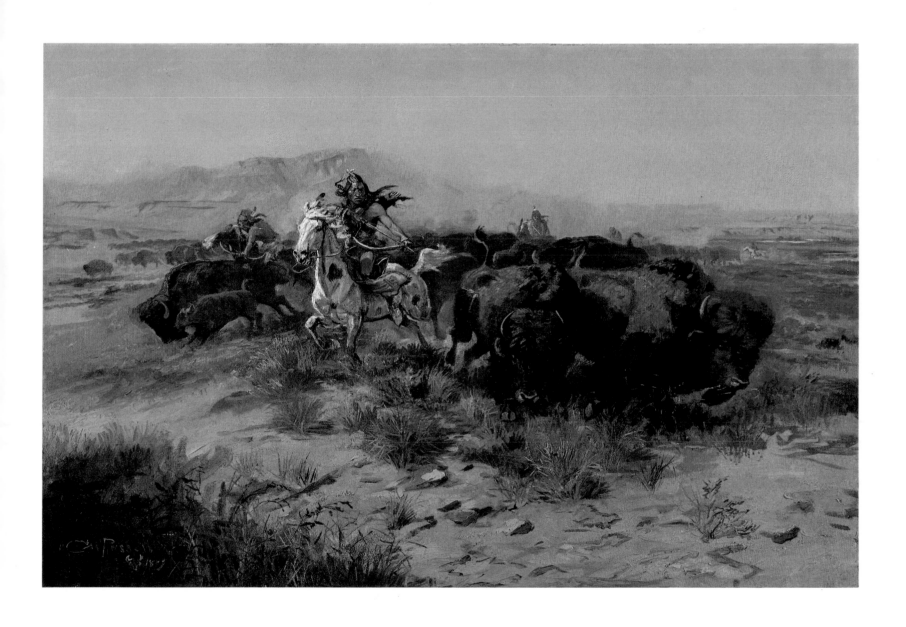

Redman's Meat

1899   Pencil, watercolor, and gouache
on paper
21 x 30 in. (53.3 x 76.2 cm.)

Signed lower left: C M Russell / (skull) 1899

In his buffalo hunt paintings Russell made no concession to delicacy. Terrified calves, cows, and bulls jam together, saliva streaming from their mouths, tongues lolling as they run for life. When an offended patron demanded that Russell alter such realistic details in an oil he had commissioned, Russell refused on the sensible grounds that, when buffalo run, they slobber.[1] Anyway, there was nothing very sportsmanlike or elevated about the chase. The white trophy hunter might single out a magnificent bull as his target, but the Indian hunter was after meat, and his techniques were designed accordingly. Russell often showed an Indian crowding a cow into a calf to slow it down and give him a better shot, though during any extended run the cows usually outdistanced the bulls while the calves were left far behind, prey to Indian boys who honed their hunting skills on them.

So natural is the action in *Redman's Meat,* and so effortlessly is it portrayed, that one must be reminded just how difficult the subject is in order to appreciate Russell's skill. His buffalo are the real thing. Here one particularly notices the foreground bull lumbering along, his "hoofs flying out below," as Francis Parkman observed, and his short tail "held rigidly erect."[2]

NOTES

1. Mrs. Charles M. Russell to Thomas F. Cole, July 17, 1918, in Adams and Britzman, *Charles M. Russell, the Cowboy Artist*, p. 282.
2. Francis Parkman, *The Oregon Trail: Sketches of Prairie and Rocky-Mountain Life*, p. 410.

EX COLLECTION

Provenance unknown.

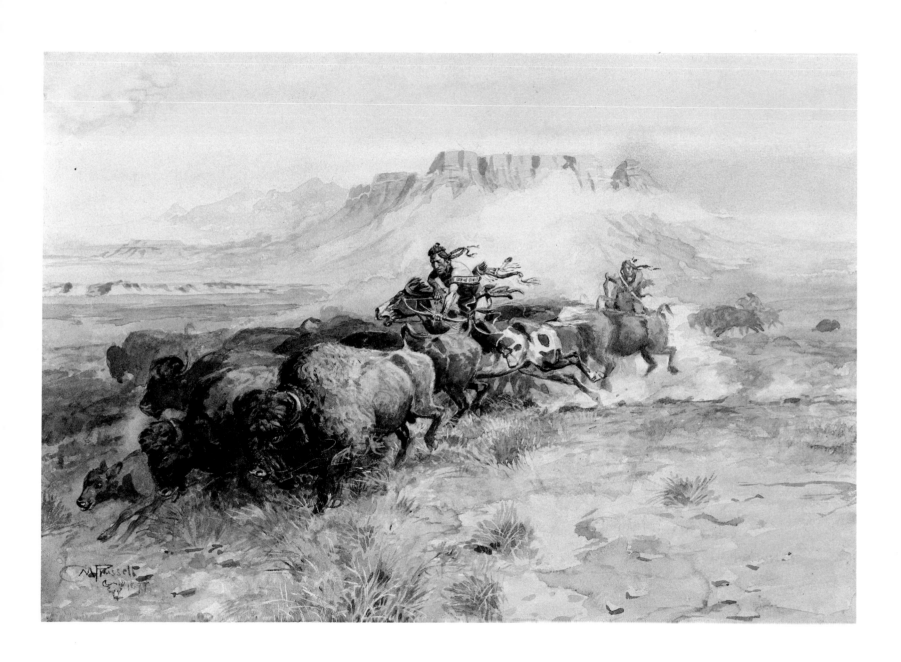

When Cowboys Get in Trouble

1899   Oil on canvas
24 x 36 in. (61.0 x 91.5 cm.)

Signed lower left: C M Russell (skull) 1899

Most cow work was routine. "Occasionally an animal would get on 'the fight' and make things interesting," the pioneer Montana cattleman Granville Stuart remembered, "but the rope horses were as clever as the men about keeping out of danger and rarely did we have a serious accident."[1] However, there were "moments of great peril in a cowboy's career," and the incident shown here was one Russell painted several times.[2] The animal, roped by the heel, has lunged at a horse and rider, backing them against the side of a cutbank. A toss of its head and the horse will be gored. The cowboy reaches for his revolver as he scrambles out of the saddle to avoid himself being gored in the leg or crushed by his rearing mount. Russell implies more trouble ahead for the cowboy, since his gun hand is about to be snagged in the loop of his rope. The third rider, preoccupied with controlling his horse, is effectively *hors de combat*. The action is tense, the composition tight. The dust cloud raised by the herd grazing calmly in the distance sets off the figure of the cowboy on the right. It has been pointed out many times that in scenes like these Russell did not generalize. The men were individuals, and so were the horses and cows. The brands tell the names of the outfits represented at the roundup and place this scene in the Big Dry country west of the Musselshell and below the Missouri.

NOTES

1. Phillips, ed., *Forty Years on the Frontier*, II, 179–180.
2. For example, *A Dangerous Situation* (1897; Stark Museum of Art, Orange, Texas); *One Down, Two to Go* (1902; The Rockwell Foundation, Corning, New York); and *A Moment of Great Peril in a Cowboy's Career* (n.d. [1904]; Amon Carter Museum of Western Art, Fort Worth).

EX COLLECTION

Provenance unknown.

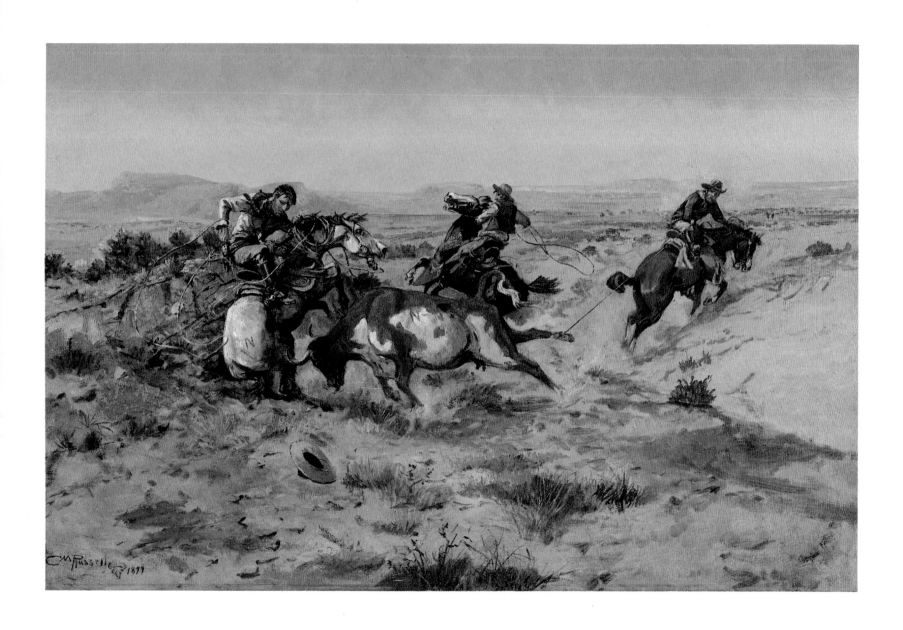

Breaking Up the Ring

1900 Pencil, watercolor, and gouache
on paper
19½ x 29⅜ in. (49.5 x 74.6 cm.)

Signed lower left: C M Russell (skull) 1900

Breaking Up the Ring is so loosely sketched and painted that it appears to have been tossed off almost casually. But it is pleasingly colored, full of dash and verve, and serves as an introduction to the composition Russell favored in his more elaborate paintings of Indians attacking stagecoaches, wagon trains, and the like. In each, a prominent central warrior, armed with a rifle and carefully rendered, is set off by two or three others clustered behind him. The action always moves from left to right, the circling braves approaching and receding on the sides of the picture; often one or more on the left fall wounded, while on the right one rides away bent low over his pony as he releases an arrow toward the embattled whites, whose individuality is lost in the dust and the distance. A critic in 1904 contended that Russell's "chief fault is a tendency to neglect portions of his picture that he considers of too little importance, and the result is often an unfinished work whose imperfections show up glaringly in a reproduction. This fact lays him liable to an accusation (that may seem partly justifiable) of carelessness . . ."[1] *Breaking Up the Ring* obviously evidences haste. At the same time, by downplaying distracting elements it successfully focuses attention on the principal figures.

NOTES

1. Kathryne Wilson, "An Artist of the Plains," *Pacific Monthly* 12 (December 1904): 343.

EX COLLECTION

Provenance unknown.

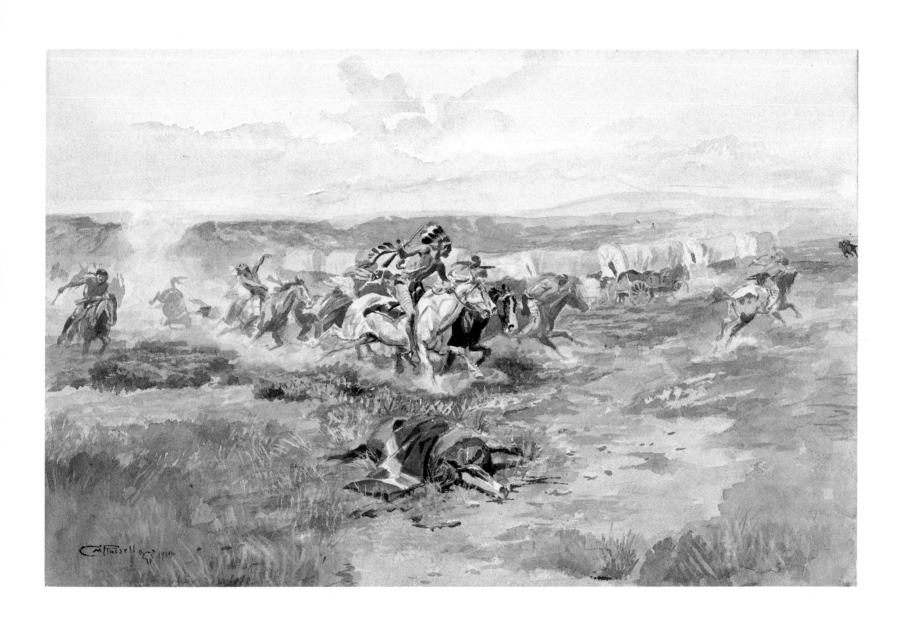

The Tenderfoot

1900   Oil on canvas
14⅛ x 20⅛ in. (35.9 x 51.1 cm.)

Signed lower left: C M Russell (skull) / 1900

If ever there was a touch of malice lurking in Charlie Russell's genial heart, it found expression in a work like this. He sketched, painted, and modeled other versions of "cowboy fun," but when it was a tenderfoot doing the dancing to the tune of a .45 he obviously took extra delight in the performance. For, unfair as the odds seem and deplorable as such bullying might be, it had the ring of an initiation rite—the West introducing itself to the East. Presumably, if the dude in *The Tenderfoot* proves himself a good sport there will be slaps on the back and a convivial round of drinks afterward. But no matter what the immediate outcome, the tenderfoot is the future, and he and his ilk will one day displace his tormentors as surely as the sun is setting behind the stage stop in Russell's painting. If the old West chose to go out with a bang and a roar of laughter, Russell as its greatest eulogist was not about to shed tears over the discomfiture of a tenderfoot or two.

Patrick T. Tucker, who rode the range with Kid Russell in the early 1880s and years later wrote a thoroughly unreliable book about their escapades together, told an anecdote that might be apocryphal but was obviously meant to describe *The Tenderfoot*. One quiet Sunday afternoon, Pat O'Hara, owner of the stage station at Geyser on Arrow Creek, decided to stir up some excitement by introducing a young English guest "looking for adventure" to a bunch of thirsty cowboys who had just ridden up "to the door branded SALOON." The Englishman

gave them all the gladhand. Pat was wiping off the bar, getting ready for business. The dude's invitation is accepted, and the boys all take a drink. Bill Bullard, a big long-legged cowpoke, pats the man with the silver on the back. That makes the Englishman feel brave, and he tells the barkeeper to fill them up again.

We all take another drink, and hurrah for the Queen.

"Give the lads another drink," the tenderfoot says.

By this time the pilgrim [traveler] is a hoss man, and steps outside to look the hosses over. Bill Bullard is trailing the dude, pulling his shooting iron as he goes. They are both walking crooked. A lone Indian buck is standing by the log shack. He can't move— too much firewater. . . . but he is still standing up and his eyes are working.

The pilgrim is traveling slow. He sees a lot of saddle hosses. Bullard is making eyes at the boys, and walking tiptoe. His legs are shaky but his aim is still good. He takes a crack at Johnny Bull's feet with his six-gun. That raised a dust. The pilgrim crowhops. Bill makes him dance the cancan while he shoots at his feet. . . .

Russell was sitting in the shade of his cow hoss on the side of a hill, taking it all in. . . . He told me afterward that this was the first time he had ever seen a man dance to the music of a six-gun.[1]

The Tenderfoot is what it appears to be, a joke, not a deathless work of art. It is populated with stock western types: the Indian, the saloonkeeper, the gambler, the Chinese cook, the stagedriver, and, sitting at the end of the bench watching intently, the Cowboy Artist himself. Arresting touches include the skillful way the setting sun is implied by the streak of light along the saloon roof and on the distant bluff, and the deep shadow cast over the foreground figures. There is also artfulness in the composition as the frightened, rearing horse carries the action from right to left along the path of the bullet to the dude's dancing feet. Since the other horses are so nonchalant about the gunfire, one can assume that the skittish animal is the dude's own mount.

NOTES

1. Patrick T. Tucker, *Riding the High Country*, ed. Grace Stone Coates, pp. 52–55. Tucker comments on the cowboy propensity, in swapping yarns, to tell "more lies than truth" (p. 69), and his book certainly proves the point.

EX COLLECTION

Newhouse Galleries, New York City.

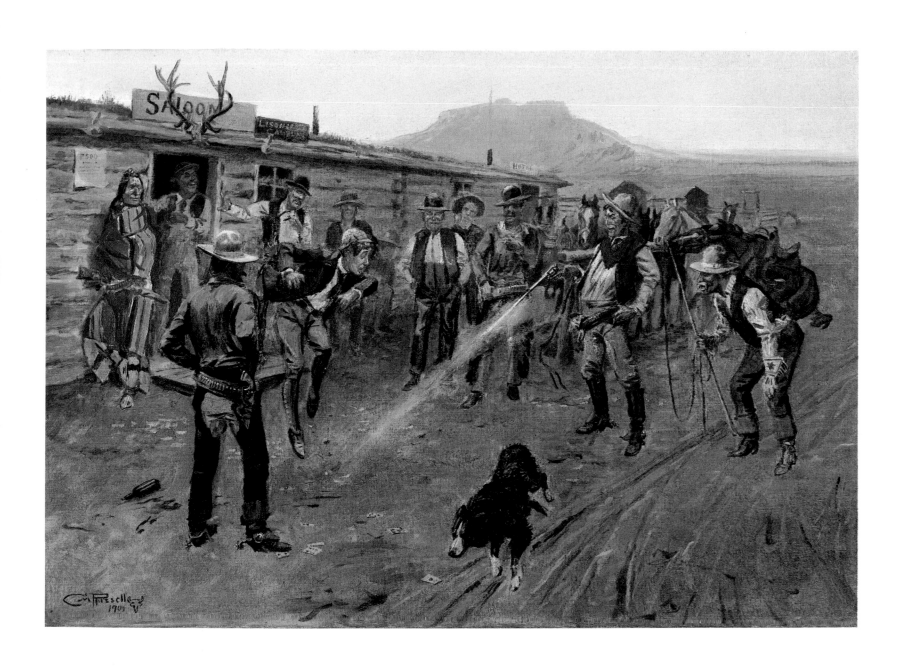

On the Attack

1901   Pencil, watercolor, and gouache
on paper
11 5/8 x 17 5/8 in. (26.5 x 44.8 cm.)

Signed lower left: C M Russell (skull) 1901

In 1889, Frederic Remington painted a mammoth (4 x 8 ft.) oil titled *A Dash for the Timber* (Amon Carter Museum of Western Art, Fort Worth) showing a band of cowboys racing pellmell for safety with Apaches hot on their heels. The painting is a dazzling exercise in Wild West theatrics, and Remington drove home the point by having all the onrushing cowboys part around the viewer except one who, coming hell bent for leather, is shown straight on. Russell occasionally painted similar groups of trappers or cowboys in full flight from pursuing warriors, the action sweeping across the picture at an angle, usually from right to left. *On the Attack* is a carefully painted and vigorous version; its riderless horses and desperate faces tell a dramatic tale. But none of Russell's paintings on the theme remotely rivals *A Dash for the Timber*. Suffice it to say, Remington owned the subject.

EX COLLECTION

Provenance unknown.

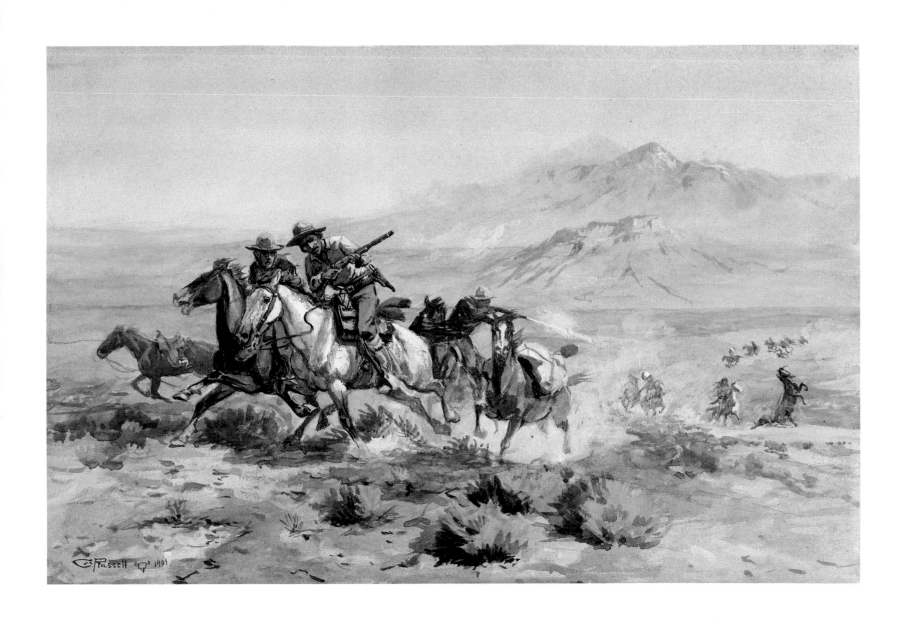

The Buffalo Hunt

1901   Oil on canvas
24⅛ x 36⅛ in. (61.3 x 91.8 cm.)

Signed lower left: C M Russell (skull) 1901

The buffalo hunt shown here has elements of the traditional surround—wherein hunters circled the herd and forced it to mill—though this is actually a parallel chase, with the bowman and the lancer pressuring the opposite flanks. Few plains Indians actually employed the lance in buffalo hunting. The Plains Cree may never have used it, while the Blackfeet had virtually abandoned it by 1870.[1] John Ewers notes that, when a Blackfoot hunter did wield a spear, he grasped it with two hands and, holding it overhead, thrust downward.[2] Russell's lancer would seem to be at a disadvantage in trying to bring down a buffalo with a spear held as shown.

The composition of *The Buffalo Hunt* (No. 30, to employ Frederic Renner's numbering system) is distinctive among Russell's many related works. Here the surging herd has been bunched so tightly by the pressure of the hunters on the flanks and at the rear that it forms a triangular mass moving directly at the viewer like an arrow in flight. *The Buffalo Hunt* and the painting that follows, *Returning to Camp*, constitute a matched set.

NOTES

1. Mandelbaum, *The Plains Cree*, p. 95; Ewers, *The Horse in Blackfoot Indian Culture*, pp. 156–157.
2. Ewers, *The Horse in Blackfoot Indian Culture*, pp. 158, 200–201.

EX COLLECTION

Maurice Weiss, Helena, Montana.

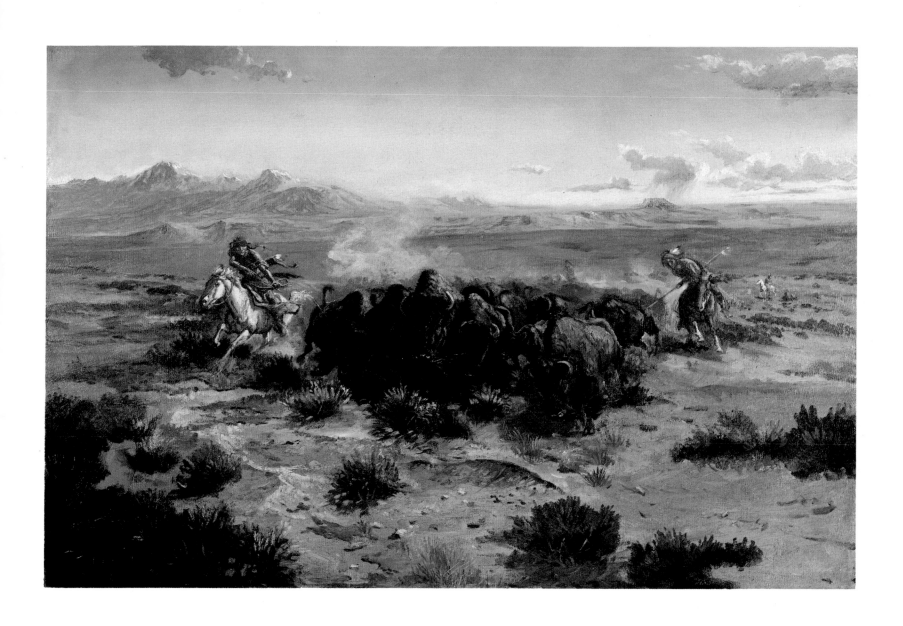

Returning to Camp

1901   Oil on canvas
24⅛ x 36 in. (61.3 x 91.5 cm.)

Signed lower left: C M Russell / (skull) 1901

In *The Buffalo Hunt*, Russell ran the action right at the viewer; in this sequel, *Returning to Camp*, the viewer trails after the women and boys transporting the spoils of the chase back to the village. The reversal in perspective complements the before-and-after story Russell set out to tell and results in another strikingly different oil. The men, who may have assisted with the butchering (about an hour per animal) have ridden off ahead on their buffalo horses, leaving the women to bring home the meat and hides by travois or slung over the backs of the pack horses.[1] Full of the kind of detail admired in Russell's work, *Returning to Camp* is also rich in human interest. A mother glances over at her young son proudly displaying the trophy of his chase; soon he too will hunt the mighty buffalo. An old woman drives off one of the wolflike dogs frustrated in its bid to partake of the feast so tantalizingly near.

The buffalo was always referred to as the plains Indians' staff of life. "It was their food, clothing, dwelling, tools," George Bird Grinnell wrote. "The needs of savage people are not many, perhaps, but whatever the Indians of the plains had, that the buffalo gave them."[2] In *Returning to Camp* Russell makes the same point visually.

NOTES

1. See Ewers, *The Horse in Blackfoot Indian Culture*, pp. 160–161; Mandelbaum, *The Plains Cree*, p. 58.
2. George Bird Grinnell, "The Last of the Buffalo," *Scribner's Magazine* 12 (September 1892): 278.

EX COLLECTION

Maurice Weiss, Helena, Montana.

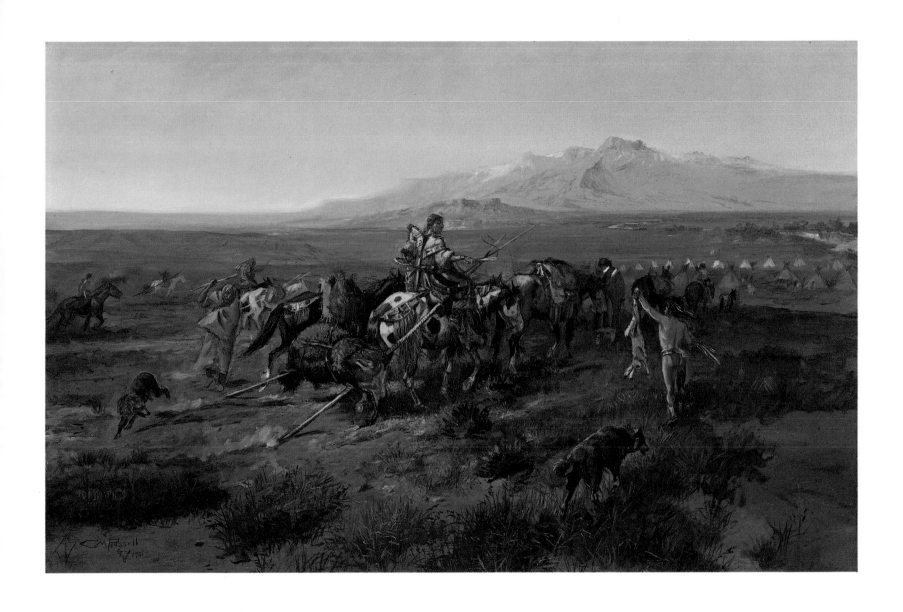

Counting Coup [The War Scars of Medicine Whip]

1902   Oil on canvas
18⅛ x 30⅛ in. (46.0 x 76.5 cm.)

Signed lower left: C M Russell / (skull) 1902

Few Russell paintings are as well documented as this stirring depiction of intertribal warfare. It was painted for a distant relative, George W. Kerr of St. Louis, and sent along with a descriptive letter. While he was a young man visiting with the Bloods, Russell sat in the lodge of Medicine Whip and heard him relate the story of his greatest war exploit:

My son, he said, fifty snows behind me the Sioux were very bad . . . At last in the moon of painted leaves a scout came in with a Sioux arrow . . . It was not long till many Bloods were on their war ponies in the tracks of the Sioux. The sun was not yet in the middle when we sighted them. It was a running fight . . . until our arrows were nearly gone . . . Now every time a Sioux bow string spoke a Blood brave was wounded or sent to shadow land . . . They had killed our Chief and our hearts were on the ground. The Sioux now called us many bad names . . . One young man called to me saying "you with the pretty pony, that is not a squaw pony, see he hangs his head in shame. He has the coup paint on his hip, but no man is on his back" . . . His words were like hot irons in my heart . . . Throwing down my bow and empty quiver I shouted "Come brothers we will show them how the Bloods kill lice . . ." My pony was strong and I was soon among them. He with the bad tongue ran in front of their Medicine Man. I made a false thrust at his throat and as he raised his shield drove under stopping his heart . . . Then quickly

changing my shield to the string hand I struck the Medicine Man across the face with my quirt. Then the Sioux crowded about me and left their war pictures on me as you see today. This scar on my face was from the tomahawk which stunned and blinged [blinded] me. I remember twisting my fingers in my pony mane. Then it was night very dark. When I awoke my people were about me. The Sioux were dead. All still their hearts slept. They were all scalped, except Bad Tongue and the Medicine Man, which were left for me. The scars on my leg are where the arrows went under my shield. That was long ago, My Son . . .[1]

Russell loved this tale of valor from the olden days on the plains. He retold it with some embellishment in "The War Scars of Medicine-Whip"[2] and based two striking oils on it: *For Supremacy* (1895; Amon Carter Museum of Western Art, Fort Worth) and *The Making of a Warrior* (1898; The Warner Collection of Gulf States Paper Corporation, Tuscaloosa). In all the related paintings and pen sketches that Russell did, he invariably placed a corpse in the foreground—a grim reminder of the cost of valor.

Russell obviously lavished care on *Counting Coup.* Every figure in it is well painted. But the color scheme, with its predominance of pinks and blues, does not do justice to the action portrayed, and for all the fine details the composition as a whole seems cluttery when compared to Russell's brilliant 1908 oil *When Blackfeet and Sioux Meet* (p. 140). It is a comparison that establishes just how much Russell's work improved over six years during this dynamically productive stage of his career.

NOTES

1. Charles M. Russell to George W. Kerr, September 29, 1902, in McCracken, *The Charles M. Russell Book,* p. 116.
2. *Trails Plowed Under,* pp. 177–186.

EX COLLECTION

Newhouse Galleries, New York City; Samuel H. Rosenthal, Jr., Los Angeles, California; Mrs. Silas Bent Russell, St. Louis, Missouri; George W. Kerr, St. Louis, Missouri.

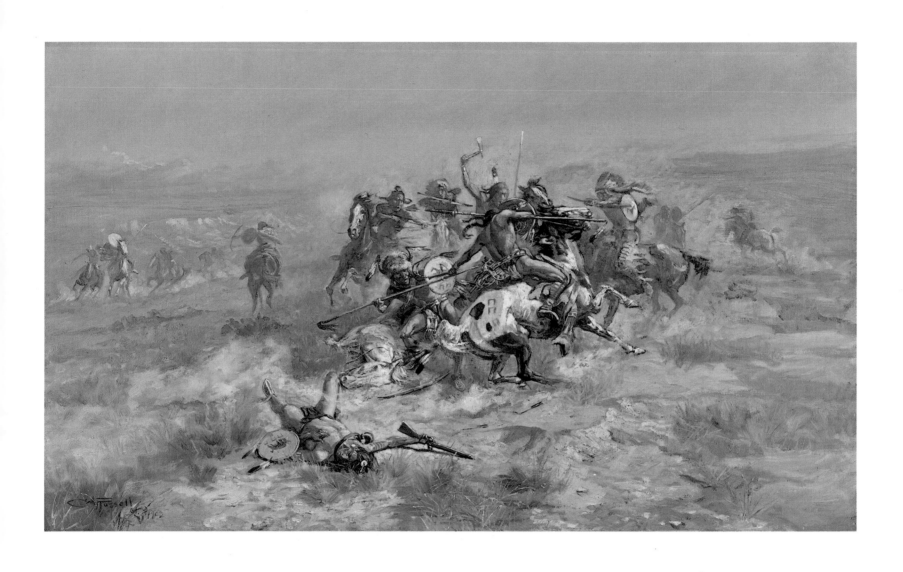

Trouble Hunters

1902   Oil on canvas
22 x 29⅛ in. (55.9 x 74.0 cm.)

Signed lower left: C M Russell (skull) 1902

Plains Indian warfare ordinarily was an individual, volunteer activity, unsystematic and unrelated to larger tribal goals. Young men followed an experienced warrior in hopes of stealing horses and, should the need arise, winning war honors, or coups, in combat with the enemy. Raiding parties tended to be small—a dozen men or less—and since the object was horses, not battle, the ideal raid was one in which the horses were taken without even arousing the owners.[1] The party in *Trouble Hunters*, however, appears very much on the prod. The men bristle with weapons—shields and lances, bows and arrows, rifle and knives—suggesting that they are out for blood and would welcome a fight. Such scalp parties were usually fairly large in size. Two or three scouts moved ahead of the main body, as Russell has shown. Apparently they have spotted something and are waiting for the others to catch up.

Russell liked the theme of *Trouble Hunters*. Eight years later he painted an oil with the identical title that could be taken as another view of the same three warriors. He often set scenes like this at day's end, and in his later work the Indians became almost unthreatening as they basked in the sun's fading warmth—perfect symbols of Russell's own nostalgia over the vanished West. This version, painted in 1902 with the artist in command of his medium, has a different aura. The sky is roseate, and the setting sun washes the men in pinks and reds, but they exude menace. They are lean, tough, and full of fight. The figure of the mounted warrior in the foreground with the distinctive fur cap obviously appealed to Russell. With minor variations it appeared in a succession of paintings from 1899 to 1903.

NOTES

1. Grinnell, *Blackfoot Lodge Tales*, p. 250; Ewers, *The Blackfeet*, pp. 126–129; Kennedy, ed., *The Assiniboines*, p. 48; Mandelbaum, *The Plains Cree*, pp. 239–247.

EX COLLECTION

Alice P. Biggs, Helena, Montana.

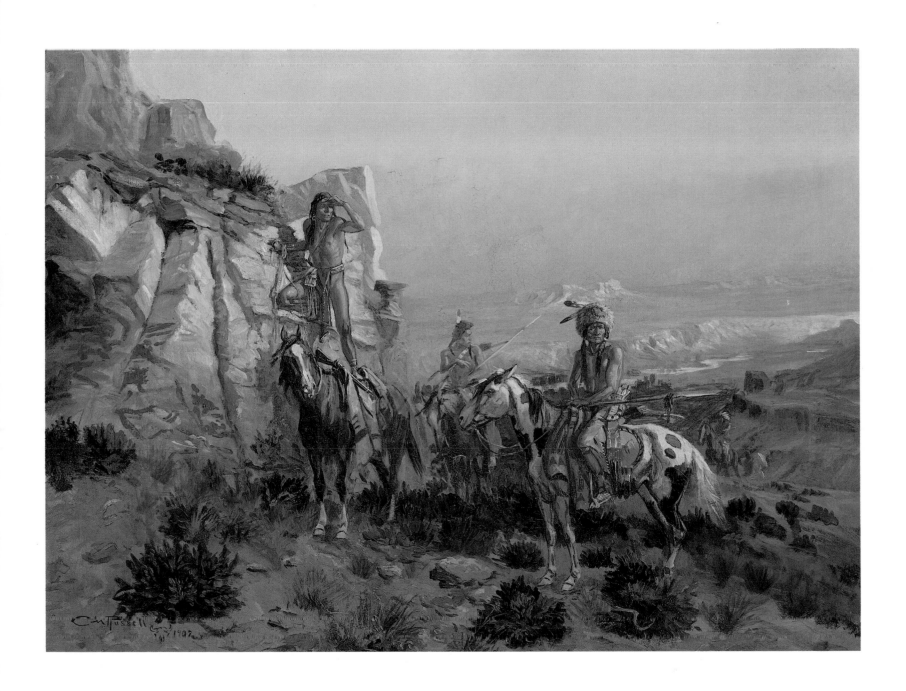

Indian Head

1904   Pencil, watercolor, and gouache
on paper
15 ¼ x 9 ¼ in. (38.7 x 23.5 cm.)

Signed lower right: C M Russell (skull) / by
E. S. Paxson— / Chas. Schatzlein / 1904.

This Indian head is the work of three Montanans: Russell, his close friend and first serious dealer Charles "Dutch" Schatzlein, owner of the Schatzlein Paint Company in Butte, and Edgar S. Paxson (1852–1919), a Missoula artist who, judging from the end result, was the guiding spirit behind this joint endeavor. His reputation rested on a few large historical oils and numerous watercolor Indian portraits, of which this one is typical. Russell respected Paxson, who arrived in Montana three years ahead of him, in 1877, as Montana's pioneer painter, and was generous in his praise. "I can't paint an Indian head with Ed Paxon [*sic*], nor can I mix his colors," he told an interviewer in 1917,[1] and when Paxson died two years later Russell commented: "Paxson has gone, but his pictures will not allow us to forget him. His work tells me that he loved the Old West, and those who love her I count as friends. Paxson was my friend . . . I am a painter, too, but Paxson has done some things that I cannot do. He was a pioneer and a pioneer painter."[2]

The circumstances under which *Indian Head* was painted in 1904 are unknown, but the same three artists collaborated again in 1906 on a mural that decorated Schatzlein's dining room.[3] Russell visited Paxson's studio two years later,[4] exhibited at the Montana State Fair in Helena with him in 1909,[5] and rode beside him in a Missoula parade celebrating Montana's past in 1915.[6] Their mutual respect adequately accounts for this particular collaboration, though Russell's contribution to it is difficult to ascertain since the pose, drawing (especially the rendering of eyes, ears, and mouth), and greenish coloration are all so characteristic of Paxson's work while nothing distinctively Russell's is evident.

NOTES

1. Noyes, *In the Land of Chinook*, p. 126.
2. C. M. Russell, November 1919, quoted in Michael Kennedy, "Frontier Vermeer," *Montana Magazine of History* 4 (Spring 1954): 38; Franz R. Stenzel, "E. S. Paxson—Montana Artist," *Montana, the Magazine of Western History* 13 (Autumn 1963): 76.
3. The section of the mural painted by Russell, *The Indian War Dance*, is in the collection of the Amon Carter Museum of Western Art, Fort Worth.
4. *Great Falls Daily Tribune*, January 15, 1933; clipping in the C. M. Russell Scrapbooks, Montana Room, Great Falls Public Library, Great Falls, Montana.
5. "Montana Fine Art," *Treasure State*, June 26, 1909, p. 5; "Best Art Exhibit Ever Collected in the West," *Great Falls Daily Tribune*, October 1, 1909, p. 10.
6. "Russell's Art in Park," *Great Falls Daily Tribune*, July 2, 1915, p. 6.

EX COLLECTION

Provenance unknown.

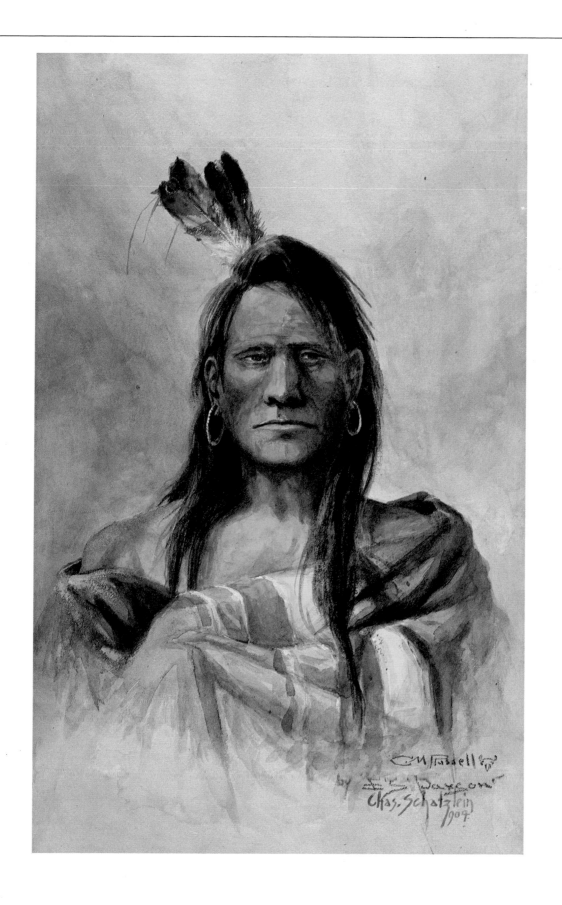

The Bucker

1904 Pencil, watercolor, and gouache
on paper
16¼ x 12¼ in. (41.3 x 31.1 cm.)

Signed lower left: C M Russell / (skull) 1904

Charlie Russell had no problem accounting for his aversion to bronc busting. It was a specialist's job during his days on the range. The average cowboy did not tackle the half-wild horses in the rough string, and those who did usually paid the price.[1] "I never got to be a bronk rider but in my youthfull days wanted to be," Russell recalled, "and while that want lasted I had a fine chance to study hoss enatimy from under and over   the under was the view a taripan gits The over while I hoverd ont the end of a Macarty rope was like the eagle sees grand but dam scary for folks without wings."[2] Elsewhere he quipped, "Never did take kindly to broncos as my mind and theirs did not seem to work in unison," but there is no denying his uncanny feel for horse anatomy, however he came to observe it.[3] Russell could twist man and animal anyway he wanted for purposes of action, yet, since he visualized the figures in the round, always make his distortions seem natural—a trick that Frederic Remington and other artists influenced by stop-action photography did not master.

Russell painted three similar watercolors in 1904: *A Bad Hoss* (or *Bronc Buster*) (Whitney Gallery of Western Art, Cody), *Powder River, Let 'er Buck* (or *The Bucking Bronco*) (Thomas Gilcrease Institute, Tulsa), and this painting, *The Bucker*. All three are virtuoso performances, and the praise that a New York critic at the time heaped on one applies to the others as well: "The artist shows here his thorough knowledge of both man and beast. The ugly temper and viciousness of the bronco is splendidly done, and all details such as trappings on the saddle, swinging of the quirt or lash by the loop instead of the handle and the dress of the cowboy are perfect."[4] Comments like these helped establish Russell's reputation in the East as a gifted painter of the West. In particular, he was praised for his realism. But the three watercolors are also artistic successes. The vertical composition of each augments its visual impact, emphasizing the towering height of the bucking horse and the rider on its back as they crowd the edges of the painting and, in their violent exertions, threaten to explode right out of it.

NOTES

1. E. C. Abbott and Helena Huntington Smith, *We Pointed Them North: Recollections of a Cowpuncher*, p. 230; Jeff C. Dykes, ed., *The West of the Texas Kid, 1881–1910: Recollections of Thomas Edgar Crawford, Cowboy, Gun Fighter, Rancher, Hunter, Miner*, p. 122; Ramon F. Adams, *The Old-time Cowhand*, chap. 36.

2. Charles M. Russell to Will James, May 12, 1920, in *Good Medicine*, p. 68.

3. Noyes, *In the Land of Chinook*, p. 120.

4. "Smart Set Lionizing a Cowboy Artist," *New York Press*, January 31, 1904, p. 4.

EX COLLECTION

Provenance unknown.

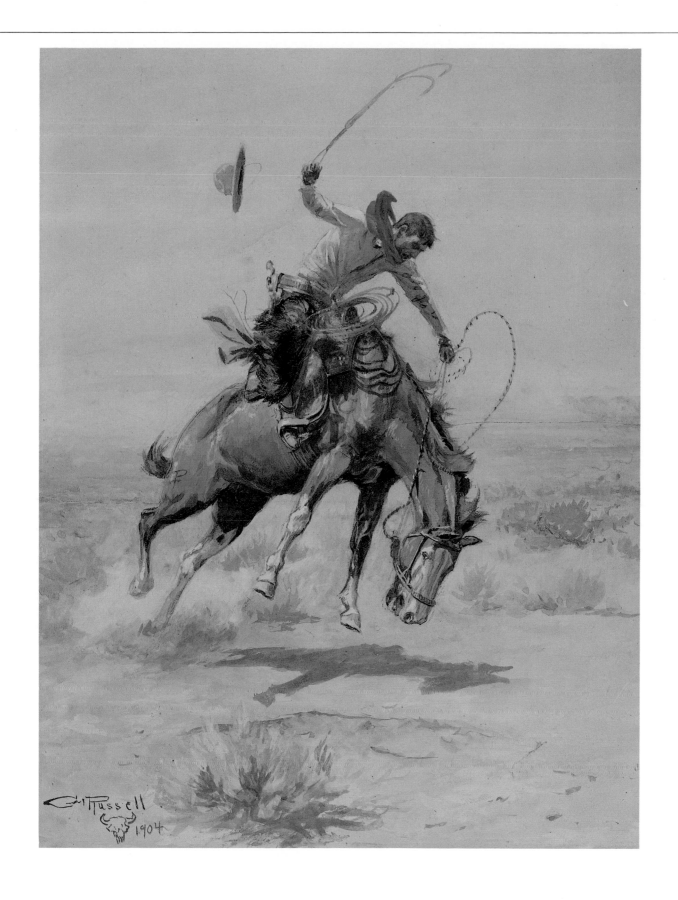

He Snaked Old Texas Pete Right Out of His Wicky-up, Gun and All

1905   Pencil, watercolor, and gouache
on paper
12⅜ x 17⅛ in. (31.4 x 45.4 cm.)

Signed lower left: C M Russell / (skull) 1905

With the encouragement of John N. Marchand, a New York illustrator he had met the previous summer in Montana, Russell spent January and part of February 1904 in New York City, passing much of his time there in the studio Marchand shared with two other artists. During his stay, he told a reporter, he did "considerable work and more than 'broke even' on expenses. I did some illustrations for Scribner's, Outing, McClure's and Leslie's magazines, and some of it will be published in a short time. . . . My friend, Marchand, took me around and introduced me to the art editors of the big publishing houses, which was mighty fine for me. Many of the editors promised me work in the future in illustrating western stories."[1]

He Snaked Old Texas Pete Right Out of His Wicky-up, Gun and All was one of the pictures that Russell painted for *McClure's Magazine* to illustrate the first two installments of Stewart Edward White's *Arizona Nights*. It is faithful to White's story about a tough named Texas Pete, "about as broad as he was long," with "big whiskers and black eyebrows," who discovered a waterhole in the middle of the Arizona desert, set up shop, and began gouging the emigrant traffic en route to California "two bits a head—man or beast" for a drink of water. Texas Pete sat outside his canvas shack, Winchester across his lap, and let a crude sign speak for him. One day two good-hearted cowboys chanced by when an emigrant, denied water because he could not meet the price, bent down to scoop up a drink for his sick child from an overflow puddle. His thirsty horses chose the same moment to dip into the trough. Texas Pete, nursing a hangover and in an uglier mood than ever,

jumped up and fired, killing one of the horses. Instantly, a cowboy grabbed his rope and "with one of the prettiest twenty-foot flip throws I ever see done he snaked old Texas Pete right out of his wicky-up, gun and all. The old renegade did his best to twist around for a shot at us; but it was no go; and I never enjoyed hog-tying a critter more in my life than I enjoyed hog-tying Texas Pete."[2] Action abounded, in short, and Russell put it all into his painting, which appeared in the February 1906 *McClure's*. For some reason N. C. Wyeth was assigned to illustrate the remaining installments of White's story. Since only his pictures were used in the book when it appeared the next year, the publishers evidently preferred his rather decorative approach to Russell's more literal one.[3]

NOTES

1. "Prefers Ulm to New York as Place of Residence," *Great Falls Daily Tribune*, February 16, 1904, p. 8.

2. Stewart Edward White, "Arizona Nights," *McClure's Magazine* 26 (February 1906): 412–419.

3. Wyeth's mentor, the great illustrator Howard Pyle, began a brief, unhappy stint as art director of *McClure's Magazine* in early March 1906. Possibly he brought Wyeth in to replace Russell as a matter of personal preference.

EX COLLECTION

Provenance unknown.

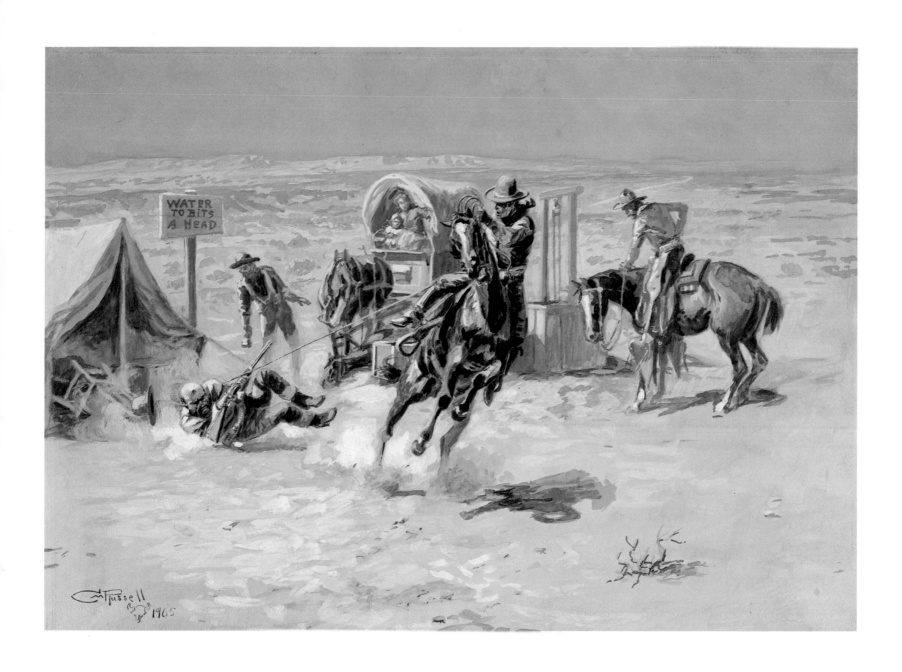

Utica [A Quiet Day in Utica]

1907 Oil on canvas
24⅛ x 36⅛ in. (61.3 x 91.8 cm.)

Signed lower left: C M Russell / (skull) 1907

Utica was a commissioned work, which accounts for its precise detail. Charles Lehman, a Lewistown merchant, purchased Utica's original mercantile store in 1886 and operated it into the 1890s before selling out.[1] In 1907 it occurred to him that it would be a fine idea to have one of his old customers, the now nationally prominent Cowboy Artist Charlie Russell, paint a picture that he could use to advertise the family store in Lewistown. None of the Lehmans inquired into price before the commission was completed. When the bill came the children hid it from their father, assuring him the painting cost a mere hundred dollars while they paid off the actual figure in installments.[2]

Utica is the work of a seasoned professional, though it is not Russell at his very best. The painting has a contrived quality, perhaps because Russell was so concerned with creating a portrait gallery for the enjoyment of the Lehmans and their customers. The cowboys and the spectators—including Charles Lehman, standing in the doorway of his establishment, and the Cowboy Artist

himself, leaning on the hitching post rail taking everything in—were all recognizable individuals. Though the colors run to pinks and blues, the picture holds together nicely, and precisely *because* Russell introduced the contrived action in the foreground, *Utica* is more than a painted advertisement. The dog, trailing its tin cans, has caused just enough commotion to enliven what would otherwise be a dull day in Utica and an even duller picture.

NOTES

1. Taurman et al., *Utica, Montana*, pp. 10, 14, 96–97.
2. McCracken, *The Charles M. Russell Book*, pp. 95, 204–205.

EX COLLECTION

Newhouse Galleries, New York City; Charles Lehman, Lewistown, Montana.

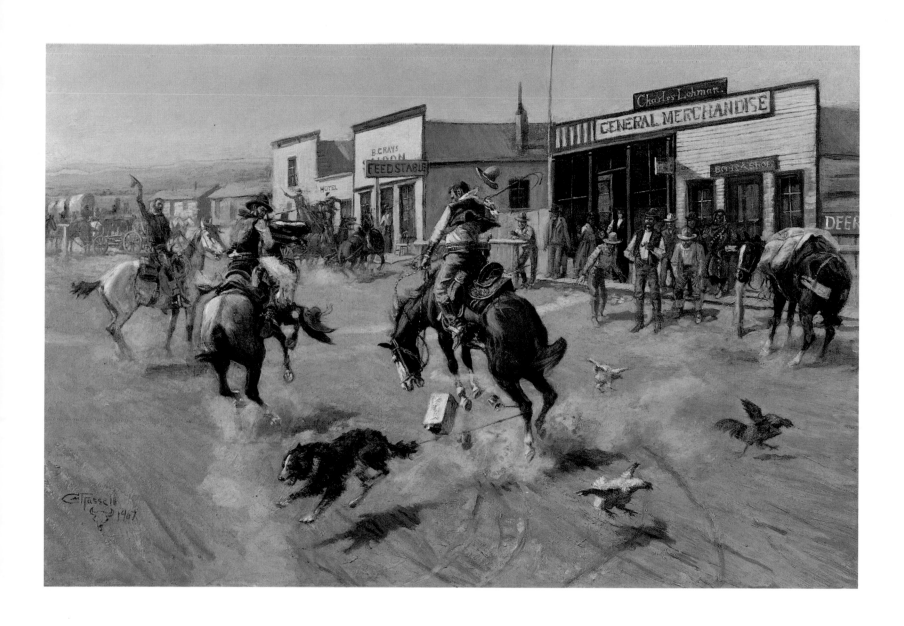

The Scout

1907 Pencil, watercolor, and gouache
on paper
16¾ x 11⅝ in. (42.6 x 29.5 cm.)

Signed lower left: C M Russell / (skull) 1907

Russell painted the Pawnees infrequently, but when he did he made them easily identifiable by showing the distinctive roach hair style favored by Pawnee men in the buffalo hunting days. Indeed, a writer in 1880 maintained that the tribe's name derived from the word for "horn" and referred to the scalp lock, which was "dressed to stand nearly erect or curving slightly backward, somewhat like a horn."[1] George Bird Grinnell, a close student of several western tribes—notably the Pawnee, Blackfoot, and Cheyenne—hypothesized that the Pawnees were known to their enemies as "wolves" in grudging recognition of their superior ability as scouts, or "prowlers."[2] They cemented this reputation in the period 1864–1876 when, under the command of Frank and Luther North, they distinguished themselves as scouts in the service of the U.S. Army. Years later, Luther North recalled the appearance of a Pawnee fighting man: "On their old Nebraska reservation in 1861–62, I saw some of the great Pawnee warriors paint their horses, particularly if they were white or had white spots on them, which would make them better marks for their enemies. They would also braid the tails of their horses, and fasten colored feathers in the tails and manes. I have known them to take at least two hours to paint their faces, tie colored feathers in

their scalp locks and prepare themselves and horses for a fight. That was in the tribal battles between the Sioux and Pawnees . . ."[3] Russell painted many solitary warriors, mounted and poised for action, including a similar watercolor also done in 1907, *Pawnee Chief* (Charles M. Russell Museum, Great Falls). But this fine study, bearing the less descriptive title *The Scout*, shows him at the top of his form.[4]

NOTES

1. John B. Dunbar, 1880, quoted in Robert Bruce, *The Fighting Norths and Pawnee Scouts: Narratives and Reminiscences of Military Service on the Old Frontier*, p. 16.

2. George Bird Grinnell, *Pawnee Hero Stories and Folk-Tales, with Notes on the Origin, Customs and Character of the Pawnee People*, pp. 244–246.

3. L. H. North (c. 1929–1932), in Bruce, *The Fighting Norths and Pawnee Scouts*, p. 71.

4. *The Scout* appeared on the cover of *Popular Magazine* 9 (August 1907).

EX COLLECTION

Newhouse Galleries, New York City.

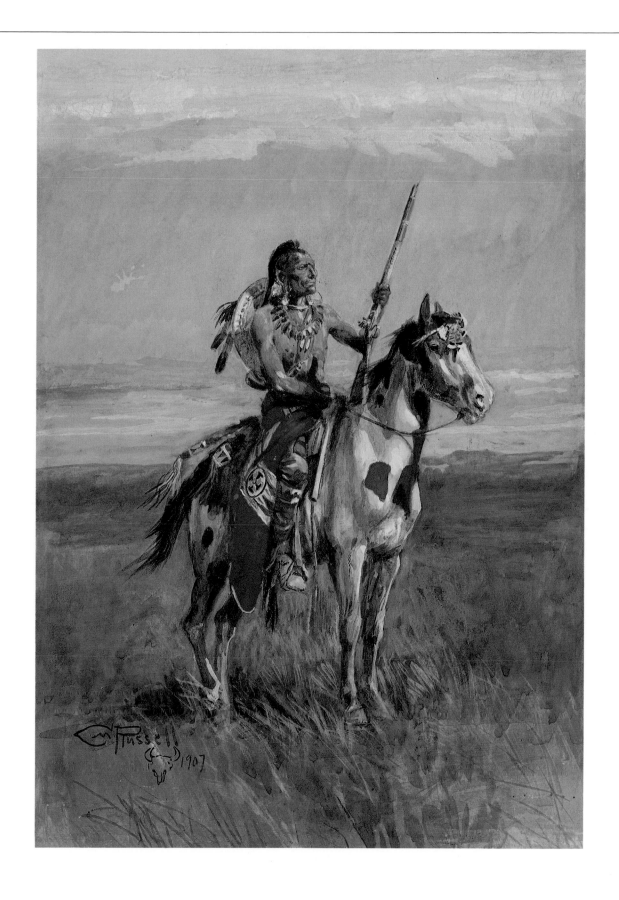

First Wagon Tracks

1908   Watercolor on paper
18¼ x 27 in. (46.4 x 68.6 cm.)

Signed lower right:
Copyright by / C M Russell (skull) 1908

1908 was a banner year for Russell. During it he painted three of his finest watercolors—*York, Bronc to Breakfast,* and this beautiful study, *First Wagon Tracks*[1]—as well as two superb oils of Indian life, *The Medicine Man* (Amon Carter Museum of Western Art, Fort Worth) and *When Blackfeet and Sioux Meet* (p. 140). The level of Russell's achievement is obvious in *First Wagon Tracks.* The colors are warm, creating a perfect twilight mood. All the figures are meticulously painted, and every aspect of the picture exhibits a mastery of the medium and care for detail and finishing. The composition is completely satisfying, and the theme an interesting one. As the West of Russell's personal experience receded into memory, he responded by going back in his imagination to an even earlier era when the Indian was in his prime and the white man an intruder on the buffalo range. "You know I have always studied the wild man from his picture side," he noted in 1918, and explained his meaning a month later when he advised a writer to "sinch your saddle on romance   hes a high headed hoss with plenty of blemishes but . . . most folks like prancers."[2] *First Wagon Tracks* would be set in the 1840s, when wagon trains heading to Oregon first cut paths across the plains. Apart from the Hudson's Bay Company blanket coat draped over one saddle, these warriors show little evidence of contact with whites. Indeed, they are puzzling over the ruts and wondering what manner of beast has left the hoofprints. The squatting warrior on the left gives the sign for buffalo, but his companion, concealing his amazement behind his hand, looks dubious. The painting's theme is carried off by the other warriors trailing in from the right,

each obviously absorbed in his own thoughts about what has left these strange markings on the ground. Red man and white usually regarded one another across a formidable cultural barrier. In paintings like *First Wagon Tracks,* Russell chose to view things from the Indian side, where it was the white man's strange ways that appeared peculiar, not the Indian's.

NOTES

1. *Bronc to Breakfast* and *First Wagon Tracks* were exhibited together in the window of the Como Company in Great Falls, where Russell had them framed, in March 1908. Accurately described in the local paper as "excellent specimens of Russell's work," they were said to be "attracting a great deal of attention" ("More Work by C. M. Russell," *Great Falls Daily Tribune,* March 26, 1908, p. 8). *York,* in turn, was deemed important enough for Russell to deed it in 1909 to the Historical Society of Montana, where *Bronc to Breakfast* has also found a permanent home. Russell painted other exceptional works in 1908, including the popular watercolor *A Disputed Trail* (Joseph T. O'Connor, Vancouver, British Columbia) showing an unexpected confrontation between a lone hunter and a grizzly bear.

2. Charles M. Russell to Harry Stanford, December 13, 1918, private collection; Russell to Frank Bird Linderman, January 18, 1919, in Dippie, ed., *"Paper Talk,"* p. 143.

EX COLLECTION

Provenance unknown.

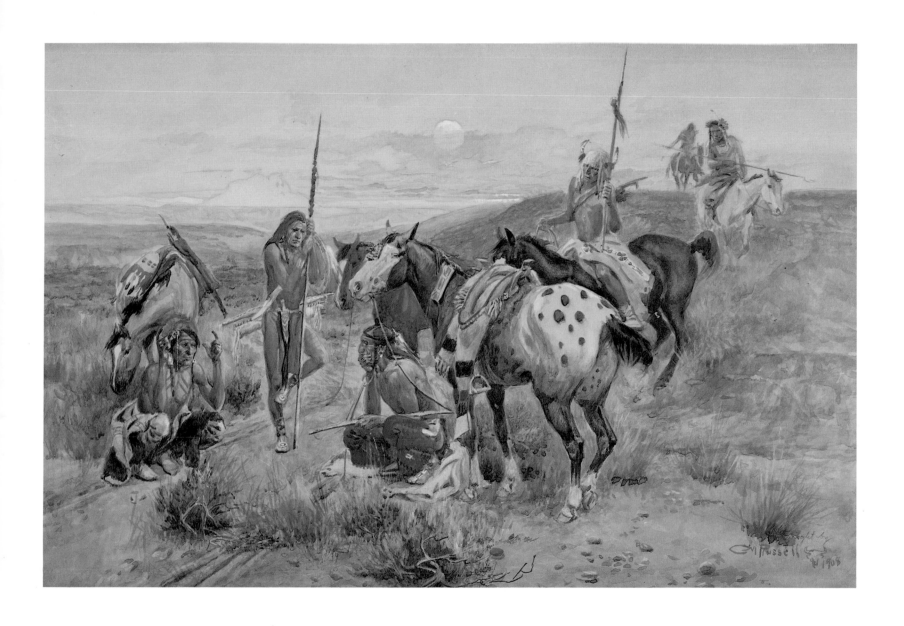

When Blackfeet and Sioux Meet

1908   Oil on canvas
20½ x 29⅞ in. (51.1 x 75.9 cm.)

Signed lower left: C M Russell / (skull) 1908

When Blackfeet and Sioux Meet is another great Russell, the summation of his work on a theme he handled often in the 1890s but rarely after executing this masterpiece in 1908, the clash of enemy tribes. In this perfectly integrated action painting he has stripped his story down to the essentials. A moment of furious fighting involving three individuals becomes in microcosm the clash between the two most feared tribes on the plains, and the whole history of war at close quarters. The outcome is uncertain as a Sioux, tomahawk upraised, attempts to intercede on behalf of his dismounted tribesman who has avoided the charging Blackfoot and now, shield raised to ward off the thrusting lance, has a chance to fire into his enemy's unprotected midriff. For the Blackfoot this is a moment of grand heroism. He has already earned a coup for striking an armed enemy with his lance, and should he ride away safely without further incident, he will receive high acclaim for his deed. The wounded pony resting on its haunches is an essential ingredient in this tale of war, while the red hand print slapped on its neck tells us something more: this dismounted warrior, now on the defensive and fighting for his life, has himself killed an enemy in hand-to-hand combat, perhaps by riding him down in battle.[1] The tables have been reversed, and he is calling upon all his martial prowess to avoid the same fate.

Of Russell's related paintings, the one most similar to *When Blackfeet and Sioux Meet* is a large 1903 watercolor showing two mounted warriors dueling at full gallop. Titled *Running Fight*, it is also known, confusingly, as *When Sioux and Blackfeet Meet* (Thomas Gilcrease Institute, Tulsa). Russell's direct inspiration for his oil was his 1905 bronze *Counting Coup*, which explains the

sculpturesque unity of the grouping and the smooth flow of the action in *When Blackfeet and Sioux Meet*. In the bronze the Blackfoot simultaneously fends off the mounted Sioux with his shield while thrusting at the dismounted Sioux with his lance, thus scoring a double coup. A final point of interest worth noting in *When Blackfeet and Sioux Meet* is the figure of the downed warrior as he both eludes and responds to his enemy's charge by twisting at the waist, his right knee bent almost to the ground, his left leg kicked out to indicate his whirling motion. Russell worked variations on this pose in many of his action pictures. See, for example, the figure of Buffalo Bill Cody in *Buffalo Bill's Duel with Yellowhand* (p. 154).

NOTES

1. Royal B. Hassrick, *The Sioux: Life and Customs of a Warrior Society*, p. 91; Ewers, *The Horse in Blackfoot Indian Culture*, p. 100.

EX COLLECTION

Newhouse Galleries, New York City; C. R. Smith, New York City; Nancy C. Russell, Pasadena, California.

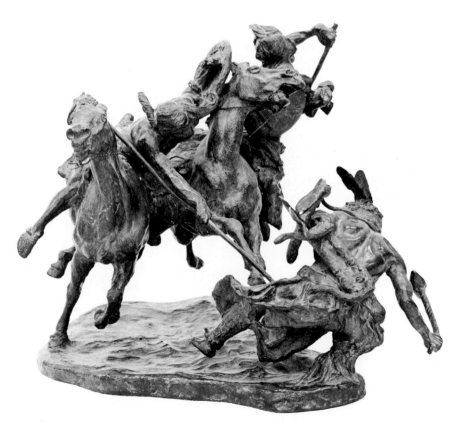

Counting Coup, 1905, Bronze
Amon Carter Museum of Western Art,
Fort Worth

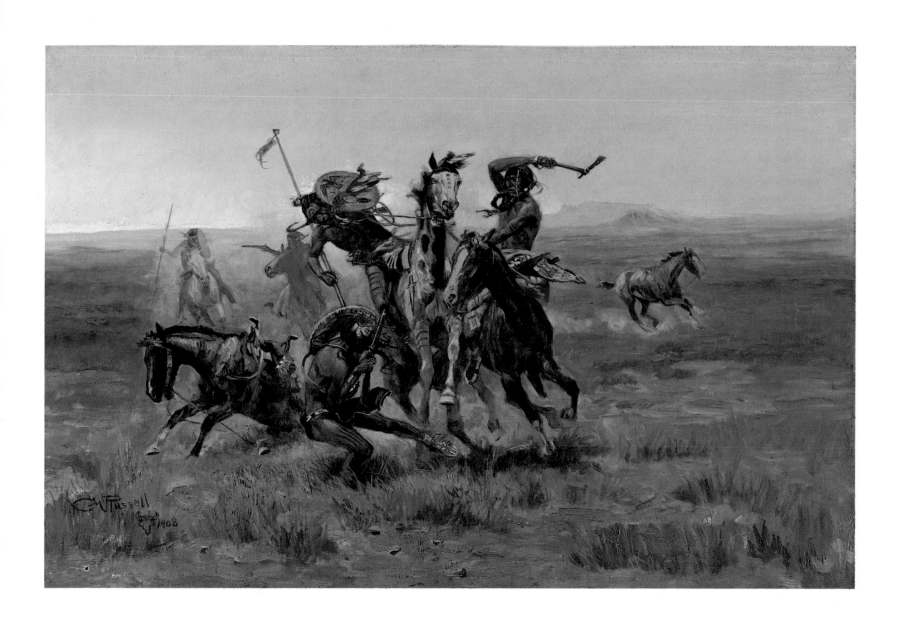

The Wounded Buffalo

1909   Oil on canvas
19⅞ x 30⅛ in. (50.5 x 76.5 cm.)

Signed lower left: C M Russell (skull) 1909;
and below: Copyright by C M Russell

In one of his short stories Russell wrote of that most prized possession of the plains Indian hunter, his buffalo horse: "In them days buffalo hosses was worth plenty of robes. This animal had to be sure-footed, long-winded, an' quick as a cat. It's no bench of a hoss that'll lay alongside of a buffalo cow, while you're droppin' arrows or lead in her. He's got to be a dodger . . . 'cause a wounded cow's liable to get ringy or on the fight, an' when she does, she's mighty handy with them black horns."[1] *The Wounded Buffalo* illustrates the point. It also shows Russell's fluent ease in painting the subject. This is not his most elaborate buffalo hunt by any means, but the snow-patched landscape, the receding flow of the chase, the frosty bite of the air, and the action—especially the aggressive charge of the cow and the frantic leap of the horse—are all expertly portrayed.

The Wounded Buffalo has an immediacy deriving from Russell's observation of in October 1908, and participation in the following spring, a roundup of buffalo on the Flathead Reservation in Montana. The privately owned herd had been purchased by the Canadian government and had to be corralled and shipped north by boxcar.[2] Russell's stint as a rider on the roundup involved a close brush with an angry bull. "Suddenly you hear a pistol shot," an eye-witness reported, "and, turning your eyes quickly towards the middle of the field, you see Charlie Russell's pony swinging about and young Pablo [son of the herd's owner] leaning from his saddle, smoking pistol in hand, over a big bull that stands quivering as if about to fall. Charlie and Young Pablo had undertaken to head-off this bull, which was running away. Charlie must have run too close, for, as you learn later, the bull suddenly turned and charged. Had Young Pablo not been ready, having anticipated the move, Charlie's cayuse at least would have been a victim."[3] Charlie remembered the incident differently. "We were on a side hill," he

wrote in January 1910, "when a bull about the size of a Murphy wagon with tassels all over him an black tung out . . . charged almost getting Peblos horse. who was bumped into mine   Peblos gun slowed him up enough so we could side step the gentelman   I dont think the led hert thi bull aney as him and his bunch swam the river an were runing the last we saw of them   but I tell you for a second or two my hair dident lay good."[4] Whoever did what, this recent, exhilarating exposure to the wild side of the buffalo obviously stimulated Russell's artistry, and he translated his own experience into this dramatic painting of a wounded cow defending its calf.[5]

NOTES

1. Charles M. Russell, "How Lindsay Turned Indian," in *Trails Plowed Under*, p. 142.

2. See John Kidder, "Montana Miracle: It Saved the Buffalo," *Montana, the Magazine of Western History* 15 (Spring 1965): 52–67; for more on Russell's involvement in the roundups, see Dippie, ed., *"Paper Talk,"* pp. 66–69.

3. Newton MacTavish, "The Last Great Roundup," *Canadian Magazine* 34 (November 1909): 33.

4. Charles M. Russell to Friend Fiddel back [Bertrand W. Sinclair], January 12, 1910, in the Stark Museum of Art, Orange, Texas.

5. Nancy Russell wrote a few years later: "Mr. Russell rode as one of the men [on the buffalo roundup] and in that way saw a great deal that was priceless. . . . You must know what all this meant to the artist. I think he rejoiced when outwitted by these grass-eaters . . ." ("Close View of Artist Russell," *Great Falls Daily Tribune*, March 1, 1914, p. 4).

EX COLLECTION

Newhouse Galleries, New York City.

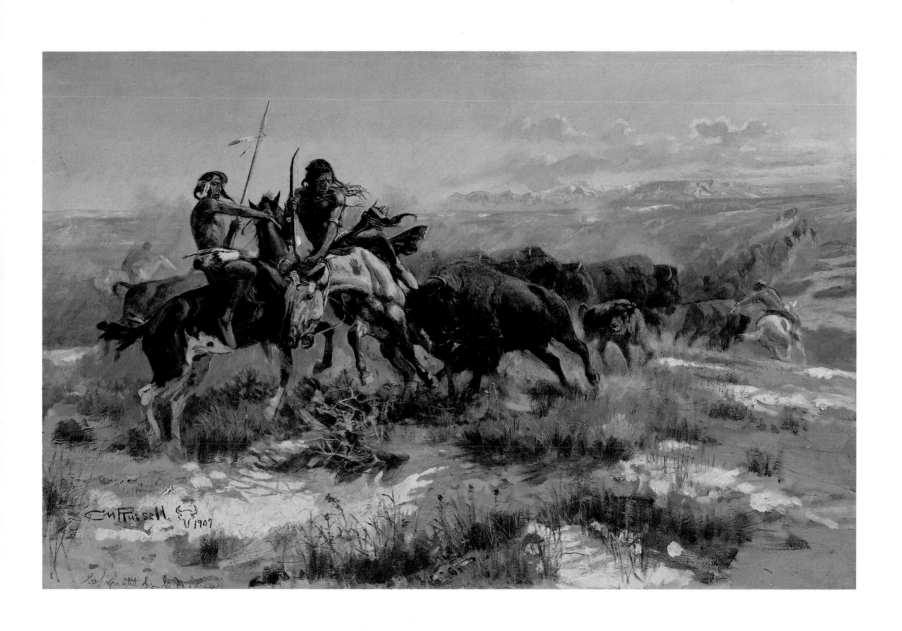

Maney Snows Have Fallen . . .
(Letter from Ah-Wa-Cous [Charles M. Russell] to Short Bull)

c. 1909–10   Pencil, watercolor, and gouache
on paper
8 x 10 in. (20.3 x 25.4 cm.)

Signed lower right: AH-WA-COUS (antelope
skull)

Contemporaries often remarked on Russell's
Indian-like features, and he was not averse to
accentuating them on occasion by dressing up
in wig, feathers, and a blanket. He also impressed others as Indian-like because of the
stern set of his mouth and his taciturnity
when working, and his engagingly expressive
storytelling style, sign language and all, when
at ease. The body of his work stands as a permanent testament to his deep respect for the
Indian as "the onley real American."[1] Though
Russell hewed to the doctrine of live and let
live and deplored reformers and moralists of
every stripe, he spoke out publicly in support
of Indian rights even when his position was
extremely unpopular. In his letters to his
many friends he reserved for a special few the
compliment that they were pure "Injun" beneath the skin, though he frequently wrote as
one Indian to another, signing off with his
Blood name Ah-Wa-Cous, the Antelope.
When he invited an easterner to come visit,
he might depict himself as a plains Indian
and his correspondent as a woodlands Indian,
while a southwesterner would appear as a
Navajo.

In this letter to Short Bull, Russell has
shown himself and his wife Nancy as Blackfeet extending the welcoming pipe to two
Sioux visitors. It is possible that Short Bull

was Jim Gabriel who, as a performer with
Buffalo Bill's Wild West when Russell saw
him in 1907, was "fighting Sioux every day."[2]
This letter and another addressed to Jim
Gabriel were sold together in 1933, suggest-
ing the possibility. But whoever Short Bull
was, this much is certain: he would receive a
very different reception from Mr. and Mrs.
Antelope than the one portrayed in *When
Blackfeet and Sioux Meet* (p. 140).

NOTES

1. Charles M. Russell to Charles N. Pray, January 5, 1914, in the Charles M. Russell Museum,
Great Falls; a portion of the letter, including this
quotation, is reproduced in Dippie, ed., *"Paper
Talk,"* p. 71.
2. Charles M. Russell to Kid Gabriel, 1909, in
Good Medicine, p. 83.

EX COLLECTION

Newhouse Galleries, New York City; Anderson
Galleries, New York City.

Maney snows have fallen since the Black feet an
Sioux smoked. and the grass has grone long
in the trail betwene there fires
but if Short Bull comes to the lodg of the Antilope
the pipe will be lit an robes
spred for him
the Antilope has spoken

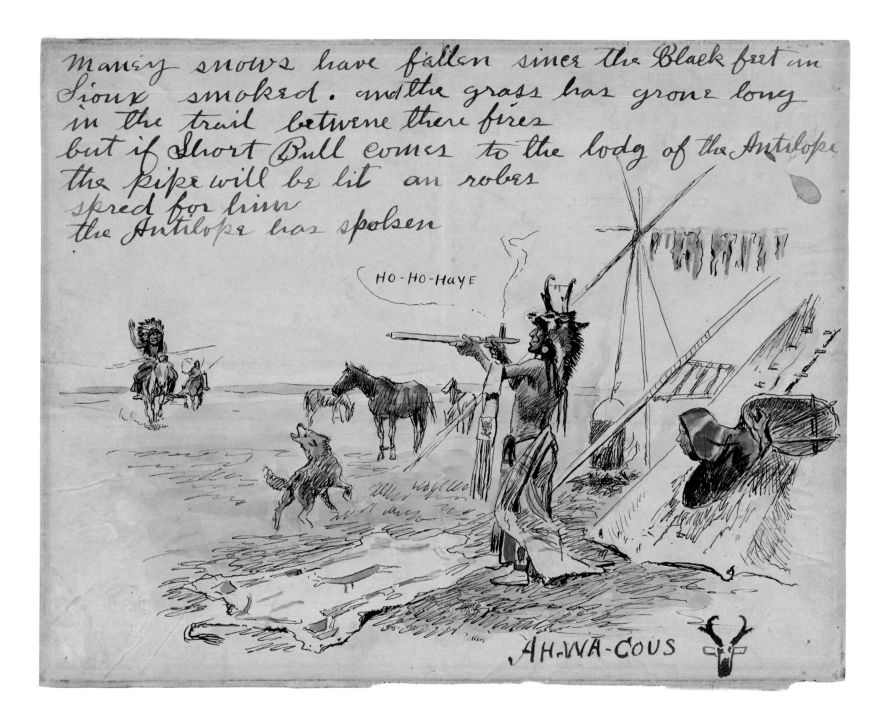

HO-HO-HAYE

AH-WA-COUS

He Tripped and Fell into a Den on a Mother Bear and Her Cubs

1910   Pencil, watercolor, and gouache
on paper
17 x 14 in. (43.2 x 35.6 cm.)

Signed lower left: C M Russell / (skull)

In 1910 Russell accepted a commission he came to regret. He agreed to illustrate Mrs. Carrie Adell Strahorn's book *Fifteen Thousand Miles by Stage: A Woman's Unique Experience during Thirty Years of Path Finding and Pioneering from the Missouri to the Pacific and from Alaska to Mexico.* Mrs. Strahorn's stagecoaching days with her husband qualified her as a bona fide pioneer since they stretched back to 1871. They also endowed her with an imperious manner, and in 1910 she set up camp near the Cowboy Artist's summer retreat on Lake McDonald to give him the benefit of her advice. Russell grumbled, but he also completed the sizable assignment, which involved four paintings in color, another thirteen in monochrome, and sixty-eight pen and inks.[1]

He Tripped and Fell into a Den on a Mother Bear and Her Cubs illustrated a story Mrs. Strahorn told at second-hand about a man from Challis, Idaho, who set out one afternoon for a few hours of hunting with his dog and inadvertently stumbled into a bear's den. He was badly mauled by the protective mother before his faithful dog distracted her long enough to allow him to crawl away. At last the bear ambled off to rejoin her cubs, and the dog, in the best tradition of *Lassie,* ran to town and brought back help. Russell has graphically depicted the moment when

the man, both arms broken, lies helpless while his dog comes to the rescue. Bears fascinated Russell. He incorporated them in several large action paintings, sculpted them frequently, and obviously found this incident congenial enough to kindle more enthusiasm in him than most of the others he was required to illustrate for Mrs. Strahorn.[2]

NOTES

1. See Austin Russell, *C.M.R.: Charles M. Russell, Cowboy Artist,* pp. 154–155. Sometime in November 1910, Russell wrote to his friend and fellow artist Philip R. Goodwin: "I have been mighty bussy with that book of Mrs. Strayhorns but am about through." This suggests a 1910 date for *He Tripped and Fell into a Den on a Mother Bear and Her Cubs* (letter in the Stark Museum of Art, Orange, Texas).

2. Carrie Adell Strahorn, *Fifteen Thousand Miles by Stage: A Woman's Unique Experience during Thirty Years of Path Finding and Pioneering from the Missouri to the Pacific and from Alaska to Mexico,* pp. 156–157.

EX COLLECTION

Provenance unknown.

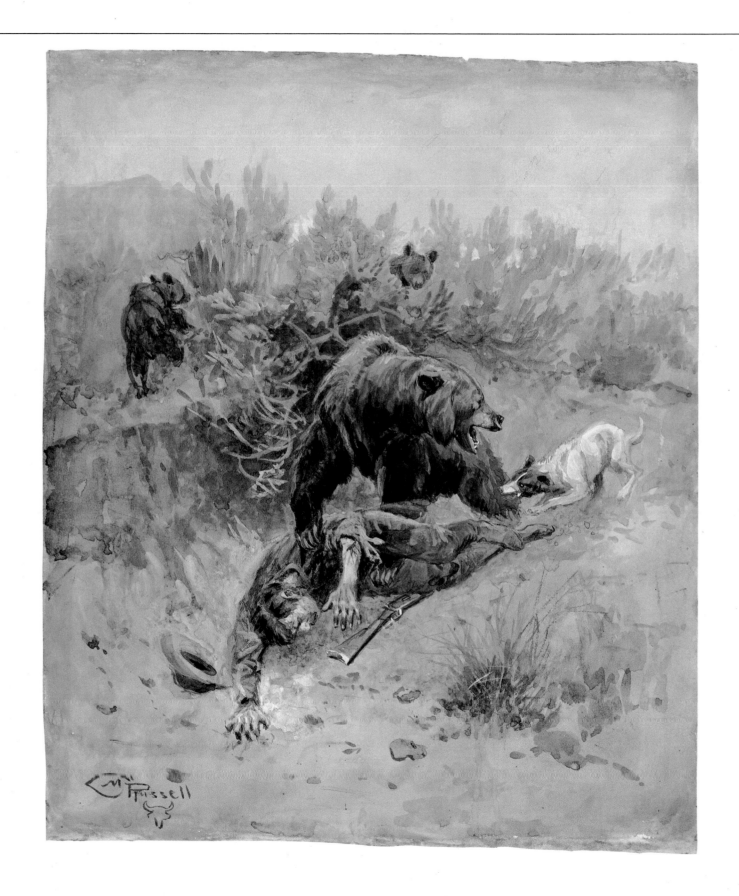

His Wealth

c. 1910   Pencil, watercolor, and gouache
on paper
6¼ x 9¼ in. (15.9 x 23.5 cm.)

Signed lower left: C M R (skull)

Before the white man came and, to Russell's way of thinking, despoiled the land, the western Indians lived a life that was simple, even spartan, yet rich beyond reckoning. "While the buffalo lasted, the Injuns counted their wealth in hosses," Russell observed.[1] Horse wealth varied from tribe to tribe—a rich Plains Cree might own five horses, a rich Blackfoot forty or fifty.[2] Another measure of status was the number of wives a man supported. Among the old-time Blackfeet it was "a very poor man" who did not claim three, George Bird Grinnell wrote in 1892. "Many had six, eight, and some more than a dozen. I have heard of one who had sixteen."[3]

In this quick sketch, with the self-explanatory title *His Wealth*, Russell shows the plains warrior at his peak. Independent, fearless, and self-sufficient, he rode with the haughty dignity befitting his station as "nature's nobleman," lord and master of a vast domain that provided his every want. After his first, fumbling campaign against plains Indians in 1867, George A. Custer offered a heartfelt tribute:

The Indian, born and bred to his prairie home, accustomed to look to it for his subsistence as well as his shelter, is never at a loss for either, let him be where he may. The buffalo supplies him with food; no bread is required; his pony, like himself, a stranger to the luxuries of civilization, seeks no better food than the wild prairie grass. . . . In addition to [the pony's] transporting the lodgepoles, which one would imagine to constitute a sufficient load, there is not unfrequently added a squaw, and from one to three pappooses, depending entirely upon the extent of the family and the wealth of the paternal head, the latter being most usually estimated by the numbers of his ponies or buffalo robes. That a small, half-starved pony, supporting such an immense load, should outmatch a large American horse with a lighter burden seems improbable, yet such is the case.[4]

Estimated according to his needs, then, the wealth of the plains warrior portrayed by Russell was substantial indeed.

NOTES

1. Charles M. Russell, "Injuns," in *Trails Plowed Under*, p. 27.
2. Ewers, *The Horse in Blackfoot Indian Culture*, pp. 30–32.
3. Grinnell, *Blackfoot Lodge Tales*, p. 218.
4. George A. Custer letter, November 11, 1867, in Brian W. Dippie, ed., *Nomad: George A. Custer in "Turf, Field and Farm,"* pp. 28–30.

EX COLLECTION

Provenance unknown.

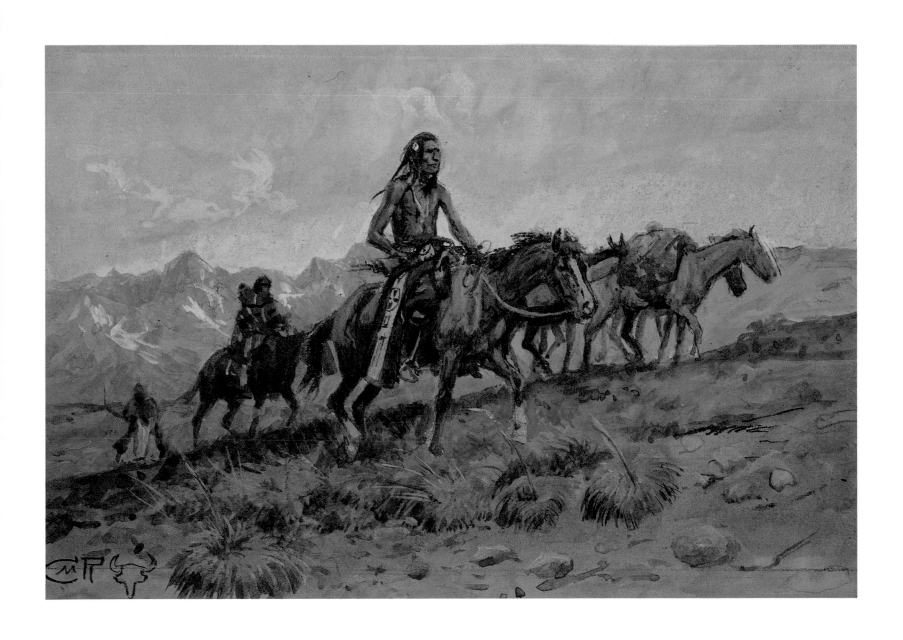

[Bucker]

1912   Pencil, watercolor, and gouache
on paper
19¾ x 28⅝ in. (50.2 x 72.7 cm.)

Signed lower left: C M Russell / © (skull)
1912

"An Injun once told me that bravery came from the hart not the head," Charlie Russell observed in 1916. "If my red brother is right Bronk riders and bull dogers are all hart above the wast band but its a good bet theres nothing under there hat but hair."[1] Russell's closest friend from his rangeland days, Con Price, was the genuine article—a first-class bronc buster. Price began cowboying in 1885 and did not retire until a kick from a horse disabled him in 1943.[2] Shortly before his death in 1958 he told a reporter a delightful tale:

> Charlie exaggerated me, he painted me riding a horse lots of times, but he never did paint me getting bucked off. I was always riding 'em in Charlie's pictures.
>
> It reminds me of a time Charlie and me was in a saloon. There was a bunch of cowboys there, all talking about what they did after a bronc made the first jump. They asked a tough looking little guy from Texas what he did after the first jump.
>
> "Me, why I don't do nothing, unless the horse tries to step on me," the Texan said.[3]

Russell painted some pretty snaky broncs over the years. The one in this watercolor would appear to be an honest bucker, the kind that gave the buster a jolting ride without resorting to tricks. In horizontal compositions like this one Russell often included other figures watching the action, with the occasional infuriated camp cook waving his fist and cursing the cowboy whose bucking horse has just carried him through the campfire and the morning's breakfast. The composition of this 1912 painting is a model of simplicity. The plain sky and unfenced prairie set off the solitary competition between horse and rider, lending the scene a timeless quality.

NOTES

1. Charles M. Russell to Guy Weadick, January 28, 1916, in *Good Medicine*, p. 137.
2. Con Price, *Memories of Old Montana* and *Trails I Rode*; Con Price to Joe Scheuerle, December 28, 1943, photocopy in my possession; Jack O'Reilly, "Con Price, Cowboy: A Personal Tribute," *Montana, the Magazine of Western History* 8 (Summer 1958): 50–53.
3. "Con Price Missed Gathering of Cowhands, but Not in Spirit; Tells Russell Stories," *Great Falls Daily Tribune*, [c. February 1958], clipping in my possession.

EX COLLECTION

Provenance unknown.

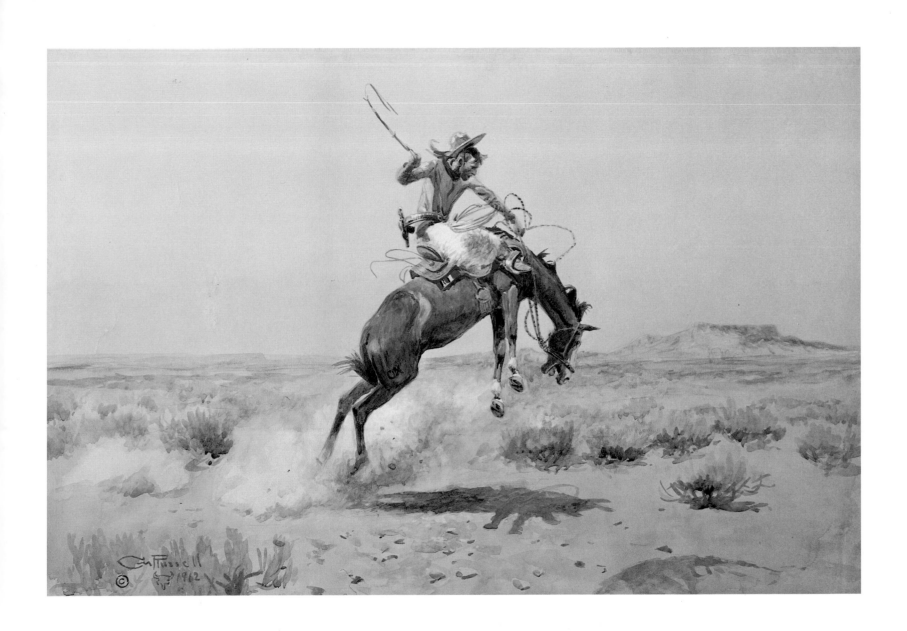

Man's Weapons Are Useless When Nature Goes Armed

1916   Oil on canvas
30 x 48⅛ in. (76.2 x 122.2 cm.)

Signed lower left: C M Russell / © (skull)
1916; *inscription:* TO HOWARD EATON / FROM
HIS FRIEND / C M Russell

This amusing oil was painted by Russell as a thank you for his good friend Howard Eaton, a pioneer dude rancher who hailed from Pittsburgh, settled near Medora in North Dakota in 1882, and then, with his dude wrangling business well established, relocated permanently on the eastern side of the Big Horn Mountains, near Wolf, Wyoming. Eaton expanded his operation to include trail rides through Glacier and Yellowstone Parks and the Grand Canyon country of the Southwest, and by the time of his death in 1922 his name was synonymous with western tourism. Russell was an honored guest on several Eaton trail rides. He accompanied camping trips through Glacier in 1915 and 1916 and made a particularly memorable excursion with an Eaton party through Arizona and along the Grand Canyon in October 1916. "In the city men shake hands and call each other friends but its the lonsome places that ties their harts together and harts do not forget," Russell wrote to one of his companions on that excursion, and in gratitude he executed this large oil for Eaton.[1]

Russell painted buffalo and bear in profusion; they were mighty symbols of the untamed West. But he also loved nature's smaller creatures, from the prairie dog to the field mouse, and, as this wry tribute suggests, had nothing but respect for the lowly skunk. Two hunters return at dusk after a day in the field to find their camp ransacked and their evening meal of pork and beans partially devoured by an invading force that they can repel only at the risk of having their nest fouled. The extravagant scale of Russell's thank you is evident when one remembers that he made the same idea the subject of a modest sketch back in 1907, *"All Who Know Me—Respect Me,"* for use on a postcard.

NOTES

1. Charles M. Russell to Santa Fe [Tom Conway], March 24, 1917, in Dippie, ed., *"Paper Talk,"* p. 130. On Eaton, see Jerome L. Rodnitzky, "Recapturing the West: The Dude Ranch in American Life," *Arizona and the West* 10 (Summer 1968): 113–114.

EX COLLECTION

Newhouse Galleries, New York City; Mary B. Eaton, Wolf, Wyoming; Howard Eaton, Wolf, Wyoming.

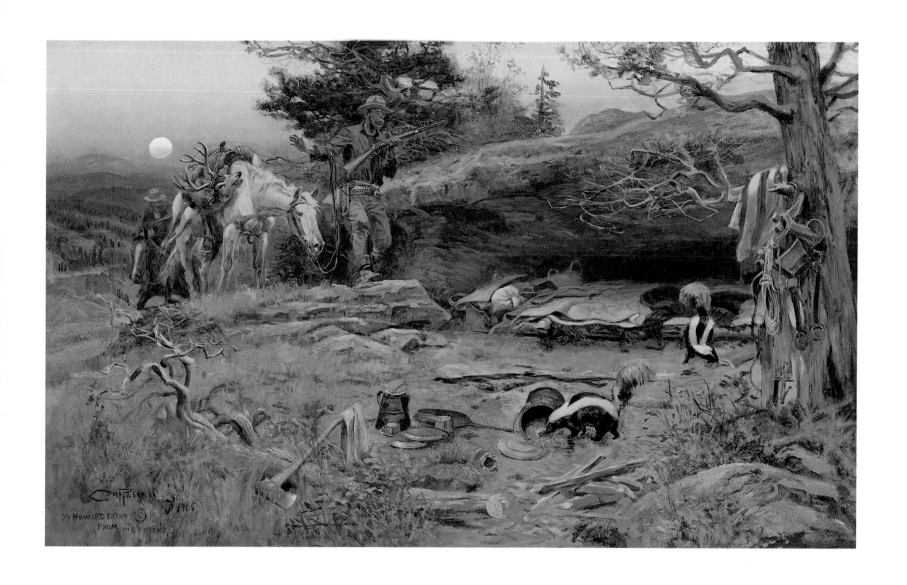

Buffalo Bill's Duel with Yellowhand

1917   Oil on canvas
29⅞ x 47⅞ in. (75.9 x 121.6 cm.)

Signed lower left: C M Russell (skull)
1917 / ©

As a boy, Charlie Russell's head was stuffed full of the kind of Wild West heroics personified for almost fifty years by William F. (Buffalo Bill) Cody. A drawing of "Bufalow Bill" stands out among the Indian and cowboy scenes Russell sketched in a notebook during his last year at school,[1] and in the Judith Basin in the early 1880s he was sometimes referred to as the "Buckskin Kid" because of the Buffalo Bill–style jacket he affected. When he saw Buffalo Bill's Wild West in New York in 1907, Russell could not suppress a note of disappointment. Cody had "lost most of his hair in the London fog," Russell wrote, and while the "show was good   real cow boys an Indians," authenticity had been sacrificed to audience appeal: "I learn here that punchers wore red shirts an indians go to ware strung with slay bells . . ."[2]

But several years after he saw his balding boyhood hero in the artificial light of Madison Square Gardens, Russell honored him in two fine oils depicting incidents in Cody's career in the 1870s at a time when he was still more plainsman than performer, *Buffalo Bill's Duel with Yellowhand* and *Running Buffalo* (1918; Thomas Gilcrease Institute, Tulsa). Russell was originally commissioned to paint a third oil showing Buffalo Bill scouting a Cheyenne camp, but his patron, Thomas F. Cole, a mining magnate resident in Duluth, Minnesota, may have canceled it because of Russell's refusal to make changes he requested in the 1918 oil.[3] *Buffalo Bill's Duel with Yellowhand* stands as a spirited re-creation of a legendary episode. In 1876, when he was already an established stage performer, Cody served as a scout with the Fifth Cavalry in the Sioux campaign that saw Custer fall on the Little Big Horn. Not only was he closely connected with the storied events of that summer's fighting, but Cody was also with the Fifth when they met a party of warlike Cheyennes on July 17 and was involved in a skirmish during which he killed a Cheyenne

named Yellow Hair or, as it has been erroneously rendered through the years, Yellow Hand, in an exchange of rifle shots. When Russell went to portray the scene in 1917, the year Cody died, he undoubtedly relied on the old scout's account of what had become through many tellings a personal duel between two warrior heroes:

. . . One of the Indians, who was handsomely decorated with all the ornaments usually worn by a war chief when engaged in a fight, sang out to me, in his own tongue:
"I know you, Pa-he-haska; if you want to fight, come ahead and fight me."
The chief was riding his horse back and forth in front of his men, as if to banter me, and I concluded to accept the challenge. I galloped towards him for fifty yards and he advanced towards me about the same distance, both of us riding at full speed, and then, when we were only about thirty yards apart, I raised my rifle and fired; his horse fell to the ground, having been killed by my bullet.
Almost at the same instant my own horse went down, he having stepped into a hole. The fall did not hurt me much, and I instantly sprang to my feet. The Indian had also recovered himself, and we were now both on foot, and not more than twenty paces apart. We fired at each other simultaneously. My usual luck did not desert me on this occasion, for his bullet missed me, while mine struck him in the breast. He reeled and fell . . .

Just so did Russell show the duel, with its grisly sequel implied by the knife riding prominently on Cody's hip. Having finished off Yellow Hair, Cody "scientifically scalped him in about five seconds" and, waving the trophy over his head, called out for the benefit of the approaching troopers, *"The first scalp for Custer."*[4]

NOTES

1. R. D. Warden, *C M Russell Boyhood Sketchbook*, p. 26.

2. Charles M. Russell to H. Percy Raban, May 3, 1907, in *Good Medicine*, p. 109.

3. For the Cole commission, see Noyes, *In the Land of Chinook*, p. 122 (Russell was working on the Yellow Hand painting while Noyes interviewed him); for their disagreement, see Adams and Britzman, *Charles M. Russell, the Cowboy Artist*, pp. 279–280, 282.

4. *The Life of Hon. William F. Cody Known as Buffalo Bill the Famous Hunter, Scout and Guide: An Autobiography*, pp. 343–344. The same account appeared in the later editions of Cody's book, accompanied by a full-page illustration, *The Duel with Yellow Hand*, that Russell probably saw; see Buffalo Bill (Hon. W. F. Cody), *Story of the Wild West and Camp-Fire Chats*, p. 676. Buffalo Bill that day was actually wearing a Mexican-style outfit of black velvet agleam with silver buttons and ornamented with lace and scarlet piping, while the Cheyenne sported a feather bonnet that Cody took, along with his shield, weapons, and scalp. For the best accounts of the whole affair, see Don Russell, *The Lives and Legends of Buffalo Bill*, chap. 17, and Paul L. Hedren, *First Scalp for Custer: The Skirmish at Warbonnet Creek, Nebraska, July 17, 1876*.

EX COLLECTION

C. Bland Jamison, Santa Fe, New Mexico; Thomas F. Cole, Duluth, Minnesota.

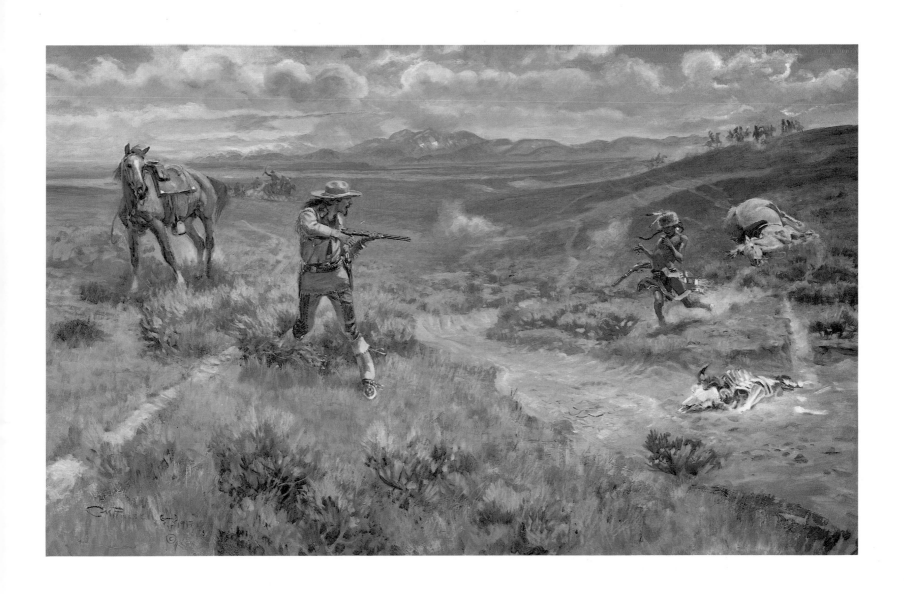

When White Men Turn Red

1922 Oil on canvas
24 x 36¼ in. (61.0 x 92.1 cm.)

Signed lower left: C M Russell / (skull) ©;
dated lower right: 1922

Russell's compassionate affection for the old-time westerners left stranded by civilization's advance extended to the so-called squawmen, objects of ridicule and contempt with the passing of the frontier period that had made red-white unions common. Russell himself had felt the lure of Indian life and knew that he, like several of his cowboy friends, would have been quick to take an Indian wife had the right woman come along. In his story "How Lindsay Turned Indian" he told the tale of a fur trapper who explained his reasons for "going Indian" in these words:

In early times when white men mixed with Injuns away from their own kind, these wild women in their paint an' beads looked mighty enticin', but to stand in with a squaw you had to turn Injun. She'd ask were your relations all dead that you cut your hair! or was you afraid the enemy'd get a hold an' lift it!—at the same time givin' you the sign for raisin' the scalp. The white man, if he liked the squaw, wouldn't stand this joshin' long till he throwed the shears away, an' by the time the hair reached his shoulders he could live without salt. He ain't long forgettin' civilization. Livin' with Nature an' her people this way, he goes backwards till he's a raw man, without any flavorin'.[1]

When White Men Turn Red, with the long-haired trapper and his wives, horses, dogs, and all trailing down from the hills to join their kinfolk camped in the valley below, could be an illustration for Russell's text.

Painted in 1922, *When White Men Turn Red* is the only example in the Richardson collection of Russell's later work in oils. Its vibrant colors are typical of his palette after 1919, while the composition is the same as that of *The Salute of the Robe Trade* (1920) and *Where Guns Were Their Passports* (1924; both Thomas Gilcrease Institute, Tulsa). Though Russell's draftsmanship remained solid till the end, his line became increasingly tentative and disjointed, while his colors ran riot. Why the sudden and pronounced change in his work, particularly his oils? Some critics think that his eyes and his color sense betrayed him. Russell himself expressed an interest in the vivid hues of Maxfield Parrish[2] and may have felt at this late juncture in his career that he could experiment freely with his own color range. Certainly the plague of minor ailments and the serious bout of sciatic rheumatism that put him on crutches in 1923 startled him into an acute awareness of his advancing age, accompanied by an almost unbearable longing for olden times that found expression in the gaudy, flaming oils of his sunset years.

NOTES

1. *Trails Plowed Under*, p. 135.
2. "Russell Exhibiting Fine Collection of His Western Paintings in the East," unidentified clipping [December 1919] in the C. M. Russell scrapbook, Amon Carter Museum of Western Art, Fort Worth.

EX COLLECTION

Newhouse Galleries, New York City; Howard Vanderslice, Kansas City, Missouri.

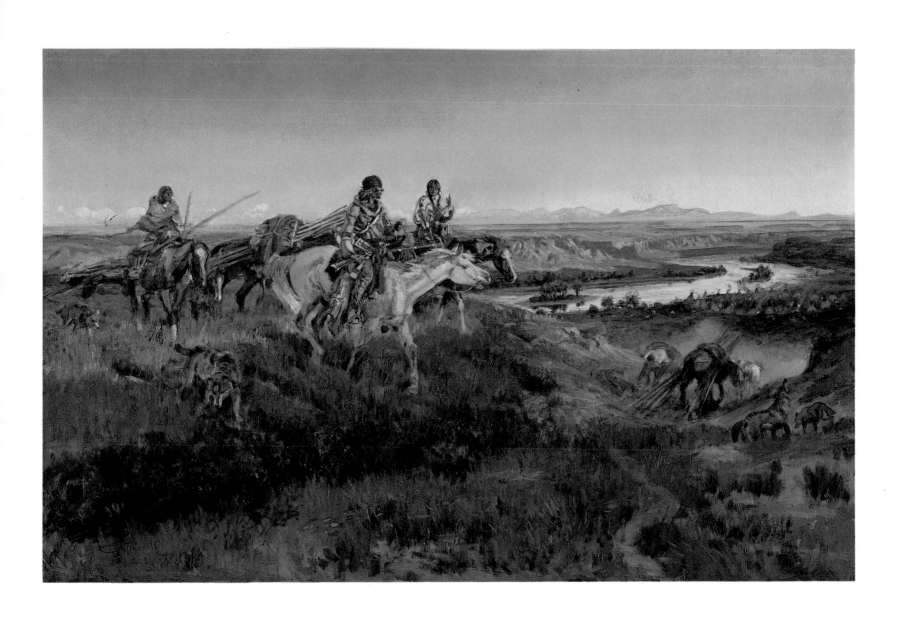

Roping

c. 1925–26 Gouache on paper
15 x 19¼ in. (38.1 x 48.9 cm.)

Unsigned

This painting, probably done around 1925–26, takes us back to Russell's years as a cowboy and his watercolor *Roping the Renegade* (p. 58)—the first and the last works by Russell in the Richardson collection. Both show a cowboy taking his "dally welts" while his partner attempts to drop a second loop on the cow. "Judgment of time and distance was half the battle in good ropin'," Ramon F. Adams has written. "Top ropers seemed to know by intuition the proper time to throw. They were experts who went 'bout the business without any fancy flourishes. In heelin' he seemed to know jes' when the loop reached the animal's feet at the split second they'd be off the ground."[1] Here the roper's problems are compounded since the cow has already been caught and is struggling to pull free. But the throw is accurate and the animal is about to have its hind feet pulled out from under it. This was a nifty piece of cow work that Russell also recorded around the turn of the century in *Throwing on the Heel Rope*,[2] in a pen-and-ink sketch, *Work on the Roundup* (c. 1922; Amon Carter Museum of Western Art, Fort Worth), and in one of his last major watercolors, *When Cows Were Wild* (c. 1926; Montana Historical Society, Helena).

NOTES

1. Adams, *The Old-Time Cowhand*, p. 230.
2. *Rocky Mountain Magazine* 1 (December 1900): 221.

EX COLLECTION

Provenance unknown.

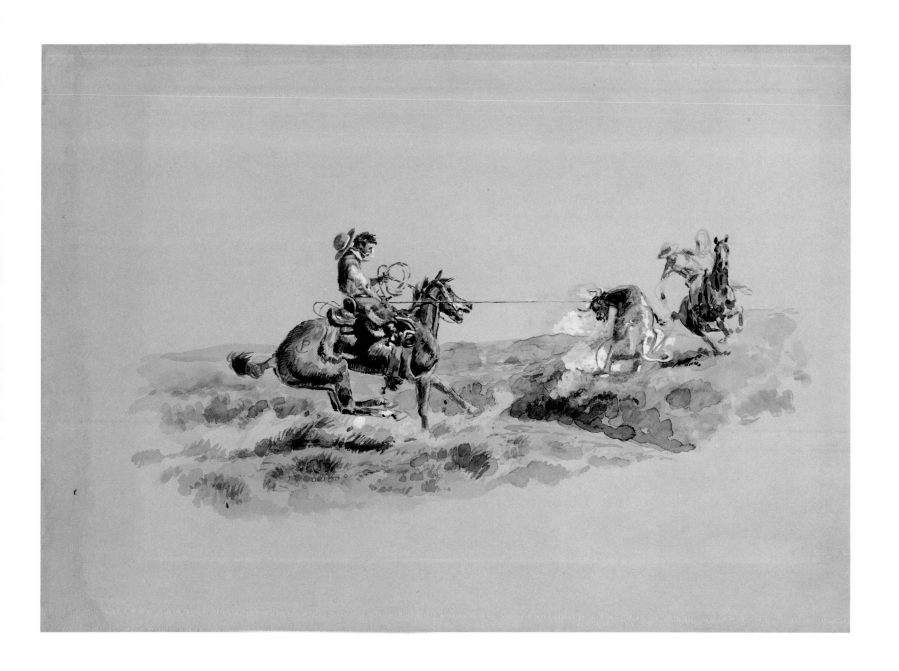

Other Western Painters

Indian Encampment

by Peter Moran (1841–1914)

c. 1880–81 Oil on panel
12⅞ x 31 in. (32.7 x 78.7 cm.)

Signed lower right: P. Moran

Compared to his long-lived brother Thomas, one of America's foremost landscape painters, Peter Moran is positively obscure.[1] The Moran family emigrated from England in 1844 and settled in Philadelphia the next year. After a brief apprenticeship as a printer, Peter followed in his brother's footsteps and turned to the study of art, eventually establishing a reputation as an accomplished etcher of animals.[2] Both Morans were drawn to the West, and Peter accompanied Thomas on a sketching trip to the Teton range in 1879. On his own two years later he made a tour of the pueblos in Arizona and New Mexico.[3] Along with four other painters (including Gilbert Gaul, who is also represented in the Richardson collection [p. 164]), Moran served as a special agent for the Eleventh Census in 1890. His published report on the Wind River Reservation in Wyoming was illustrated with three of his paintings. One in particular, a study of the slaughterhouse at the Shoshone agency on beef issue day, provides a striking contrast to *Indian Encampment*.[4] The title of this painting tells us nothing, but its details do. The Indians that Moran saw in 1890 had lost all vestiges of independence and were reduced to living on government handouts. But the natives in *Indian Encampment* were still armed, rich in horses, and living in the traditional way, suggesting that Moran completed the painting a decade before, following his trip to the Tetons.[5]

NOTES

1. Scattered information about Peter Moran can be found in three books on his brother's work: Fritiof Fryxell, ed., *Thomas Moran: Explorer in Search of Beauty*; Thurman Wilkins, *Thomas Moran: Artist of the Mountains*; and Carol Clark, *Thomas Moran: Watercolors of the American West*.

2. W[illiam] H[owe] D[ownes], "Peter Moran," *Dictionary of American Biography*, VII, 152.

3. Wilkins, *Thomas Moran*, pp. 123–128; and Robert Taft, *Artists and Illustrators of the Old West, 1850–1900*, p. 216.

4. "Report of Special Agent Peter Moran on the Indians of the Wind River Reservation, Shoshone Agency, Wyoming, July and August, 1890," in *Report on Indians Taxed and Indians Not Taxed in the United States (Except Alaska) at the Eleventh Census: 1890*, H. of R. Misc. Doc. No. 340, Pt. 15, 52 Cong., 1 sess. (Washington: Government Printing Office, 1894), pp. 629–634.

5. See Taft, *Artists and Illustrators of the Old West*, p. 366 n. 13.

EX COLLECTION

Newhouse Galleries, New York City.

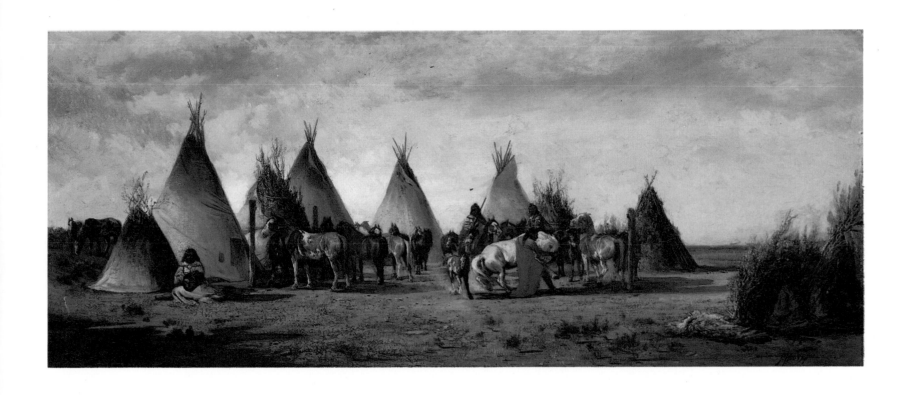

The Pow-Wow
by William Gilbert Gaul (1855–1919)

c. 1890   Oil on canvas
18⅛ x 24⅛ in. (46.0 x 61.3 cm.)

Signed lower right: Gilbert GAUL.

Gilbert Gaul, a New York-based artist, was once described as "the most capable of American military painters."[1] His reputation in his day was sufficient to earn him election as a National Academician in 1882. A busy illustrator, Gaul specialized in western subjects too. He traveled extensively, gathering impressions at first-hand, and in 1890 offered an unvarnished picture of life on the Sioux reservation in the oils he prepared while serving as a special agent for the Eleventh Census. He did not dress up his Indians or show them engaged in the activities of an earlier day. Rather, exhibiting the concern for detailed accuracy characteristic of military artists, Gaul recorded exactly what he saw.[2] "None of Mr. Gaul's pictures are 'studio' pictures," a contemporary noted. "All his sketches are made from life out on the frontier . . . Of course he does not paint his pictures out in the open; he uses a camera and a color-box, and makes his notes from life, but paints his picture in his studio . . ."[3]

What makes an oil like *The Pow-Wow* more than a painted photograph is Gaul's distinctive, loose brushwork and his sensitivity to color effects, evident here in the treatment of the early evening light. The tone of *The Pow-Wow* gives it a dimension beyond the literal, making it a statement on the plains Indian in transition. "The appearance of the Indian is fast changing," Gaul observed in his report on his visit to the Standing Rock Reservation in North Dakota in August 1890. "The day of buffalo robes and buckskins is passing away. With the Sioux breechcloths are

no more. The Indian is no longer a gaily bedecked individual. Most of his furs and feathers have disappeared simultaneously with the deerskin. When he lost his picturesque buckskins he had to make his leggings of army blankets, red and blue." Most of the Sioux men that Gaul saw were dressed in military clothing and sported felt hats with a decorative feather or two and red handkerchiefs knotted about their necks. They exhibited some sartorial variety, unlike the women who were "very uniform" in dress. "Invariably the shawl is worn, which is made to answer the purpose of head covering . . . They wear loose robes to the ankles, with flowing sleeves. . . . The dresses are usually of bright colors, red being greatly worn, and of the brightest kind. . . . As ornaments they wear brass bands at the wrists, earrings, strings of beads, necklaces of calves' teeth, supposed to be of the elk, and painted porcupine quills."[4] Gaul's comments on the ersatz elks' teeth necklaces make a point expressed graphically in *The Pow-Wow*, where elements of the old and the new stand in uneasy juxtaposition. The tipis ("now all of canvas or muslin") with the meat (beef, not buffalo) drying on the rack contrast with the wagon, coffee pot, kettle, and clothing worn by the huddled men. There is a fine feeling for the expanse of the Dakotas here, but also a sense of confinement, a realization that the horizon has permanently shrunk for the buffalo-hunting warriors of yesteryear who now listlessly wait at the agency to receive their beef rations on issue day.[5]

NOTES

1. W[illiam] H[owe] D[ownes], "William Gilbert Gaul," *Dictionary of American Biography*, IV, 193.

2. Gaul's paintings stand as historical records when compared, for example, to the photographs of the Brulé Sioux taken by John A. Anderson in the same period. See Paul Dyck, *Brulé: The Sioux People of the Rosebud*, and Henry W. Hamilton and Jean Tyree Hamilton, *The Sioux of the Rosebud: A History in Pictures*.

3. Jeannette L. Gilder, "A Painter of Soldiers," *Outlook*, July 2, 1898, p. 570.

4. "Report of Special Agent Gilbert Gaul on the Indians of Standing Rock Reservation, Standing Rock Agency, Fort Yates, North Dakota, August, 1890," in *Report on Indians Taxed and Indians Not Taxed in the United States (Except Alaska) at the Eleventh Census: 1890, H. of R. Misc. Doc. No. 340, Pt. 15, 52 Cong., 1 sess.* (Washington: Government Printing Office, 1894), p. 526.

5. Ibid., p. 524; and "Report of Special Agent Gilbert Gaul, on the Indians of the Cheyenne River Reservation, Cheyenne River Agency, South Dakota, July and August, 1890," in *Report on Indians Taxed and Not Taxed*, p. 585.

EX COLLECTION

Provenance unknown.

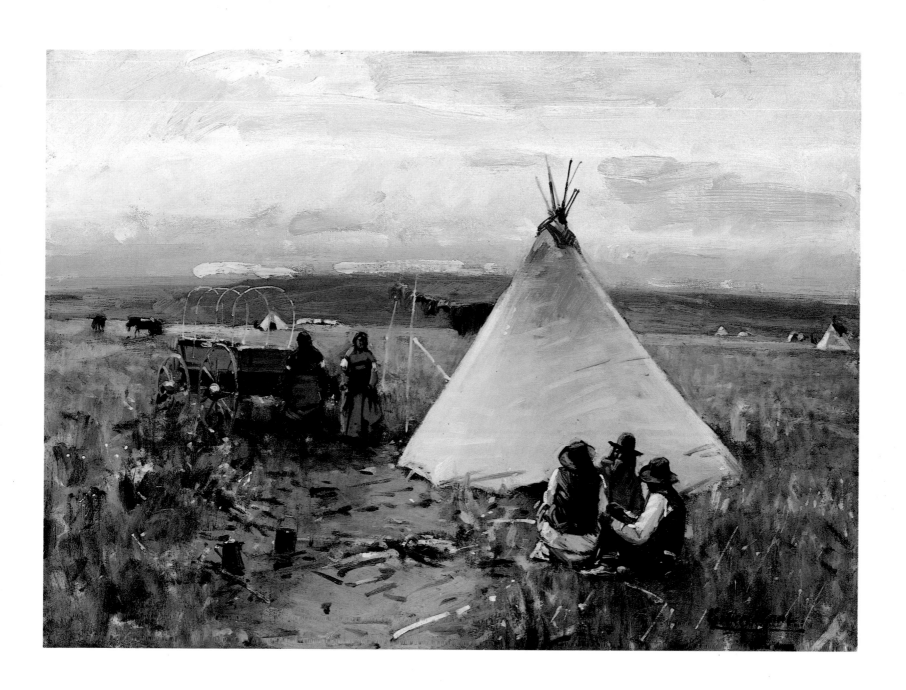

Naí-U-Chi: Chief of the Bow, Zuni 1895   by Charles Francis Browne (1859–1920)

1895   Oil on canvas
18½ x 12¾ in. (47.0 x 32.4 cm.)

Signed lower left: C. F. Browne / 1895;
inscription upper left: NAÍ-U-CHI / CHIEF OF
THE BOW / ZUNI 1895

In the summer of 1895 three friends from Chicago—writer Hamlin Garland, sculptor Hermon A. MacNeil, and his studio mate, painter Charles Francis Browne—embarked on an adventure in the West, a tour of the Indian country of Colorado, Arizona, and New Mexico.[1] At Walpi on the Hopi reservation, they witnessed the snake dance— "without doubt the strangest, most weird and perhaps most ancient ceremonial dance-drama in all our American domain," according to Browne—before going on to Zuñi, "the largest native city under our flag, and . . . now, practically, what it was when the first white man saw it over three centuries ago."[2] The tour "profoundly influenced" Garland's subsequent career, marking a turning point in his writing from prairie tales to stories of the high country. "In truth every page of my work thereafter was colored by the experiences of this glorious savage splendid summer," he recalled.[3] MacNeil was similarly affected. Over the next decade, following his return to Chicago, he devoted himself to Indian subjects, including two much-admired sculptures inspired by the Hopi snake dance.[4] While Browne also was attracted "by the strangeness, picturesqueness and real interest" of the natives, he was least influenced by the tour.[5] Landscape, not genre painting or portraiture, was his teaching speciality at the Chicago Art Institute, and it was his work in this field that earned him election as an associate in the National Academy of Design in 1913. Nevertheless, Browne did paint Indians in 1895, including this creditable likeness of the Zuñi notable Naiuchi, elder brother in the most prestigious and secretive of the Zuñi esoteric orders, the priesthood of the Bow. Naiuchi held this office until 1903, the year before his death.[6]

NOTES

1. Lonnie E. Underhill and Daniel F. Littlefield, Jr., eds., *Hamlin Garland's Observations on the American Indian, 1895–1905*, pp. 12–18.

2. Charles Francis Browne, "Elbridge Ayer Burbank: A Painter of Indian Portraits," *Brush and Pencil* 3 (October 1898): 33.

3. Hamlin Garland, *A Daughter of the Middle Border*, pp. 29, 31.

4. Jean Stansbury Holden, "The Sculptors Mac-Neil," *World's Work* 14 (October 1907): 9408–9417; "Notes," *Craftsman* 16 (September 1909): 710; and J. Walker McSpadden, *Famous Sculptors of America*, pp. 311–317.

5. Browne, "Elbridge Ayer Burbank," p. 16.

6. Matilda Coxe Stevenson, "The Zuñi Indians," in *Twenty-Third Annual Report, Bureau of American Ethnology*, pp. 20, 576–577. Also see Jesse Green, ed., *Zuñi: Selected Writings of Frank Hamilton Cushing*, esp. pp. 96–98, 149–150; the illustrations include (p. 79) Henry F. Farny's 1882 portrait *Chief Priest of the Bow*. Taft, *Artists and Illustrators of the Old West*, pp. 368–369, n. 37, confirms that this was a likeness of Naiuchi, though a comparison between it and Browne's portrait of thirteen years later is sufficient to establish the fact.

EX COLLECTION

Charles P. Everitt, New York City.

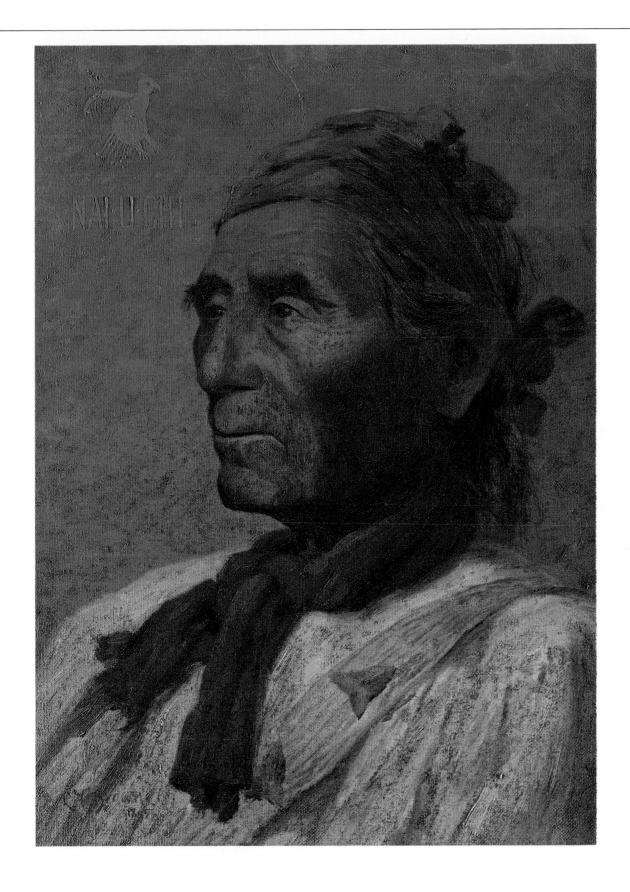

Indians

c. 1910   Oil on canvas
20⅛ x 28⅛ in. (51.1 x 71.4 cm.)

Signed lower left: (shield) E W DEMING

Edwin Willard Deming enjoyed a long, productive career as artist and illustrator. He was best known as a muralist. "I haven't a bit of that decorative feeling and must go on doing easel pictures," Frederic Remington wrote him in 1909 in a letter stating his intention to have Deming do "a panel or two" for the dining room of the Remingtons' new house in Connecticut.[1] But in the same period Deming's smaller canvases were also winning recognition for their evocation of the spiritual side of Indian life.[2] Raised on a homestead in Illinois, Deming had traveled extensively among the western tribes in the late 1880s and through the 1890s before turning to a study of the eastern tribes.[3] His contemporaries thought that he had managed to penetrate the mystery of the Indian mind and could present the world through their eyes.

It was a judgment that Deming happily accepted. He saw himself as the interpreter of the Indian's soul and was given to quoting Remington to the effect, "Deming, the difference between your Indians and mine is that I saw my Indians through the sights of a rifle and you saw yours from inside his blanket in his tipi."[4]

Indians differs from the stylized, allegorical studies, rich in folkloric elements, upon which Deming's reputation rested. As an action picture, it exhibits some of his limitations—despite formal training in New York and Paris, Deming was not always a careful draftsman[5]—and it also indicates a sizable debt to Remington's great oil *Ridden Down*. The situations are identical. A brave, pursued by an enemy war party, can flee no further.

Dismounted, he braces for his last stand. Club in hand, imperturbable in the face of death, he is the model of the stoical warrior. While Remington showed a meeting between hostile plains tribes, Deming chose to underline the clash of different Indian cultures by giving his lone warrior the roach cut usually associated with the woodland tribes.

NOTES

1. Frederic Remington to E. W. Deming, [1909], in Therese O. Deming, comp., *Edwin Willard Deming*, ed. Henry Collins Walsh, p. 25.

2. See "Folk-lore of a Vanishing Race Preserved in the Paintings of Edwin Willard Deming—Artist-Historian of the American Indian," *Craftsman* 10 (May 1906): 150–167.

3. With artist DeCost Smith, Deming co-authored three articles recounting western experiences in *Outing* 23–25 (October 1893, May 1894, February 1895): "Sketching among the Sioux," "Sketching among the Crow Indians," and "With Gun and Palette among the Red-skins." Also see Deming's "Custer's Last Stand: The Indians' Version of the Massacre," *Mentor* 14 (July 1926): 56–57.

4. Quoted in Thomas G. Lamb, *Eight Bears: A Biography of E. W. Deming, 1860–1942*, p. 28. Since the same remark appeared in a piece by a journalist in the *New York Post*, one wonders if the words that Deming recalled were his rather than Remington's (see Deming, *Edwin Willard Deming*, p. 43). Either way, the description is apt.

5. Lamb, *Eight Bears*, p. 97.

EX COLLECTION

Provenance unknown.

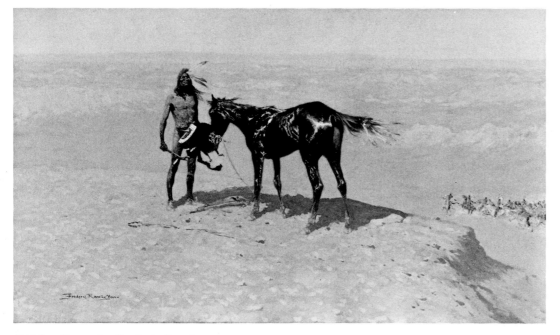

Ridden Down by Frederic Remington, 1905
Amon Carter Museum of Western Art,
Fort Worth

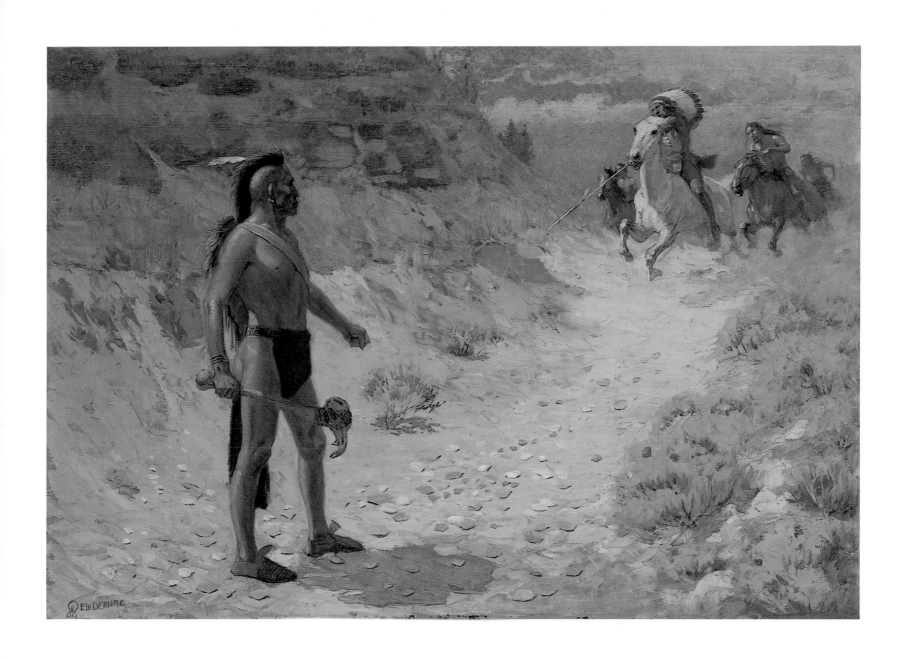

Attack on the Herd [Close Call]

by Charles Schreyvogel (1861–1912)

c. 1907   Oil on canvas
25⅛ x 34¼ in. (63.8 x 87.0 cm.)

Signed lower left: Chas Schreyvogel.

Charles Schreyvogel's work, apart from a scattering of portraits and a few tranquil scenes, constitutes a sustained tribute to the Wild West. In his paintings, troopers charge, Indians dodge and whoop, rifles and pistols discharge, sabres swing, bodies crash to the ground, and horses are always at full gallop. Though others—notably Rufus F. Zogbaum—portrayed the Indian-fighting army, only Schreyvogel rivaled Remington in the public's esteem, and only that duo tried to elevate the subject from illustration to art. Because Remington thought that Schreyvogel was poaching on his turf—and in the oil that first brought him critical recognition, *My Bunkie* (1899), was directly stealing his ideas—he launched an attack on Schreyvogel's work in 1903 on the grounds of historical inaccuracy.[1] Typically, Remington was talking about details of dress and accoutrements in a Schreyvogel cavalry scene, with the result that his criticisms seemed petty and his motive in making them mere envy. Had he not been so committed to Wild West action himself, he might more pertinently have charged Schreyvogel with misrepresenting what life in the Indian-fighting army was all about, for, based on his own experience, it had precious little to do with fighting and a great deal to do with boredom and drudgery. Schreyvogel, because he was unfamiliar with it and because it was irrelevant to his interests anyway, simply eliminated the greater part of reality from his work and presented an unadulterated vision of constant, violent action. It was a vision that reflected his particular circumstances. Like Remington, he was a life-long easterner. Born in New York in 1861, trained in Munich (1886–1890), and a resident of Hoboken, New Jersey, until his death in 1912, Schreyvogel made regular visits to the West beginning in 1893. On these he gathered inspiration and satisfied an obsession with accuracy of detail no less pronounced than Remington's own. This concern with verisimilitude has even persuaded his biographer that his work was realistic despite its obvious commitment to the fantasy West served up by that master showman, Schreyvogel's friend William F. (Buffalo Bill) Cody.[2]

Attack on the Herd is in most respects a typical Schreyvogel. Many of his oils isolate two or three figures engaged in a deadly duel. This one is distinctive, however, in that its white protagonist is a cowboy rather than a cavalryman. The only comparable Schreyvogel is a 1907 oil, *Hard Pushed*, showing a cowboy in identical costume—red shirt,[3] chaps, and a hat with the rim rolled back—trying to elude two warriors armed with bow and spear. It is possible that *Attack on the Herd* was originally known as *Close Call*, though the present title is more descriptive. The Indians have successfully separated the cowboy from the herd, while another warrior can be seen in the background stampeding the cattle by flapping a blanket.

NOTES

1. See Horan, *The Life and Art of Charles Schreyvogel*, pp. 31–40, and R. C. Wilson, "The Great Custer Battle of 1903," *Mankind* 5 (February 1976): 52–59. Interestingly, the painting that Remington chose to attack, *Custer's Demand* (1903; Thomas Gilcrease Institute, Tulsa), was one Schreyvogel *not* concerned with an Indian-white skirmish.

2. See Horan, *The Life and Art of Charles Schreyvogel*, pp. 40, 49–50, 56, and, for Schreyvogel and Cody, pp. 46–47.

3. This detail probably came from Buffalo Bill's Wild West—note Charlie Russell's comment on the subject in the commentary with *Buffalo Bill's Duel with Yellowhand* (p. 154). Similar red shirts pop up in paintings by Remington and William R. Leigh (pp. 172 and 174) done in the same period.

EX COLLECTION

Newhouse Galleries, New York City; Jacob Ullrich, Hoboken, New Jersey [?].

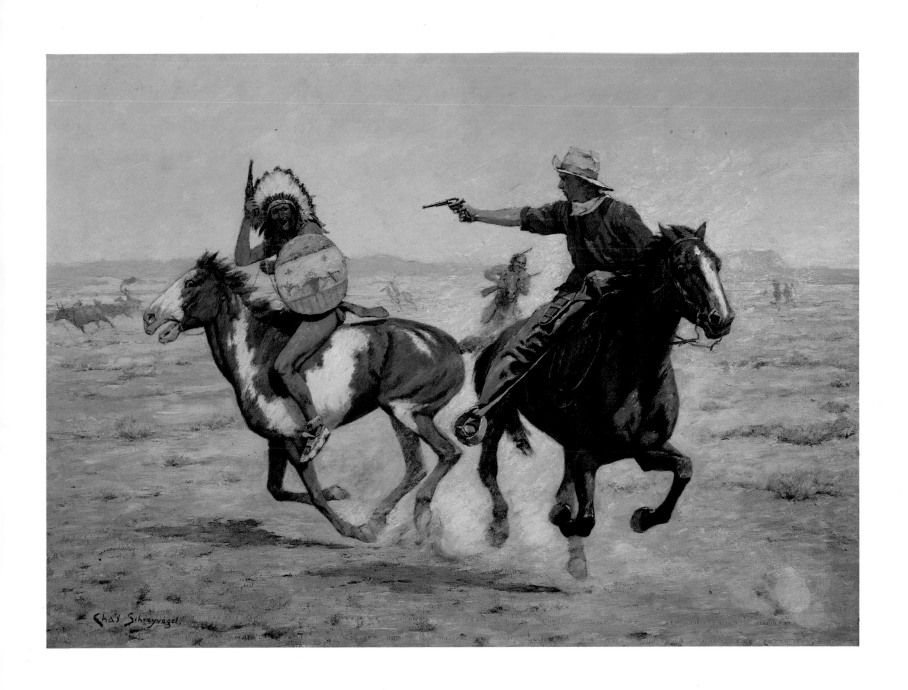

The Hold Up [The Ambush]   by William Robinson Leigh (1866–1955)

1903   Oil on canvas
32¾ x 22¾ in. (83.2 x 57.8 cm.)

Signed lower right: W. R. LEIGH. / 1903.;
inscription lower left:
Copyright 1904 / By Am. Litho Co. N.Y.

Of the painters who gained fame as delineators of the American West around the turn of the century, William Robinson Leigh is routinely cited as the most thoroughly trained.[1] A native of West Virginia, he spent fifteen years studying drawing, painting, and composition in Baltimore and Munich and apprenticing as a mural painter before establishing himself as an artist and illustrator in New York City in 1896. A decade later, fulfilling "a desire that has been in me since boyhood," Leigh went west and fell in love with the desert country.[2] "I saw Acoma and the Grand Canyon," he recalled years later. "I knew that some of the most distinctive—characteristic—dramatic—poetic—unique motives in the world were here in this virgin country waiting an adequate hand to do them justice."[3] Leigh never doubted that his was the hand adequate to the task, and while he would venture into other areas over the next half-century, he was primarily a western artist. Since he was a crusty, opinionated man, he occasionally painted allegorical pieces intended to embody his views. They were, with few exceptions, disasters. For all his technical sophistication, Leigh displayed a pedestrian imagination and abysmal taste in his allegories, and they principally serve to foster a renewed appreciation for less pretentious, more successful western oils like *The Hold Up*.[4]

NOTES

1. Remington was proud to say that he was a drop-out from Yale's School of Fine Arts, while Russell may have enrolled in a St. Louis art school but stayed only long enough to realize he could learn nothing drawing from a plaster cast of a foot.

2. *Mentor*, June 15, 1915, notes on the back of plate 6, *An Argument with the Sheriff* by William R. Leigh.

3. W. R. Leigh, "My America," *Arizona Highways* 24 (February 1948): 25.

4. Examples of Leigh's allegorical work are reproduced in June DuBois, *W. R. Leigh: The Definitive Illustrated Biography*, and D. Duane Cummins, *William Robinson Leigh: Western Artist*. Cummins provides a more critical, searching treatment of Leigh's views, but neither biographer comments extensively on artistic merit.

EX COLLECTION

Newhouse Galleries, New York City.

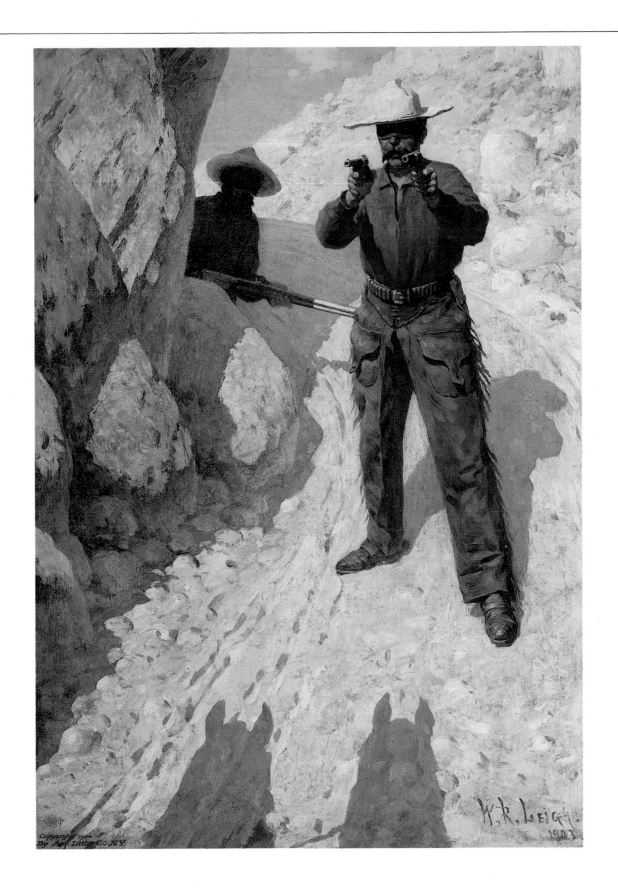

Copyright 1904
By Am. Litho Co. N.Y.

W.R. Leigh.
1903

173

Bears in the Path [Surprise]

by William Robinson Leigh (1866–1955)

1904   Oil on canvas
21⅛ x 33⅛ in. (53.7 x 84.2 cm.)

Signed lower left: W. R. LEIGH / 1904

In preparing for a major painting, Leigh worked out each compositional element separately in meticulous drawings. Then he laboriously transferred them to canvas to produce finished works short on spontaneity but notable for their polish, vibrant colors, and aura of make-believe. Leigh never permitted factual considerations to dim "the sunlight and thrill of the glorious West."[1] But he bristled at the charge that his western paintings were merely gaudy illustrations, and he waged a passionate war against what he deemed the scandal of modern art without ever recognizing that his own old-fashioned approach clashed with the subject matter of many of his oils, particularly the astonishing action scenes he executed in his seventies and eighties in which he sent men and horses flying about the canvas with little regard for probability but with an unflagging sense of the dramatic.

Bears in the Path, like *The Hold Up*, is interesting as a western subject done before Leigh ever saw the West of his childhood dreams. Both paintings capture moments of suspense, anticipating rather than showing the violence that might momentarily occur. And both confront the viewer face on. In *The Hold Up* an outlaw costumed in a red shirt, chaps, white hat, and an unlikely Lone Ranger–style mask trains his revolvers on the stagecoach indicated by the shadows cast by the horses. The viewer's angle of vision is that of the driver. In *Bears in the Path*, Leigh depicts another confrontation much favored by western painters—Russell did several—though none took more pride in his rendering of bears than Leigh, who painted them often and was not about to leave them to the viewer's imagination here. Like the bandit, the surprised man stands with left leg extended, his weight planted on the right, poised for swift action, another study in suspense. Since he is also decked out in a red shirt and chaps, it would appear that these were props in Leigh's New York studio. Of course, it is just as likely that Leigh had been doing research at Buffalo Bill's Wild West and had reached the same conclusions as Schreyvogel about what the average westerner wore.

NOTES

1. W. R. Leigh, "My America," *Arizona Highways* 24 (February 1948): 26.

EX COLLECTION

Newhouse Galleries, New York City.

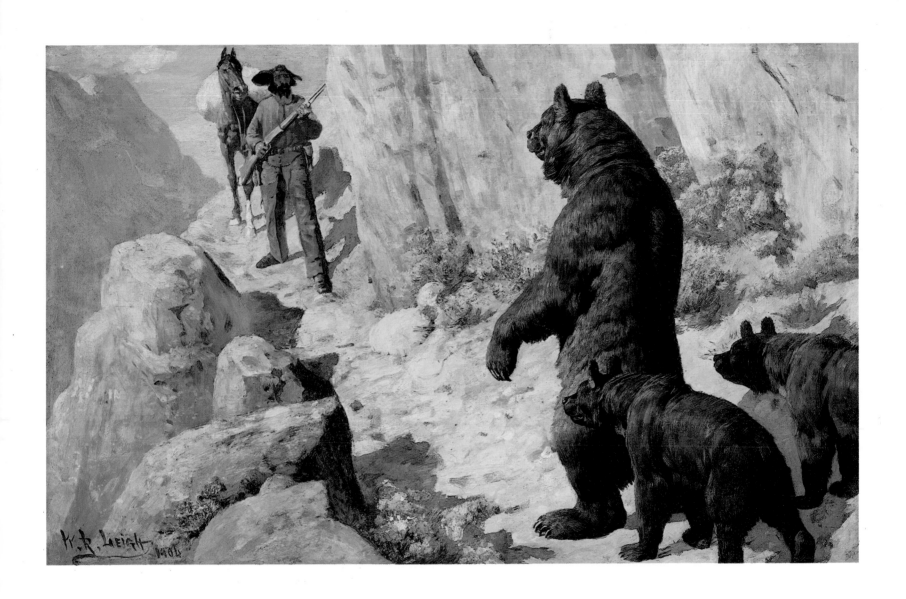

Trouble on the Pony Express
by Frank Tenney Johnson (1874–1939)

c. 1910–20   Oil on canvas
36 ¼ x 28 ¼ in. (92.1 x 71.8 cm.)

Signed lower left: Frank Tenney Johnson

Frank Tenney Johnson was born on a farm in Iowa where he spent his childhood "along the Oregon Trail upon the wild rolling prairie."[1] The Johnsons moved to Milwaukee in 1888, and Frank studied art there and in New York City until 1904 when he realized his youthful ambition to see the far West. A five-month stay in Colorado, Wyoming, and the desert Southwest filled his reference files with oil sketches and hundreds of photographs of the subjects that would preoccupy him: cowboys, Mexicans, and southwestern Indians. Subsequent trips expanded his repertoire—in 1912, for example, he joined Charlie Russell on a sketching expedition to the Blackfoot reservation east of Glacier Park in Montana—though he never strayed far from his original concerns. Johnson's reputation is based on his painterly oils notable for their use of color. He favored nocturnals and sun-splashed scenes capturing the light early in the morning and late in the day when shadows and warm orange tones replace the floodlit clarity of mid-day.

NOTES

1. Babcock Galleries, "Paintings of the West," *El Palacio* 8 (July 1920): 237.

EX COLLECTION

Provenance unknown.

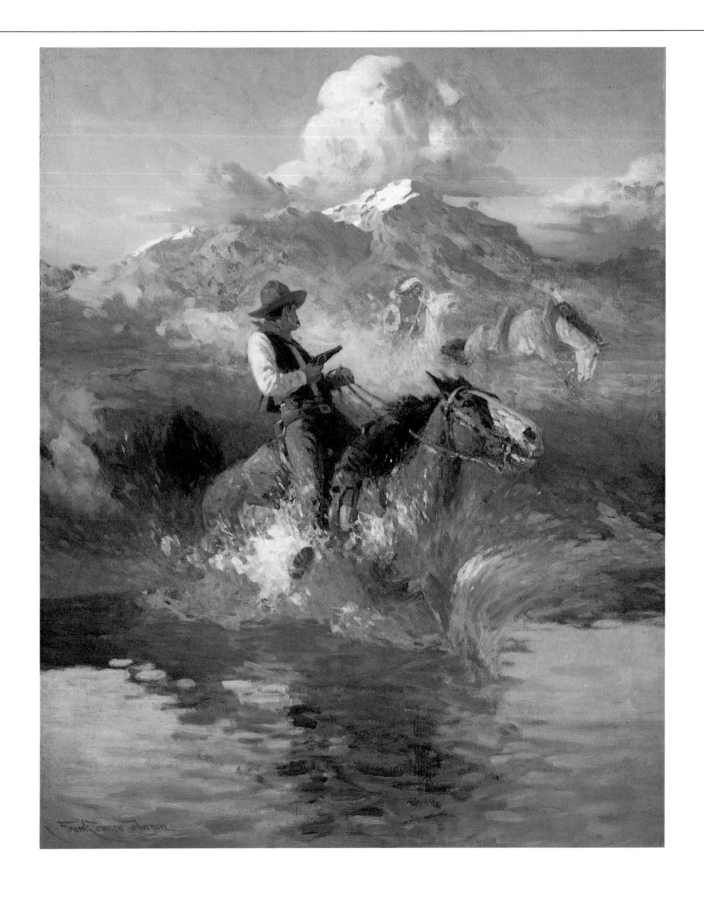

Contrabandista a la Frontera

by Frank Tenney Johnson (1874–1939)

1925   Oil on canvas
36⅛ x 45⅛ in. (91.7 x 114.6 cm.)

Signed lower right: F. Tenney Johnson—
/ 1925

Contrabandista a la Frontera and *Trouble on the Pony Express* are unusual in portraying violence—a point made by Johnson's biographer[1]—but representative in showing his two favorite color schemes. They suggest why Johnson's reputation as a pure painter—that is, to adopt the terminology of the times, as an artist rather than an illustrator—was sufficiently elevated to secure his election as an associate in the National Academy of Design in 1929 and as a full member eight years later, a distinction conferred upon only three other artists represented in the Richardson collection, Gilbert Gaul, William R. Leigh, and Peter Hurd. Nevertheless, Johnson's paintings, individually so striking, collectively exhibit definite limitations. There is too much striving after a few patented effects, too many scenes with clouds piled column high over the central figure, too many night scenes of a solitary cowboy, head bent, hands cupped, lighting up a cigarette. There is a vague, generalized quality to Johnson's work, an absence of the concrete detail and exact observation characteristic of most popular western art, and this very quality accentuates the similarity of his paintings and the paucity of creative imagination behind them. All western artists repeat themes and figures, but the best do not copy themselves. In this respect, Johnson is kin to another, much-admired western painter, Henry F. Farny; both seemed better before their works were brought together between two covers, where the redundancies become glaringly apparent. The figure on the left of *Contrabandista a la Frontera*, for example, is lifted straight out of Johnson's 1924 oil *Cattle Rustlers*.[2] There is a second, more troubling problem with Johnson's work. Many of his paintings indicate a deep, unacknowledged debt to Remington. The composition of *Contrabandista a la Frontera* is reminiscent of Remington's great oil *Fired On* (1908; National Collection of Fine Arts, Smithsonian Institution, Washington, D.C.), while the figure on the right could have ridden straight out of Remington's painting *The Scout* (1902). Similarly, the rider in *Trouble on the Pony Express* seems to have stolen his costume and pose from the foreground figure in Remington's *His Last Stand* (p. 28), while the color scheme owes much to the work of one of Johnson's first instructors in Milwaukee, Richard Lorenz.

Sid W. Richardson owned four Frank Tenney Johnson oils at one time but traded two of them for William R. Leigh's *The Hold Up* and *Bears in the Path* (pp. 172 and 174). In terms of his collection's quality, it was the right decision.

NOTES

1. Harold McCracken, *The Frank Tenney Johnson Book: A Master Painter of the Old West*, p. 12.
2. Ibid., p. 125.

EX COLLECTION

Provenance unknown.

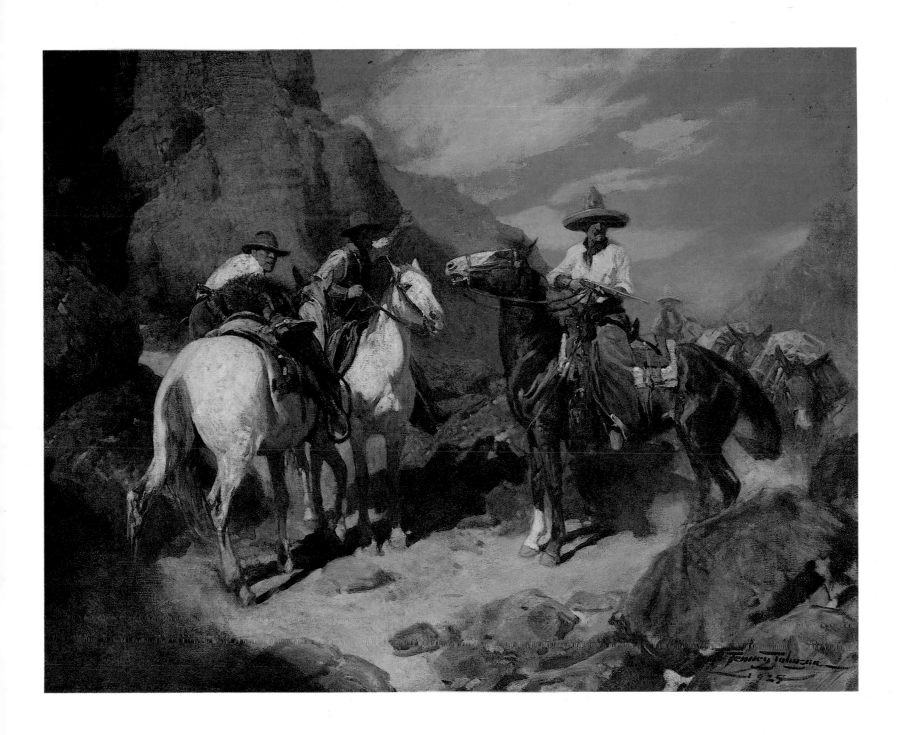

The Forty-niners

by Oscar E. Berninghaus (1874–1952)

Before 1942   Oil on canvas
26¼ x 36¼ in. (66.7 x 92.1 cm.)

Signed lower left: O E BERNINGHAUS

Oscar E. Berninghaus is the only member of the famous Taos artists' colony represented in the Richardson collection. St. Louis born and raised, Berninghaus was an established commercial artist when he visited New Mexico in 1899 and "became infected with the Taos germ."[1] He established a pattern: winters in St. Louis, summers in Taos, and though a charter member of the Taos Society of Artists (1912), he did not move to Taos permanently until 1925. A generous, popular man, Berninghaus was also a diligent professional. He exhibited regularly, won major prizes, held office in such organizations as the Society of Western Artists (serving as secretary during one year of Charles F. Browne's presidential term),[2] and in 1926 was elected an associate of the National Academy.

Like such Taos friends as Ernest L. Blumenschein and Victor Higgins, Berninghaus is known for his strong sense of place. In many of his canvases, horses and Indians become inconspicuous elements, dwarfed by the spectacular, mountainous landscape that lured so many painters to northern New Mexico.[3] But Berninghaus also painted historical pictures—notably a series of oils for the Anheuser-Busch Brewing Company of St. Louis on the theme of early western transportation[4] and five murals for the Missouri State Capitol at Jefferson City.[5] *The Forty-niners*, in subject matter and style, forms part of this less familiar body of his work.

NOTES

1. Oscar E. Berninghaus, letter, April 12, 1950, in Laura M. Bickerstaff, *Pioneer Artists of Taos*, p. 9.

2. *Seventeenth Annual Exhibition of The Society of Western Artists, December 11 to December 29, 1912* (Chicago: Art Institute of Chicago, 1912).

3. For a representative sampling of Berninghaus' work, see Mary Carroll Nelson, "Oscar E. Berninghaus: Modesty and Expertise," *American Artist* 42 (January 1978): 42–47; for an intelligent appraisal of his artistry, see Van Deren Coke, *Taos and Santa Fe: The Artist's Environment, 1882–1942*, p. 18.

4. Roland Krebs, in collaboration with Percy J. Orthwein, *Making Friends Is Our Business: 100 Years of Anheuser-Busch*, pp. 337, 341–342.

5. Bickerstaff, *Pioneer Artists of Taos*, pp. 13–14.

EX COLLECTION

Newhouse Galleries, New York City.

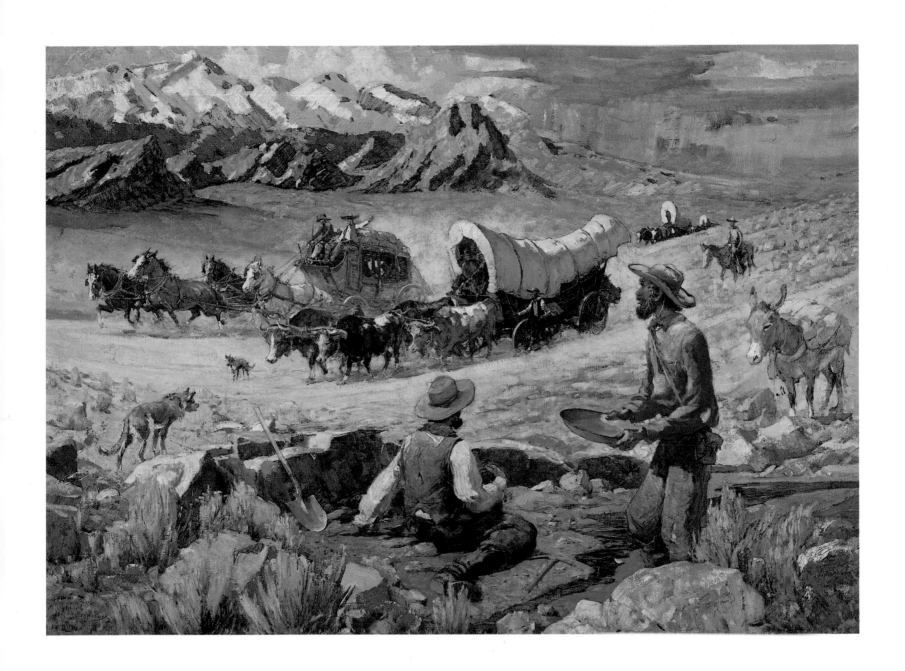

Portrait of Sid Richardson

1958   Oil on panel
32 x 48 in. (81.3 x 121.9 cm.)

Signed lower left: PETER HURD

Peter Hurd, a native of New Mexico, ventured from his home state in 1921 to attend West Point but resigned to study art instead. In 1924 he became a pupil of the renowned illustrator N. C. Wyeth at Chadds Ford, Pennsylvania, and five years later a member of the Wyeth family circle when he married his mentor's daughter Henriette. The Hurds, both artists, lived on at Chadds Ford until 1939, then settled in New Mexico where Peter Hurd has earned distinction as one of the outstanding painters of the Southwest. Though his watercolors and etchings are much admired, his reputation rests on his work in egg tempera, an exacting medium perfectly suited to his tight, precise brushstroking since it allows his heavily reworked surface to retain an airy glow. Though best known for his spare, evocative studies of the light, the landscape, the people, and the quiet charm of his native state, Hurd is also an accomplished portraitist.[1]

This painting of Sid W. Richardson was executed in 1958. As in most Hurd portraits, its carefully wrought background showing the palm trees of San José Island, off Rockport, Texas, and the herds of cattle and horses tells us something about the subject—*who* this man is—while the likeness speaks volumes about character. Hurd captured Richardson at sixty-seven, a year before his death. He reveals him to be a man of substance and vision. Richardson sits, self-assured and comfortable, but his warmth comes through even in this rather pensive study.

NOTES

1. For a brief overview of Hurd's career, see Susan E. Myer, "Peter Hurd," *American Artist* 39 (February 1975): 46–51, 100, 104; for Hurd and the Wyeth family circle, see Henry C. Pitz, "N. C. Wyeth," *American Heritage* 16 (October 1965): 52–54; for a personal statement of Hurd's relationship to New Mexico, see his "A Southwestern Heritage," *Arizona Highways* 29 (November 1953): 14–27; for a biography written by a friend, see Paul Horgan, *Peter Hurd: A Portrait Sketch from Life.*

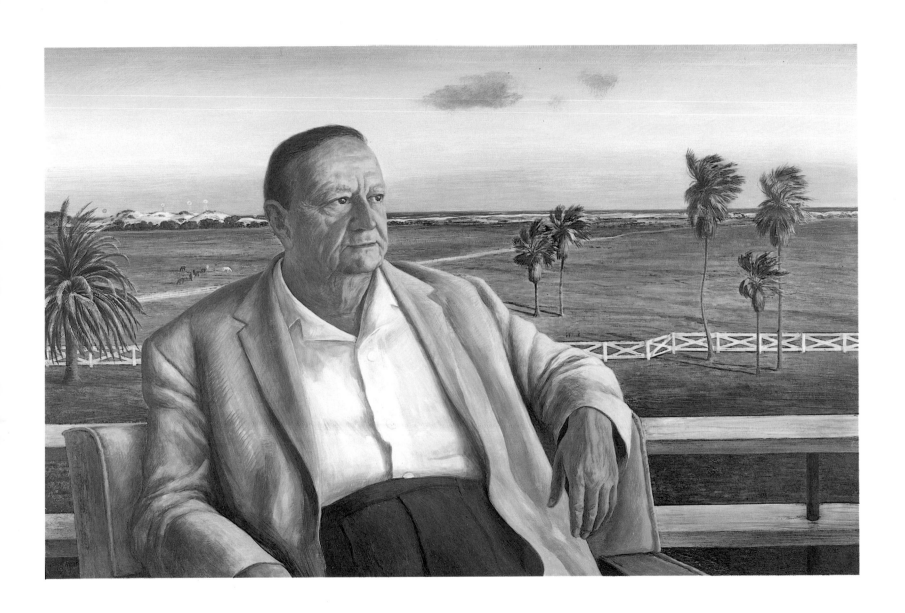

Selected Bibliography

Abbott, E. C., and Helena Huntington Smith. *We Pointed Them North: Recollections of a Cowpuncher.* Norman: University of Oklahoma Press, 1955; reprint of 1939 edition.

Adams, Ramon F. *The Old-time Cowhand.* New York: Macmillan, 1961.

————, and Homer E. Britzman. *Charles M. Russell, the Cowboy Artist: A Biography.* Pasadena, Calif.: Trail's End Publishing Co., 1948.

Ahenakew, Edward. *Voices of the Plains Cree.* Edited by Ruth M. Buck. Toronto: McClelland and Stewart, 1973.

Allen, William A. *Adventures with Indians and Game; or, Twenty Years in the Rocky Mountains.* Chicago: A. W. Bowen & Co., 1903.

Bickerstaff, Laura M. *Pioneer Artists of Taos.* Denver: Sage Books, 1955.

Bollinger, James W. *Old Montana and Her Cowboy Artist: A Paper Read before The Contemporary Club, Davenport, Iowa, January Thirtieth, Nineteen Hundred Fifty.* Shenandoah, Iowa: World Publishing Co., 1963.

Brown, Mark H., and W. R. Felton. *The Frontier Years: L. A. Huffman, Photographer of the Plains.* New York: Henry Holt and Co., 1955.

Bruce, Robert. *The Fighting Norths and Pawnee Scouts: Narratives and Reminiscences of Military Service on the Old Frontier.* New York: Robert Bruce, 1932.

Buffalo Bill (Hon. W. F. Cody). *The Life of Hon. William F. Cody Known as Buffalo Bill the Famous Hunter, Scout and Guide: An Autobiography.* Hartford: Frank E. Bliss, 1879.

————. *Story of the Wild West and Camp-Fire Chats.* N.p., 1888.

Burnside, Wesley M. *Maynard Dixon: Artist of the West.* Provo: Brigham Young University Press, 1974.

Clark, Carol. *Thomas Moran: Watercolors of the American West.* Austin: University of Texas Press for the Amon Carter Museum of Western Art, Fort Worth, 1980.

Coke, Van Deren. *Taos and Santa Fe: The Artist's Environment, 1882–1942.* Albuquerque: University of New Mexico Press for the Amon Carter Museum of Western Art, Fort Worth, and the Art Gallery, University of New Mexico, Albuquerque, 1963.

Cummins, D. Duane. *William Robinson Leigh: Western Artist.* Norman: University of Oklahoma Press and Thomas Gilcrease Institute, Tulsa, 1980.

Deming, Therese O., comp. *Edwin Willard Deming.* Edited by Henry Collins Walsh. New York: Privately printed, 1925.

Dentzel, Carl S. "The Roots of Russell: The Earliest Known Frontier Sketches of Charles Marion Russell." In *The Westerners Brand Book, Number 14.* Los Angeles: Los Angeles Corral, 1974.

Dippie, Brian W., ed. *Nomad: George A. Custer in "Turf, Field and Farm."* Austin: University of Texas Press, 1980.

————. *"Paper Talk": Charlie Russell's American West.* New York: Alfred A. Knopf in association with the Amon Carter Museum of Western Art, Fort Worth, 1979.

Dobie, J. Frank. "A Summary Introduction to Frederic Remington." In *Pony Tracks*, by Frederic Remington. Norman: University of Oklahoma Press, 1961; reprint of 1895 edition.

DuBois, June. *W. R. Leigh: The Definitive Illustrated Biography.* Kansas City: Lowell Press, 1977.

Dyck, Paul. *Brulé: The Sioux People of the Rosebud.* Flagstaff: Northland Press, 1971.

Dykes, Jeff C., ed. *The West of the Texas Kid, 1881–1910: Recollections of Thomas Edgar Crawford, Cowboy, Gun Fighter, Rancher, Hunter, Miner.* Norman: University of Oklahoma Press, 1962.

Ewers, John C. *Artists of the Old West.* Garden City, N.Y.: Doubleday and Co., 1965.

————. *The Blackfeet: Raiders on the Northwestern Plains.* Norman: University of Oklahoma Press, 1958.

———. "Fact and Fiction in the Documentary Art of the American West." In *The Frontier Re-examined*, edited by John Francis McDermott. Urbana: University of Illinois Press, 1967.

———. *The Horse in Blackfoot Indian Culture, with Comparative Material from Other Western Tribes*. Smithsonian Institution, Bureau of American Ethnology Bulletin 159. Washington: Government Printing Office, 1955.

Frederic Remington (1861–1909): Paintings, Drawings, and Sculpture in the Collection of The R. W. Norton Art Gallery, Shreveport, Louisiana. Shreveport: R. W. Norton Art Gallery, 1979.

Fryxell, Fritiof, ed. *Thomas Moran: Explorer in Search of Beauty*. East Hampton, Long Island: East Hampton Free Library, 1958.

Garland, Hamlin. *A Daughter of the Middle Border*. New York: Grosset and Dunlap, 1921.

———. *Roadside Meetings*. New York: Macmillan Co., 1930.

Green, Jesse, ed. *Zuñi: Selected Writings of Frank Hamilton Cushing*. Lincoln: University of Nebraska Press, 1979.

Grinnell, George Bird. *Blackfoot Lodge Tales: The Story of a Prairie People*. New York: Charles Scribner's Sons, 1892.

———. *Pawnee Hero Stories and Folk-Tales, with Notes on the Origin, Customs and Character of the Pawnee People*. New York: Forest and Stream Publishing Co., 1889.

Hale, Horatio. "Report on the Blackfoot Tribes." In *Report on the North-Western Tribes of Canada*. London: Office of the British Association for the Advancement of Science, 1885.

Hamilton, Henry W., and Jean Tyree Hamilton. *The Sioux of the Rosebud: A History in Pictures*. Norman: University of Oklahoma Press, 1971.

Hassrick, Peter H. *Frederic Remington: Paintings, Drawings, and Sculpture in the Amon Carter Museum and the Sid W. Richardson Foundation Collections*. New York: Harry N. Abrams in association with the Amon Carter Museum of Western Art, Fort Worth, 1973.

———. *The Way West: Art of Frontier America*. New York: Harry N. Abrams, 1977.

Hassrick, Royal B. *The Sioux: Life and Customs of a Warrior Society*. Norman: University of Oklahoma Press, 1964.

Hedren, Paul L. *First Scalp for Custer: The Skirmish at Warbonnet Creek, Nebraska, July 17, 1876*. Glendale, Calif.: Arthur H. Clark Co., 1980.

Horan, James D. *The Life and Art of Charles Schreyvogel: Painter-Historian of the Indian-Fighting Army of the American West*. New York: Crown Publishers, 1969.

Horgan, Paul. *Peter Hurd: A Portrait Sketch from Life*. Austin: University of Texas Press for the Amon Carter Museum of Western Art, Fort Worth, 1965.

"How The West Was Won": Paintings, Watercolors, Bronzes by Frederic Remington and Charles M. Russell, for the Benefit of the Hospital for Special Surgery. New York: Wildenstein, 1968.

Jacobs, Wilbur R., ed. *Letters of Francis Parkman*. 2 vols. Norman: University of Oklahoma Press, 1960.

Jussim, Estelle. *Visual Communication and the Graphic Arts: Photographic Technologies in the Nineteenth Century*. New York: R. R. Bowker Co., 1974.

Kennedy, Michael S., ed. *The Assiniboines: From the Accounts of the Old Ones Told to First Boy (James Larpenteur Long)*. Norman: University of Oklahoma Press, 1961.

Krebs, Roland, and Percy J. Orthwein. *Making Friends Is Our Business: 100 Years of Anheuser-Busch*. St. Louis: Anheuser-Busch, 1953.

Lamb, Thomas G. *Eight Bears: A Biography of E. W. Deming, 1860–1942*. Oklahoma City: Griffin Books, 1978.

Linderman, Frank Bird. *Recollections of Charley Russell*. Edited by H. G. Meriam. Norman: University of Oklahoma Press, 1963.

McCracken, Harold. *A Catalogue of the Fred-
eric Remington Memorial Collection*. New
York: Knoedler Galleries for the Remington
Art Memorial, Ogdensburg, N.Y., 1954.
———. *The Charles M. Russell Book: The
Life and Work of the Cowboy Artist*. Gar-
den City, N.Y.: Doubleday and Co., 1957.
———. *The Frank Tenney Johnson Book: A
Master Painter of the Old West*. Garden
City, N.Y.: Doubleday and Co., 1974.
———. *Frederic Remington: Artist of the Old
West*. Philadelphia: J. B. Lippincott Co.,
1947.
McSpadden, J. Walker. *Famous Sculptors of
America*. Freeport, N.Y.: Books for Libraries
Press, 1968.
Mandelbaum, David G. *The Plains Cree: An
Ethnographic, Historical, and Comparative
Study*. Canadian Plains Studies, 9. Regina:
Canadian Plains Research Center, Univer-
sity of Regina, 1979.
Manley, Atwood. *Some of Frederic Reming-
ton's North Country Associations*. Og-
densburg: Northern New York Publishing
Co., 1961.
Marlin Guns for 1963. New Haven: Marlin
Firearms Co., 1963.
Noyes, Al. J. (Ajax). *In the Land of Chinook;
or, the Story of Blaine County*. Helena,
Mon.: State Publishing Co., 1917.
Parkman, Francis. *The Oregon Trail: Sketches
of Prairie and Rocky-Mountain Life*.
Toronto: George N. Morang and Co. (Fron-
tenac Edition), 1900.
Phillips, Paul C., ed. *Forty Years on the Fron-
tier: The Reminiscences and Journals of
Granville Stuart*. 2 vols. Cleveland: Arthur
H. Clark Co., 1925.
Poesch, Jessie. *Titian Ramsay Peale and His
Journals of the Wilkes Expedition,
1799–1885*. American Philosophical So-
ciety Memoirs, 52. Philadelphia, 1961.
Price, Con. *Memories of Old Montana*. Hol-
lywood: Highland Press, 1945.
———. *Trails I Rode*. Pasadena, Calif.: Trails
End Publishing Co., 1947.

Renner, Frederic G. *Charles M. Russell:
Paintings, Drawings, and Sculpture in the
Amon G. Carter Collection*. Austin: Uni-
versity of Texas Press for the Amon Carter
Museum of Fine Arts, Fort Worth, 1966.
Rush, N. Orwin. "Frederic Remington and
Owen Wister: The Story of a Friendship,
1893–1909." In *The Diversions of a West-
erner*. Amarillo, Tex.: South Pass Press,
1979.
Russell, Austin. *C. M. R.: Charles M. Russell,
Cowboy Artist*. New York: Twayne Pub-
lishers, 1956.
Russell, Charles M. *Good Medicine: The Il-
lustrated Letters of Charles M. Russell*.
Garden City, N.Y.: Doubleday, Doran, and
Co., 1929.
———. *Studies of Western Life*. 2d ed. New
York: Albertype Co., 1890.
———. *Trails Plowed Under*. Garden City,
N.Y.: Doubleday, Page and Co., 1927.
Russell, Don. *The Lives and Legends of Buf-
falo Bill*. Norman: University of Oklahoma
Press, 1960.
Samuels, Peggy and Harold, eds. *The Col-
lected Writings of Frederic Remington*.
Garden City, N.Y.: Doubleday and Co.,
1979.
Spring, Agnes Wright. *The Cheyenne and
Black Hills Stage and Express Routes*. Lin-
coln: University of Nebraska Press, n.d.; re-
print of 1948 ed.
Strahorn, Carrie Adell. *Fifteen Thousand
Miles by Stage: A Woman's Unique Experi-
ence during Thirty Years of Path Finding
and Pioneering from the Missouri to the
Pacific and from Alaska to Mexico*. New
York: G. P. Putnam's Sons, 1911.
Taft, Robert. *Artists and Illustrators of the
Old West, 1850–1900*. New York: Charles
Scribner's Sons, 1953.
Taurman, Mildred, et al. *Utica, Montana*.
N.p., 1968.
Tucker, Patrick T. *Riding the High Country*.
Edited by Grace Stone Coates. Caldwell,
Idaho: Caxton Printers, 1933.
Underhill, Lonnie E., and Daniel F. Littlefield,
Jr., eds. *Hamlin Garland's Observations on*

the American Indian, 1895–1905. Tucson: University of Arizona Press, 1976.

Vaughn, Robert. *Then and Now; or, Thirty-Six Years in the Rockies.* Minneapolis: Tribune Printing Co., 1900.

Vorpahl, Ben Merchant. *Frederic Remington and the West: With the Eye of the Mind.* Austin: University of Texas Press, 1978.

———. *My Dear Wister—: The Frederic Remington–Owen Wister Letters.* Palo Alto, Calif.: American West Publishing Co., 1972.

Warden, R. D. *C M Russell Boyhood Sketchbook.* Bozeman, Mon.: Treasure Products, 1972.

Wilkins, Thurman. *Thomas Moran: Artist of the Mountains.* Norman: University of Oklahoma Press, 1966.

Wyeth, Betsy James, ed. *The Wyeths: The Letters of N. C. Wyeth, 1901–1945.* Boston: Gambit, 1971.